ONCE UPON AN ISLAND

Books by Elizabeth Piechocinski

The Old Burying Ground: Colonial Park Cemetery,
Savannah, Georgia 1750 - 1853

ONCE UPON AN ISLAND

The Barrier and Marsh Islands of Chatham County, Georgia

by

ELIZABETH CARPENTER PIECHOCINSKI

THE OGLETHORPE PRESS
Savannah, Georgia
2003

Copyright 2003
Elizabeth Carpenter Piechocinski, Savannah, Georgia
Cover photograph is courtesy of Georgia Historical Society.
Cover design by J. M. Connan

All rights reserved. No part of this publication may be reproduced in any form or by any means without the prior written permission of The Oglethorpe Press, Inc., 326 Bull Street, Savannah GA 31401.

Elizabeth Carpenter Piechocinski
Once Upon an Island - The Barrier and Marsh Islands of Chatham County, Georgia

ISBN 1-891495-10-0

1. Genealogy, Savannah GA, 18th and 19th century. 2. History, barrier and marsh islands, Chatham County GA. 3. Early settlement sites and graveyards. 4. Storms and hurricanes.

Library of Congress Control Number 2002109192

DEDICATION

This book is for John Piechocinski, my husband of many years. He was long suffering during the writing process, and assisted me with some of the research. It is also offered as a tribute to my brother, William H. Carpenter, for whom investigative writing and reporting was a lifelong pursuit.

TABLE OF CONTENTS

Foreword	xii
Acknowledgements	ix
Introduction	xv
Crown Land Grants	xix
The Colonial Period	1
Early Agriculture	4
Whitemarsh Island	9
The War Between the States	11
Camp Walleila	14
Saffold Airfield	16
The Gibson Family	20
Personal Reminiscences Regarding the Amorous and Goette Families	24
Free Range Livestock and Fence Laws	33
Turner's Rock	35
Wilmington Island	38
The Bryan and Screven Families	43
The Barnard Family	48
The Shad Family	52
The Oemler Family	57
Mr. Barstow and the Cuban Filibustering Attempt	66
Citrus Fruits and Melons	72

Vandalism	73
Island Legends	75
The Turn of the Century	79
Land Development	81
Wilmington Island Tragedies	90
The General Oglethorpe Hotel	98
Skidaway Island	105
The Waters Family	110
The Delegal Family	111
The Lightenstone/Lichtenstein Family	113
The Odingsells Family	115
Old Bones and Other Things	115
The Benedictines	120
Modern History	123
Tybee Island, Cockspur Island, and Little Tybee Island	126
Thomas Arkwright	132
Military History	134
The Immortal Six Hundred	136
The Hurricane of 1881	139
The Fresh Air Home	142
Wassaw Island and George Parsons	146
The Recluse of Wassaw Island	150
A Wildlife Refuge	152
Anthony Odingsells and His Family	153
Ossabaw Island	156
The Ossabaw Foundation	162
The Morel Family	165
Dutch Island/Liberty Island	170
Rita Mae Duncan Riley	172
Matthew Batson and the Wonderful Aero Yacht	178
The Marshes	184

Hurricanes	189
Shipwrecks	195
Prohibition	199
Author's Comments	205
Appendices	207
A. Island Marriages	207
B. Vital Records of Island Families	217
C. Island-Born Blacks Who Later Moved to Sandfly, Pin Point, and Other Mainland Locations.	231
D. Gravesites on the Islands	233
E. Island Victims of the Major Hurricanes	235
F. Union Soldiers Killed or Wounded in the Skirmish on Whitemarsh Island	238
G. Island Plantation Owners Whose Land Was Confiscated by the Freedmen's Bureau	240
H. Freed Negroes Who Were Given Acreage on the Islands by the Freedmen's Bureau	241
I. Negro Slaves Buried in Laurel Grove South Who Belonged to Island Families	244
J. Some Additional Biographical Sketches	248
Bibliography	251
General Index	263
Full Name Index	275

ACKNOWLEDGEMENTS

This book would have been impossible to write without the assistance of a very large number of people. There were many people who welcomed me into their homes and offices and provided me with materials, information, personal family data, and photographs for this book. There were just as many others who provided technical assistance, research, and their expertise in various fields.

A special thanks goes to Jane Martin Bragg, Joan Martin, and Joanne Martin Lukacher, who spent many hours locating interviewees, provided old maps and offered valuable suggestions for the content of this book. They were also the inspiration for this book, believing as they did that the islands' stories needed to be told.

John Albert and Jewell Anderson of the Georgia Historical Society helped enormously by searching for material in rather obscure corners of that venerable institution, and made hundreds of copies of old pictures and documents.

Frank W. "Sonny" Seiler not only provided rare photographs, but also took the time to show me the site of Matthew Batson's old airplane factory.

Thanks also to William F. Lynes for permitting me to use old family photographs.

A special thanks to Rita Harper DeLorme who can solve the toughest research problems with ease, and who did so whenever I called upon her to do so. I also wish to thank Rita's friend, Gillian Brown, at the Catholic Diocese Archives, for her help.

Cheryl and Ron Horton, Joy Waters, and Estelle Wheatley, all of whom permitted me to invade their property, not once, but several times to take photographs, in addition to providing me with information on the Bryan and Gibson families.

Emma W. Adler and Mary G. O'Malley both allowed me to use personal family archives, as did Miss Mildred Gartelmann and Loretto Lominack. John Duncan of V & J, Antique Maps, Prints and Books, kindly lent images from his personal collection.

Arnold S. Goldstein, M.S., Farris Cadle, and Judy Walet offered their expertise in the Records Room of the Chatham County Courthouse, and Cindy Wainwright at the Metropolitan Planning Commission helped me locate some missing information on the islands.

Special thanks goes to Pinya Lindroos and Paula Patolinna, my computer and scanning experts, who not only provided technical assistance, but also a camera when mine failed to function properly.

Allison Thurlow and Joe Shaffell, the Computer Wiz, graciously found time to scan old photographs for me, and I wish to thank them as well.

And then there were those who allowed me to interview them, and those who provided needed information, technical help with photographs, and valuable suggestions when I ran into dead ends: Lawrence E. Babits, PhD. at East Carolina University; Curtis Bragg, who gave up a Sunday to take his boat around Wilmington Island so I could take pictures. Elizabeth DuBose, Coordinator of Ossabaw Island Foundation; Katherine Keena, of the Juliette Gordon Low Birthplace; Eda S. Kenney, Interpretative Ranger at Skidaway Island State Park, and Jean Shomaker; Talley Kirkland, Ranger at Fort Pulaski, and Leon Lovett of Wrightsville, the artillery experts; Det. William S. "Billy" Ray of the Chatham County Police who directed me to information sources; Terry Shaw of the Bonaventure Historical Society who provided me with personal research information; Herbert H. Kemp of Sandfly; Frank R. Cullum; Harry King and Julian Space of Turner's Rock; William S. "Rusty" Fleetwood; John Saffold; Joseph Saffold; Judy W. Durden; Rita Mae Riley; Steven Williams; Walter Schaaf; Johnny Gammert; Tina Pope; Leonora S. Kuhn; Carl Weeks; Estelle Wheatley; Newell Turner Parr; Herschel Siebert; David Via; Sam Roberts; Miss Leila Norton; Marion E. Boyd; Lisa Evans

Murdock; David J. Killick, Ph.D of the Department of Anthropology, University of Arizona; Gloria Stettler and her brother, Tommy Solomon, who risked life and limb for some photographs; Sharen Lee at the Chatham County Library on Bull Street; and Margaret Waters.

I also want to thank Esther Shaver, who promoted my first book and who has offered encouragement in the writing of this one as well.

A very special thanks goes to my editor, publisher, and friend, Stephanie Jackel, who very patiently corrected my many errors and offered invaluable advice and suggestions. Her input and technical expertise made the publication of this book not only possible, but a reality.

FOREWORD

This book is not so much a history of the islands of Chatham County, as it is a story of the people who once lived on the islands, as well as those who live on them today. This attempt to create an accurate and readable history of the islands was difficult to achieve since little primary source material exists. True, there are the old land records for some of the people who received land grants, and who bought and sold land on the islands, and there are some military records and Colonial records available. Personal accounts could only come in interviews with people who were able to recall certain events and incidents that occurred during their lifetime.

It was, therefore, understandable that old newspaper accounts became of paramount importance in reconstructing some of these events. One instance of this reliance was evident in the use of newspaper articles written in the late 1960's by my brother, Bill Carpenter, then a staff writer for the *Savannah Evening Press*. Although he died more than thirty years ago, I remember listening to him express his views and give his account regarding the destruction of the marshlands in order to mine phosphates. While he tried very hard to be impartial and objective in his writing, it was difficult due to his overriding concern for preservation and conservation of our natural resources.

The fact that the phosphate-mining plan failed and the mining leases were not issued was due in part to his coverage, and that of others, of the plan, which brought the whole scheme to the attention of the public. It made the public aware of the value and importance of preserving the marshes. The value of these marshes has not diminished. If anything, their value to our well-being has increased, especially since they provide a major portion of the very oxygen we breathe, as well as a nursery for the shell and fin fish which spawn in their meandering tidal creeks.

Other news items from old newspapers were not only informative, but entertaining as well. They provided an insight into the lives of the people who were associated with the islands in various capacities and time periods. By including these items, I hoped to give readers stories that would make interesting reading. These were things that were buried in various archived collections, and ones which the average person would not be likely to search out. I felt that the resurrection of these fascinating vignettes of turn-of-the-century life on the islands would provide a glimpse of an era when life was much simpler.

Georgia has one of the most stringent sets of laws pertaining to the protection of human burials and old gravesites. Unfortunately, these laws have not always existed, nor have they always been honored. Wilmington Island, as well as the others, had burial grounds, which no longer exist. There are numerous references to vaults and gravesites that have since disappeared. Only a very few scattered burial sites remain, and often they have been vandalized. Frequently old burial grounds and old graves interfered with commercial and residential development, and often developers were prone to ignore the regulations and bulldoze burial sites.

I hope this practice has vanished, but there are fairly recent occurrences of graves being discovered and quickly destroyed in order to avoid the legal procedures outlined in the state statutes, which include the notification of any surviving family members, and may also involve the services of a state archaeologist. In any event, such graves must be noted, and, if the graves are to be moved, they must be properly moved and records kept, listing pertinent information regarding the graves.

This book attempts to give the reader an idea of what the marsh islands were like during the early days of the colony, and later as part of the state of Georgia. Many of the earliest settlers on the islands have left little, if any, trace to show that they were once here. A few names survive in old deed books and in a few place names. I have tried to resurrect some of these old names so that their place in the history of the area is remembered. A scholarly approach was not deemed to be the best way to do this. I hope this book will stir old memories, and perhaps give newer residents on the islands a much broader picture of the place they chose to make their homes, and their own sense of place in the history of this land of Chatham County, Georgia. With these thoughts in mind, let us begin our island journey.

INTRODUCTION

Situated approximately eight miles southeast of the sprawling city of Savannah, the islands of Whitemarsh and Wilmington appear to float above the tidal waters and marshes that define them as distinct and separate entities from the surrounding wetlands. The spartina, cordgrass, and other marsh grasses and reeds that form the protective savannas that lend their name to the city a short distance to the west give sanctuary to the various life forms that shelter there. The marshes themselves are composed primarily of salt-tolerant sediments that provide biologically rich habitats for many species of life.

Shimmering lush green in late spring and summer, richly golden brown in the cooler months, the savannas provide nourishing habitats to the nesting low country birds and marine life that exist within those vast expanses, threaded by the tidal waters that meander through their domain. It is here that shrimp, oysters and other shell and fin fish spawn. Defined by the major rivers -- the Savannah, the Bull, and the Wilmington -- which make their way to the sea, and also by the lesser streams -- St. Augustine, Richardson, Turner, Half Moon, and Shad -- the savannas or marshes provide a buffer zone from the raging storms that can and often do move inland from the sea. The islands that arise from these same marshes have also been populated throughout much of their prehistory.

The first humans to visit these islands were likely the ancestors of the various Indian tribes who paddled their dugouts along the small creeks, searching for game in the marine forests and shellfish in the mud flats of the estuaries. The mild climate encouraged small settlements, probably temporary or seasonal at first, on the higher points of land. The food supply was plentiful, and many fresh water springs flowed from pure artesian sources. The waterways provided a quick and easy access to the mainland and to the other small islands. Villages eventually sprang up from those first temporary and seasonal camps, and, with the passage of time, a more sophisticated culture developed.

These early villages have long disappeared. We know of them only in the shell middens that remain, the occasional pottery shards that may make their way to the surface, the odd flint points that a curious child occasionally finds. Or perhaps it is a brief reference in an archaeological report or survey, or a chance remark that jogs someone's memory of playing near such a site in a long ago childhood and discovering an ancient bird point or stone implement or pottery shard.

Archaeological excavations have revealed more information about those early islanders. They hunted the game, fished the streams, gathered oysters from the mud flats, and collected berries, nuts, and edible plants in the forest. These early inhabitants cultivated the rich soil and stored food for the winter months. They made pottery and primitive tools, and traded goods with other nomadic people who passed through. They also buried their dead here, in little-understood ceremonies. By the time the first Europeans arrived to settle on the islands, these people had long vanished, with little or no trace to mark their stay other than some mounds and middens.

Between 1938 and 1940, the Works Project Administration conducted a number of archaeological surveys in Chatham County. Some of these lasted only a few days, while others extended over a period of several months. Several of these surveys were located on the islands.

In the fall of 1938, archaeologists Preston Holder and Antonio J. Waring, a Savannah native, excavated a site on the southern tip of Wilmington Island between Little Half Moon Creek and the Wilmington River. This site was given the designation Meldrim Site. Few notes were kept, there were no site maps or photos, and the artifacts recovered from the site have since disappeared from extant Works Project Administration records.[1]

The site itself was an oyster shell mound about ten feet high and one hundred feet in circumference. The two test pits that were dug yielded only pottery shards.

Between 1939 and 1940, three additional sites on Wilmington Island and one on Whitemarsh Island were excavated by Dr. Caldwell and Dr. McCann. Two of these were given the name Walthour Site, and consisted primarily of shell middens. The third Wilmington Island site was located on land belonging to Miss Mary Oemler, whose family had lived on the land since the late 1700's. It was located near a tidal creek in the north central part of the island. Upon excavation, this last site revealed a large village that was occupied between 2000 B. C. and 1250 A. D. Many storage pits were uncovered as well. Evidence uncovered by the archaeological excavations indicated that these sites were ones of continuous occupation for more than two thousand years. Burials with offerings, cremated burials, pottery artifacts and stone artifacts were found. Other finds included bone tools, celts, projectile points, and net sinkers. Unfortunately, many of these artifacts are no longer in the W.P.A. collection. Sketches made by the archaeologists on the site at that time have also disappeared.[2]

The Whitemarsh Island excavation by Dr. H. T. Cain in 1939[3] was designated as the Budreau Site as it was located on property belonging to J. L. Budreau who owned a large truck farm on the island. The site was located off of Battery Point Road. There were three large areas, which showed evidence of aboriginal occupation. Pottery shards were recovered from this site as well.

Conclusions drawn from all of these excavations suggested that while some of the mentioned sites on the islands were only occupied seasonally by mobile populations, there were also some large, more or less permanent settlements surrounded by smaller nuclear settlements.[4] The pottery fragments found in these sites were distinct types of pottery, with decorations of crossed and linear designs, check-stamped, and some with fine cord markings, as well as plain pottery. Single locations were used as cemeteries, resulting in burial mounds. Unfortunately, many of the documents, maps, and artifacts pertaining to these sites have disappeared. Indeed, the sites themselves have vanished due to the encroachment of suburban development. New homes dot the landscape that was once the sole domain of the early native inhabitants.

In addition to the prehistoric sites, which have been identified, other sites of archaeological importance also exist. One of these sites, Long Point on Whitemarsh Island, was surveyed and excavated by Dr. Lawrence E. Babits, Principal Investigator of the Center for Low County Studies at Armstrong State College in 1983.[5] This particular site was originally owned by a supporter of the Crown, but was obtained by Lyman Hall in 1783 as a "Confiscated Estate." The few artifacts recovered from this site were mostly of nineteenth century origin.

Oyster shell mound, Wilmington Island, Savannah.

[1] DePratter, Chester B. W. P. A. *Archaeological Excavations in Chatham County, Georgia: 1937-1942*, Laboratory of Archaeology Series, Report No. 29, p. 15

[2] *The Waring Papers, The Collected Works of Antonio J. Waring, Jr.*, ed. by Stephen Williams. The University of Georgia Press. No date, p. 182.

[3] DePratter. p. 15

[4] Crook, Morgan R. *Mississippi Period Archaeology of the Georgia Coastal Zone*. University of Georgia, Laboratory of Archaeology Series, Report No. 23, p. 36.

[5] Babits, Lawrence E. *Phase II Archaeological Investigation: Long Point, Whitemarsh Island, Chatham County, Georgia. October 1983.*

Crown Land Grants

Although these areas may have been visited briefly by Spanish and French explorers, the first Europeans to actually live on these islands were Englishmen who arrived with James Edward Oglethorpe and who obtained Crown grants to settle these wilderness islands. Until about 1741, the Trustees in London issued the land grants in *tail male*. They believed that this policy was necessary in order to maintain an equal number of planters or soldiers to the number of lots of land. Fifty acres of land was considered sufficient and would prevent the accumulation of several lots by one person into a large estate, because the Trustees did not feel that the colonists were capable of managing large tracts of land. This policy was a means by which the Crown maintained sovereignty and control in the Georgia colony.

After 1741, the officials of the colony were given authority to grant land. Over a period of time, larger grants of land were permitted and were issued in *fee simple title*. Eventually, in 1750, a policy was established whereby land could be bought, sold, and transferred through inheritance as were other properties.

Of the early settlers, the following are listed in the Schreck Indices at the Chatham County Courthouse, as well as in the colonial records and Crown grants[6] as receiving or owning land on the islands:

John Barnard — October 1, 1744. Barnard petitioned the board for 500 acres on Wilmington Island

Captain Adam Mackdonald — September 29, 1744. Captain Mackdonald petitioned the board for a 500-acre tract on Wilmington Island, and was granted this tract.

Peter Baillou — January 1746. Baillou petitioned for 450 acres at the north end of Whitemarsh Island. Petition was denied because he already possessed a town, garden, and farm lot in town. He eventually did acquire acreage on Whitemarsh Island.

John Penrose — March 26, 1747. Penrose petitioned for 300 acres on Whitemarsh Island. He already owned a small island containing fifty or sixty acres near Whitemarsh Island where he built a schooner. John Penrose was one of the first settlers on Whitemarsh.

John Penrose — March 20, 1749. Penrose surveyed three hundred acres on Penrose Island (a part of Whitemarsh Island).

George Siegfrit — April 1755. George Siegfrit, a planter, received 150 acres on White Marsh Island in the Warsaw River opposite Thunderbolt.

John Barnard — April 1755. Barnard received six hundred acres on the southeast end of Wilmington Island. According to his petition there were twenty-five persons in his family, consisting of his wife, four children and nineteen Negroes.

Thomas Palmer — June 1755. Palmer was granted two hundred fifty acres on White Marsh Island, adjoining the lands of Siegfrit.

Adam Crandie — August 1755. Adam Crandie acquired one hundred fifty acres on White Marsh Island at Jenkins' Creek.

Henry Yonge, Esq. — November 1755. Yonge was granted three hundred acres on Wilmington Island. Yonge already owned one thousand acres, and describes himself as having a wife, five children, and eighteen Negroes.

William Dews — May 15, 1756. Dews was granted one hundred fifty acres on Wilmington Island, bounded on the east by a branch of Tybee Creek, and on the north by the property of Anthony Camuse.

John Helvenstine — January 1757. Helvenstine petitioned and received two hundred acres on White Marsh Island, adjoining Thomas Palmer's lands. Jacob and Jeremiah Helvenstine were to follow on Wilmington Island. (Jacob Helvenstine was to establish a school on the island.)

Jonathan Gasper Betz — 1757. Betz received two hundred acres on Wilmington Island.

John Michael Betz — 1757. This Betz brother received one hundred acres on Wilmington Island.

Jane Barnard — July 7, 1759. She had one hundred acres surveyed on Baillou's Island; bounded on the west by John Helvenstine, on the north by Peter Baillou, on the east by Thomas

Bruce. The original warrant and original plat says that Jane Barnard is a widow, and this grant is in trust for her infant son, Robert Barnard.

Thomas Bruce — May 1, 1759. Thomas Bruce was granted a tract of two hundred acres on Whitemarsh Island, bounded on the north by Peter Baillou, on the south and east by Thomas Bruce, and on the west by vacant land.

John Morel — 1760. Morel received seven hundred eighty acres of land as a Crown land grant legally described as being on Wilmington Island, a part that later became known as Screven's Island, now called Talahi Island. This property was later acquired by the Bryan family and passed down to the Screven family by marriage. In 1947, Claude Falligant, who divided the property into lots, subsequently sold to various individuals, purchased Screven.

Isaac Young — 1760. Young received six hundred acres on Wilmington Island.

James Houstoun — November 3, 1761. Houstoun received two hundred eighty-five acres on Whitemarsh Island, bounded by the land of John Helvenstine on the south, and by marshes on the other sides.

Thomas Vincent— December 1757. Thomas Vincent, Merchant and Representative in the General Assembly for the town of Savannah, received three hundred fifty acres on Wilmington Island. Vincent died in 1767 and his wife Hannah inherited the property. In 1768, Hannah Vincent sold these 350 acres to Frederick Herb and Frederick Fahm.

In 1770 and 1782, Frederick Fahm and Frederick Herb conveyed land on Wilmington Island to Catherine Shad. Herb died on his plantation near Savannah in 1790; Frederick Fahm died in 1796, the oldest inhabitant of Savannah.

William Gilbert — June 1759. Gilbert died in Savannah in 1795. His property went to John Jarvis who died in 1795 on Skidaway Island. His executors, Charles Odingsells and Robert Bolton, transferred this property to Jane Jarvis and her children in August of 1818.

Thomas Green — October 1759. Green received four hundred acres. He died in Liberty County about June 1790, and David Delegal was named as his next of kin.

George Siegfrit — October 1759 and 1760. Siegfrit received one hundred fifty acres on Whitemarsh Island.

Jonathan Morel — September 1760. He received five hundred acres on the islands.

Jonathan Gasper Betz — December 1760

Timothy Barnard — April 1761. Barnard received five hundred acres on Wilmington Island.

James Houstoun — November 1761. He received two hundred eighty-five acres

Grey Elliott — November 1764. Elliott petitioned for two separate grants of one hundred acres each on White Marsh Island. Grey Elliott, Esq., died in London in August of 1798. William Mein, a merchant in Savannah published Letters of Administration for Elliott's estate on January 5, 1802.

John Barnard — February 1775. In September of 1778, John Barnard and his wife sold these one hundred acres to Samuel Elbert. This property was located northeast of William Dews' land on Whitemarsh Island.

In August 1781, Jane Barnard transferred title of one hundred acres to Frederick Treutlen. Jane Barnard died in 1794 at White Bluff.

Isaac Young — August 1760. Young received six hundred acres from the estate of John Barnard in August of 1760. The property was on the southeast side of Wilmington Island, and was bounded on the north and west by a Mr. Rentz and the Wassaw River. Young died at Little Ogeechee in May 1799.

[6] Hemperley, Marion R. *English Crown Grants in Christ Church Parish in Georgia 1755-1775*. State Printing Office, Atlanta.

ONCE UPON AN ISLAND

THE BARRIER AND MARSH ISLANDS
OF
CHATHAM COUNTY, GEORGIA

THE COLONIAL PERIOD

During the Colonial period, the islands were given over primarily to the production of indigo. This plant was used to produce blue dyes, which were then sent to England. This crop was heavily subsidized by the Crown. The processing was rather complicated. Other crops also grown here during this period were rice and some cotton, although at first the strictures against slavery in the colony made the production of these crops unprofitable. Both of these crops required a larger work force to produce, and the European settlers did not adapt well to the labor conditions imposed by the climate these crops demanded. Sea Island cotton, also known as blackseed cotton, was grown on Wilmington Island as early as 1791, and shipments of the cotton were sent to England.[7]

Eventually, with the Repealing Act of 1750, the ban against slavery was revoked, and the island planters, now permitted to bring slaves into the colony, turned more to rice and cotton, particularly the Sea Island cotton which was noted for its long fibers and easily visible black seeds. With the larger work force, made possible by the African slaves, cotton became highly profitable. This cotton was extremely well suited for the light sandy soil of the coastal islands. The invention of the cotton gin by Eli Whitney in 1793 encouraged its production, and the demand for land for this purpose increased dramatically. The planters also continued to grow indigo, as well as corn and rice.

Several early landowners also undertook some shipbuilding, some of the more notable of whom were John Penrose, Joseph Bryan, and a few others. There were no roads to the islands, and all travel to and from the islands was by boat. Generally, water transportation fell into three categories: dugouts, periaguas, and boat-canoes. Of these, the periagua was used almost exclusively along the inside waterways. It was a two-masted, oar-powered vessel. Rusty Fleetwood in *Tidecraft* refers to the periagua as "the workhorse of the coast."[8] It had a small cabin, and carried freight as well as passengers. The dugout types were mainly used in the small tidal creeks and rivers. Most of the early planters had larger craft such as Bermuda sloops or schooners for shipping cargoes overseas. Coastal travel was carried out mainly through the winding creeks and streams that threaded their way between islands and hammocks. Thus, it was possible to travel up and down the coast without venturing into the ocean itself. Today, the intracoastal waterway follows many of these old coastal trading routes.

Schools were established on the islands for the children of the families living there. In 1757, Jacob Helvenstine was to establish a school on Wilmington Island. While little is known about this first school, or even whether or not it was actually established, certainly the next earliest one was a special school for boys established by Slaughter Cowling, a highly respected schoolmaster. Cowling opened this school in 1798 with an enrollment of twenty-five boys from the planters' families.[9] The location of Cowling's school is not known for certain, but early plat maps indicate a plot known as the "School House" plot. Cowling married Miss Betsey Herb or Hext, the daughter of one of the old island families, in 1783.

By 1802, Mr. Cowling had acquired considerable acreage on Wilmington Island. The *Georgia Gazette* carried a notice in its November 30, 1802, issue, stating that Slaughter Cowling was offering one hundred and one acres of cotton land, a good dwelling house, a cotton house, kitchen, Negro houses, and additional outhouses and spring for sale. By 1803, Cowling had moved his boarding school from Wilmington Island into Savannah, to the Eppinger house, and later, to Broughton Street where he continued to operate it until about 1811.[10] There was a school located on Turner's Rock which was for the younger children. They arrived by boat from the plantations to attend the school. The older children were usually sent away to boarding schools in the North.[11]

[7] Terry Shaw.

[8] Fleetwood, William C., Jr., *Tidecraft*, WBG Marine Press, 1995, p. 301.

[9] Bowden, Haygood S., *Two Hundred Years of Education, 1733-1933, Savannah, Chatham County, Georgia.* The Dietz Printing Company, Publishers. Richmond, Va. 1932.

[10] *Ibid.*

[11] Smith, Fae Oemler, *A Sea Island Plantation. China Grove, Wilmington Island, Georgia.* A paper. Georgia Historical Society, Savannah, Georgia. Undated, but probably 1959.

EARLY AGRICULTURE

It has long been known by most Georgia school children that one of the crops experimented with in the young Georgia colony was the production of silk. Silk culture required silk worms to spin the cocoons, the threads of which were then unwound from the cocoons and wound onto spools or bobbins in the filature house. This crop was dependent on mulberry trees to provide food for the silk worms. It was therefore necessary to plant groves of mulberry trees on which the silk worms could feed. Early planters such as John Penrose, Robert Gibson, and others planted some mulberry trees on Whitemarsh Island, but this effort was soon abandoned, as this venture did not turn out to be a significantly profitable crop. It is very likely that such groves were also planted on Wilmington Island, and inevitably met the same fate as those in other areas of the colony, since it was obvious that this would not be the economic success originally envisioned.

Indigo was an important crop in the colonies as it was the source for the highly prized blue dye used to color cotton and woolen fabrics. It was first introduced in South Carolina by Elizabeth Lucas in 1736.[12] It was very quickly adopted into the agricultural pursuits in Georgia, where it was learned that indigo was much easier to cultivate than rice and was much less expensive to grow.

While the plant itself is a legume, there are over three hundred known species. Of these, the one of greatest interest to the planter was the *Indigofera suffructiosa,* a plant consisting of a single semi-wood stem with dark green, oval-shaped leaves and red flowers which then formed pea pods. This plant could reach a height of two to six feet. The dye obtained from the plant was produced by a rather involved process of harvesting the plant in late summer, and bundling the stems (the leaves having been removed), which were then placed in large tubs and covered with water. Fermentation occurred within less than eighteen hours, and the resulting liquid, blue in color, was drawn off into another tub. This process produced extremely noxious odors.[13]

The second tub was agitated with specially designed wooden paddles, resulting in a mash being deposited in the bottom of the tub, leaving a top layer of clear liquid. This clear liquid was then carefully removed, leaving the sediment in the bottom of the tub. This sediment was shaped into small bricks and put into shallow pans to dry. The dark blue bricks, when dry, were then ready for export to European markets. It would not be until 1897 that a German firm would produce a synthetic form of indigo that finally would displace the natural product, although by this time the cultivation of indigo in Georgia had long been replaced with rice, cotton, and other crops which did not require the tedious steps involved in the production of indigo.

Rice was another staple crop that could be grown on the islands. The cultivation of this crop depended on a readily available supply of fresh water, the amount and level of which could be controlled by a system of dikes in order to periodically flood the rice fields. It was a crop that could be grown in conjunction with indigo. Although some cotton and rice were grown, indigo was the primary crop in the early days of the colony. It was in great demand in Europe, and what was produced in Georgia was exported to England. The British demand for the dye ended with the American Revolution, and the planters turned to cotton and other crops.[14] There are said to be a few sites on Wilmington Island today where wild indigo has survived the encroachment of modern development and progress.

When Sea Island cotton was introduced in the colony, it was quickly determined that the soil on the islands was quite suited for its culture. This type of cotton had very long fibers and black seeds, which were easily visible and thus could be removed more quickly by hand. Nicholas Turnbull, who had a plantation on Whitemarsh Island, was one of the first planters who raised this Sea Island cotton from seed given him by Josiah Tattnall, and shipped it to England in 1787, according to a letter published in the *Georgia Gazette* in 1799.[15]

Slave cabins such as these dotted the landscape on many of the islands.
Courtesy V & J Duncan, Antique Maps, Prints & Books, Savannah GA.

This letter was to dispute the claim that Wilmington Island produced the first significant shipment of cotton to England in 1799. It was not long before this cotton replaced indigo as a primary crop, and, in order to produce great quantities of cotton, slaves were brought in by the planters.

The invention of the cotton gin in 1793 by Eli Whitney at Mulberry Grove Plantation created rapid changes in the prices of cotton. The Sea Island cotton, because of its superiority, was in great demand, and the period between 1800 and 1860 was a time of great prosperity in Georgia.

One important natural resource, found in great abundance on the islands, was the *Quercus virginiana*. This magnificent tree possesses the qualities which gave it the name by which we know it, the live oak. The wood from this tree has a toughness and density that did not escape the notice of the early shipbuilders. It is resistant to most diseases that attack other trees and is able to thrive in areas of coastal sandy soil which are exposed to saltwater.[16] Its only natural enemy is fire, which leaves it vulnerable to insects. The live oak's habitat is limited to the coastal areas extending from Virginia south to Florida and along the Gulf coast to Texas.

Virginia Steele Wood, in her book *Live Oaking,* states that John Morel, who owned a plantation on Ossabaw as well as a shipyard and plantation at Beaulieu, was one of a very few people in Georgia who was engaged in shipbuilding and selling ships' timbers. He employed a master shipwright named Daniel Giroud. Business was evidently good because Giroud advertised for ship carpenters, and offered good wages with the promise of punctual payment in cash every month. In 1774, Morel's shipbuilding yard completed the *Bewlie,* a ship of two hundred tons. He also offered for sale live oak frames for ships which would be cut to specifications of the buyer. Other items pertaining to shipbuilding such as sterns, stern posts, transoms, bow timbers, and futtocks could also be obtained from his plantation.[17]

The great live oak forest that once covered the islands of Chatham County has been mostly destroyed by various commercial endeavors and residential development. The wood was used by early settlers for houses, ships, and even fuel. Some of the planters cut and sold the wood to shipbuilders in the North. By the early 1800's, a thriving business in the obtaining and cutting of hundreds of tons of live oaks for ships' timbers was well established. John James Audubon decried the destruction of the forest because of the huge waste involved in harvesting the timber, and he predicted that the timber would become so valuable because of its scarcity that the cost would be prohibitive.[18]

By the late 1880's steel had replaced much of the wood in ships and the market for the wood declined rapidly. Wilmington Island provided oak and pine timbers for ships during World War I. Mary Amorous Goette sold some of her timber on Whitemarsh Island to be used for ships' masts. Her granddaughter, Mary Goette O'Malley, said that it was the only time she ever cut or sold any of the timber on her property. Shipbuilders in Savannah used the curved limbs of the giant live oaks to construct the curved keels of ships, and the tall pines were cut for deck planking. So many trees were cut that the forests never fully recovered. Further cutting of the trees for residential and commercial uses have depleted the huge forest that once covered much of the islands.

[12] *The World Book Encyclopedia.* "Indigo," Vol. 10, 1998 Edition, p. 223.

[13] *The Encyclopedia Brittanica,* "Indigo," 15th Edition, Volume 6, page 294.

[14] Smith, Julia Floyd, *Slavery and Rice Culture in Low County Georgia, 1750-1860.* University of Tennessee Press: Knoxville, 1985, page 28.

[15] Shaw, Terry.

[16] Wood, Virginia Steele, *Live Oaking: Southern Timber for Tall Ships.* Northeastern University Press, Boston, 1981.

[17] *Ibid.*

[18] *Ibid.*

WHITEMARSH ISLAND

White Marsh, Whitemarsh, Whitmarsh Island, however you choose to spell it — or say it, for that matter — lies approximately twelve miles southeast of Savannah. The island is bounded by the Wilmington River on the west and south, Richardson Creek on the north, and Turner's Creek on the east. A smaller island, it covers an area of approximately 4,298 acres of high ground.

Here, as on its big sister to the east, Wilmington Island, native Americans established temporary, and later, permanent settlements. Some of their villages have been noted by archaeologists, and at least one archaeological excavation was made in the 1930's.[19] Most of these early native people on the island were seasonal residents, moving on as the seasons changed.

Early European colonists who received land grants of property on the island were Peter Baillou, John Penrose, George Siegfrit, Robert Gibson, Adam Crandie, Thomas Palmer, John Helvenstine, Lewis Turner, Richard Bradley, Langdon Cheves, Josiah Tatnall, and John Barnard. Some of these men built homes here and lived on the island with their families, while others acquired the acreage there for farming or as additional holdings.

Peter Baillou was a French hat maker who came to Georgia soon after Oglethorpe's colonists. He established a business as a hatter in Savannah. The first mention of a fire in Savannah was recorded on October 19, 1738, when Baillou's house, along with that of Giles Becu, a French baker, caught fire and burned.[20]

In 1755, Peter Baillou requested three hundred fifty acres on Whitemarsh Island. Baillou's land was bounded on the southeast by the lands of John Penrose, and on the northeast by the lands belonging to Thomas Palmer. The record is silent as to whether or not Baillou actually built a house on the property, nor is there any record of his cultivating his land, although it is reasonably safe to assume that he did plant crops on at least some of his land, if only for a brief time.

Those who established themselves on the island -- Gibson, Penrose, Palmer, and others -- probably first attempted to grow mulberry trees, as this was one of the requirements of the Trustees. They may have also grown small crops of indigo and rice, as these commodities were important to English markets overseas. Most likely they depended on the rivers for much of their food, and the easy access to deep water enabled men like Penrose to engage in some shipbuilding and trading up and down the waterways. Indeed, minutes found in the Colonial records state that in August of 1743, John Penrose asked the board of the Trustees for an advance of funds to finish and to fit out a sea schooner he was building in the river at Whitemarsh Island.[21] Penrose gave bond and also a bill of sale, and on August 8, 1744, the vessel was loaded with rice to ship to New York.

Many of the early planters maintained other residences in the city and engaged in various other occupations as well. Such was the case of Green Fleetwood who owned a plantation on Whitemarsh, but also had a home on Columbia Square in Savannah. Green Fleetwood was born in Savannah in 1812. He made his living as a ship's captain and a harbor pilot. In 1840, he married Miss Mary Morgan of Effingham County. Seven children were born of this marriage. Fleetwood died on his plantation on Whitemarsh Island in 1856. His brother, John Fleetwood, who was also a ship captain and a pilot, took over the ownership of the Whitemarsh plantation. John married Miss Mary Thompson. They had no children, and John Fleetwood died in 1859. The island plantation was confiscated by Federal authorities after the War Between the States to make reparations to the slaves. The plantation land was divided into three large parcels and allocated to three black families.[22]

The island was an area where livestock roamed freely. There was good hunting in the forests. Larger open areas of land were suitable for growing corn, and later, some cotton. By 1852, a variety of melons was being grown by R. T. Gibson who was shipping them to the markets in the North at a substantial profit.

In 1858, an article appeared in the *Daily Morning News* describing the large vegetables, which were being grown on the Matthew Amorous farm on the southwest end of Whitemarsh Island, that portion of the island known as Long Point. Of particular interest were the very large cucumbers, the largest of which was eighteen inches long.

The War Between the States

Whitemarsh Island was strategically important for the early militia, and outposts were no doubt in place to guard against intrusion by the Spanish coming up from the southern territories which were under Spanish rule. Walter Schaaf, a current resident on Whitemarsh Island, believes that one such outpost may have been on his property, which faces Richardson Creek. When the census of the United States was taken in 1860, there were only three households listed on Whitemarsh Island. These were the households of Edgar M. McDonell on Long Point; John S. Turner on Turner's Rock; and R. T. Gibson on the northern portion of the island.

By the time the American Civil War broke out, Whitemarsh's military importance had been noted, and it became the scene of numerous earthworks and gun emplacements. Some of the earthworks stretched from Gibson's Point, now known as Battery Point, across to what is now the Tybee Road. Eventually several minor skirmishes would take place here. The first military action to take place on the island occurred the last of March in 1862. The Thirteenth Georgia Infantry, under the command of Captain J. T. Crawford, came upon an enemy barge carrying a six-pounder cannon. Crawford's regiment killed one enemy soldier and took eighteen prisoners. They also captured the cannon. Only one of Crawford's men was severely wounded in this encounter.[23]

The second skirmish took place on April 16, 1862, when the Eighth Michigan Infantry, under the command of Colonel W. M.

Fenton, was attacked by Captain Crawford's Thirteenth Georgia.[24] This time Federal reinforcements arrived and routed the Georgians.

According to Lieutenant J. H. Wilson, Topographical Engineer in the United States Army, who led seven companies of the Eighth Michigan on a reconnaissance of Wilmington Island, the steamer *Honduras* made its way through Lazaretto Creek to the Tybee River and the Wilmington Narrows to Nonchalance Plantation (referred to in the Rebellion Record Document Number 140 as Screven's Plantation), where two companies disembarked. This group, under the command of Captain Minor Pratt, was to move to the southwest end of Whitemarsh Island, skirting Turner's Creek on the right. They would be responsible for covering the soldiers on the *Honduras*, which was following that creek to the Wilmington River. The other five companies of Union soldiers, approximately three hundred men, were put ashore at Gibson's Plantation. The steamer, with a six-pounder cannon, was in charge of Lieutenant Caldwell and sixteen of the Rhode Island Volunteers. They had been unable to land the gun from the boat, and thus, when attacked by the Thirteenth Georgia troops under Colonel Douglas, the six-pounder was of little use as there was danger of hitting their own men. Lieutenant Wilson stated in his report of the skirmish that the Thirteenth Georgia numbered about eight hundred men, armed with Enfield rifles.[25]

Other sources put the number at less than one hundred Confederate soldiers of the Thirteenth Georgia, of which four were killed and fifteen wounded. Wilson's report indicated that his troops confused the bugle call for "Charge" for that of "Retreat," and as a result, Federal troops retreated toward their reserves.[26] The dead and wounded were loaded aboard the *Honduras*. The Federal troops, consisting of a total of three hundred men, suffered the loss of ten men, with thirty-five wounded.

On February 22, 1864, a large Federal contingent once more attacked Whitemarsh Island. Once more, Confederate troops, this time a detachment of the Fifty-seventh Georgia, under the command of Captains Tucker and Turner, along with part of Maxwell's battery under Lieutenant Richardson, repelled these invaders.[27]

Some of these large old earthworks still remain around Battery

Crescent and Penrose Drive. One location off Penrose Drive near the eastern end of the island was most likely a Confederate infirmary, if the old medicine bottles found there a number of years ago are any indication of such use. It was in this same general area that a skeleton was discovered in 1937 by Mr. C. A. Dulmage.[28] This was in the vicinity of the Confederate breastworks, and was evidently not the first time human remains were uncovered on the eastern part of the island at Battery Point. Although no weapons or identifying items were discovered, the theory was proffered that these remains were that of a soldier of the Civil War era. Of the disposition of this discovery there is no mention, nor is there any mention regarding other skeletal remains found on the island.

In 1939, as part of a movement to locate, survey, and map the Confederate fortifications around Savannah, W.P.A. workers cleared the underbrush away from the 1862 Confederate defense fortifications on Whitemarsh Island.[29] When the task of clearing the site was completed so that the engineers could survey and map the site, it was determined that the fortification mounds ran from Battery Point to Tybee Road.

By the end of the war, few people remained on the island, and some freed slaves came and established small settlements along a few of the creeks where they earned a frugal living by fishing, shrimping, and crabbing the marshes, fur trapping, and taking their products by boat into Savannah to sell. Small truck farms eventually were established as well. The making of moonshine in stills hidden in the impenetrable forests also offered a lucrative livelihood.

[19] DePratter, p.94

[20] *A Chronological History of Savannah*, compiled by A. E. Sholes, 1900, p.46.

[21] *Colonial Records of Georgia*, p. 92-93.

[22] Nancy F. Miller

[23] Smith, Derek, *Civil War Savannah*, Frederic C. Beil, Savannah, p.74.

[24] *The Rebellion Records.*

[25] *Ibid.*

[26] *Ibid.*

[27] Smith, p.130
[28] "Finds Skeleton on Whitmarsh," *Savannah Morning News*, July 30, 1937, p.14
[29] "Finish Survey of Historical Forts," *Savannah Morning News*, February 8, 1939.

CAMP WALLEILA

Around 1922, Leila W. Espy donated fourteen acres of land, situated on Whitmarsh Island on Richardson Creek, to the Savannah Girl Scouts. This property became the Girl Scout Camp Walleila. The camp operated for more than thirty years, serving the Girl Scouts in Savannah as well as those who came from as far away as Charleston, Atlanta, Macon, and other states to spend a portion of the summer at Camp Walleila.

Brochures advertising the camp in 1936 describe Camp Walleila as being "a well established Girl Scout camp equipped with modern camping facilities and programs."[30] The brochure goes on to describe the camp as being located near the edge of Richardson Creek, a salt water stream. The central building was a "well-screened house set among picturesque live oaks hung with long streamers of moss."[31] Screened huts were arranged in units to accommodate eight to twenty girls per unit. Each unit planned its own program according to the wishes and the interests of the campers.

A wide variety of activities were available. Swimming, hiking, handicrafts, nature studies, fishing, crabbing, outdoor cooking, and gardening were only some of the many activities offered. The brochure further stated, "The only rules are the Girl Scout Laws."[32] Swimming pens or "cribs" were provided for non-swimmers. These strange-looking contraptions were constructed with a floor that rose and fell with the fluctuations of the tides, and they enabled non-swimmers to enjoy the water without being in danger of drowning or being swept downstream with an outgoing tide. On Sundays parents and friends could visit the camp for the special visitors' day program.

Undated photo of the swimming crib for non-swimmers at Girl Scout Camp Walleila on Whitemarsh Island. Photo courtesy of the Juliette Low Birthplace.

Some of the early activities offered to the Girl Scouts were boat trips to Wassaw Island and Pigeon Island. These often included overnight and three-day camping trips. Other interesting offerings were horseback riding, hikes to Battery Point, Indian legends, and at least one group participated in a hike to the mounds, which may have referred to the Confederate earthworks, or it may have been a reference to Indian mounds.

Most camp sessions were two weeks in length, but some campers stayed for additional camp sessions. The only requirement was that the girl had to be a registered Girl Scout, in good standing. Ages ranged from ten to eighteen years old. Girls could attend for the season or for one session. In 1936, the fees for attending the camp were a one-dollar registration fee, and seven dollars per week for board. A special twenty-five dollar rate was offered for four weeks. These were the local rates. The out-of-town Scouts paid eight dollars per week, unless twenty or more came from the same community, and were thus privileged to be charged the local rate.

A camp nurse was on the premises, and, looking at some of the old records kept by the nurse, much of her time was spent dispensing bandages, dealing with homesick girls, and, when all else failed, supervising the doses of Milk of Magnesia for appropriate purposes.

By 1942, a notice advertising Camp Walleila was prepared for airing over WTOC, a radio station in Savannah, which appealed to mothers who were seeking a safe and inexpensive vacation for their teenaged daughters. It emphasized that young girls need "peace…and freedom from tension and anxiety." It went on to add a grim reminder of those times, "When black-out sirens blow in Savannah this summer, wouldn't you like to know that *your daughter* is a member of a happy group gathered around a responsible adult who is telling a bed-time story?"[33] The announcement went on to inform the reader that Camp Walleila offered freedom from the "war-time frenzy" in the safety of Whitmarsh Island, and would be of inestimable benefit to young girls by virtue of the fact that it would strengthen their "inner defenses against the strain of city life during war times."[34]

Camp Walleila finally closed its doors in 1953 after more than thirty years of meeting the desires of Girl Scouts to spend part of a summer enjoying the variety of activities open to them on Whitemarsh Island. The Girl Scouts had purchased Rose Dhu property for a new camp, and old Camp Walleila was sold to a local attorney for private use.

[30] "Camp Waleila" brochure, 1936. Georgia Historical Society.
[31] *Ibid.*
[32] *Ibid.*
[33] *WTOC* Spot Announcement, 1942.
[34] *Ibid.*

Saffold Airfield

Thomas Peter Saffold was born in Davisboro, Georgia, in 1888. He eventually made his way to Savannah where he worked as an agent for the New York Life Insurance Company, a career at which he became very successful. In the 1920s, Mr. Saffold, Raymond Demere, and other prominent investors from Savannah, organized an investment group which they called the Investment Corporation of Savannah, the purpose of which was to purchase and develop real estate. Thomas P. Saffold became the president of The General Oglethorpe Hotel Corporation.

When the Investment Corporation of Savannah was dissolved by mutual agreement in the late 1930's, the members of this investment group received tracts of land in compensation for their investments. Thomas P. Saffold received one such tract of land on Whitemarsh Island. An avid sportsman, Thomas Saffold raced cars and boats, hunted, and played golf. He was reputed to own the fastest speedboat in Savannah and also had the first gasoline-powered golf cart in Savannah.

At the age of fifty-four, Mr. Saffold became interested in aviation, and in 1940, he cleared some of the land he had received from the investment company and built an airfield which began actual operations in 1943. This airfield was a private business, and became a stopover for crop dusters who were on their way to Florida, golfers who flew in to play golf at the General Oglethorpe on Wilmington Island, and others who owned their own planes and needed hangar or tie-down space. There were two runways built. The north-south runway was 3500 feet in length, while the east-west one was 2750 feet in length.

In addition to its being an airfield, there was also a driving range where golfers could improve their game. They drove balls across the north-south runway, and the lights that lined the area were not for the purpose of directing planes to the runway, because there were no night flights into Saffold Field. The lights were used instead for the driving range so it could be used after dark. Flying lessons were also offered at the airfield.

Thomas Saffold's son, Joseph Claghorn Saffold, learned to fly at age sixteen from a deaf mute named Bee Gordon, an aviationist who was well-known to that generation of Savannahians. A second son, Rex Saffold, became a test pilot for the Army during World War II.

Joseph C. Saffold, who was born in 1913, married Katherine Miller Calhoun in 1942, and the couple produced three children: Joseph Jr., Katherine Calhoun, and John Barnard Saffold. Joseph Sr. was a member of the Society of the Cincinnati, tracing his lineage from Major John Barnard. He was also a descendant of Solomon Shad as well.

18

An aerial view of Saffold Field, ca. 1940's. The old Tybee Road, now Johnny Mercer Blvd., is seen in the background. The hangars are seen on the lower left. Photo courtesy John Saffold.

Saffold Field offered a number of amenities to those who utilized its facilities. Here a budding young pilot waits patiently for the advertised curb service. Ca. 1950's. Photo courtesy John Saffold.

This family moved to Whitemarsh from Beaulieu about 1960, and lived in the old airfield manager's house. Joe and John both helped out around the airfield. John said that there was one job his father would not let him do because of the danger involved. That was propping a plane when its electrical starter failed. The job required someone on the ground in front of the plane turning the plane's prop by hand, while another person sat in the cockpit operating the throttle and starter. Sometimes, the starter would suddenly fire up unexpectedly, and the sudden spinning of the prop could seriously injure the unwary person in front of it. John finally managed to learn the process and successfully propped a plane one day when his father was not nearby. He said that his father made little comment, so thankful was he that John had escaped injury.

John recalled how his brother Joe was working at the airfield after school one day when a number of planes began arriving, one after the other. Joe was kept busy helping tie down planes, but they still kept coming in, and Joe had used up all of the tie-down lines. He ran into the house, shouting to his mother to hurry down to the hardware store and buy some rope. It seems that the Airplane Pilots' Association was having a convention at the hotel, and dozens of planes were landing at Saffold Field. Both boys were kept busy taking care of the planes that day.

In addition to the driving range and the airfield, Saffold Field also boasted two target ranges. General Frank O'Driscoll Hunter, known as "Monk," a local World War I hero, and Billy Otto of Savannah used to come out to the airfield and shoot pennies nailed to trees at 100 yards. John and his brother Joe would bring out their guns and shoot at targets with them. The men would regale the boys with old war stories.

Over the years, storms took out most of the hangars. The last hangar, which was also the newest, was destroyed by a tornado in 1973. The tornado skipped its way across the island, touching down briefly at the hangar just moments after Joseph Sr., had left to get a soft drink from the house. The hangar, where he had been working, was totally destroyed, as were the antique cars -- a 1923 Packard, a 1951 Ford, and a 1961 Thunderbird -- which were stored in the hangar, along with several private planes. The tornado next touched down at Talahi Island where it uprooted a tree that fell and destroyed one house. It then headed out to sea where it dissipated. The only damages caused by the storm were at Saffold Field and the one house on Talahi.

In the early 1990's the Chatham County Board of Education wanted a portion of the Saffold Airfield in order to build a school on the island. They had the land condemned, and a lengthy court battle followed that lasted four or five years. When this case was finally settled, the Board of Education came back a year later after the first condemnation proceedings and wanted the rest of the property. A more equitable settlement was agreed upon this time.

The old Saffold Field is gone, and the children who attend Islands Elementary School or Coastal Middle School are unaware that once this was an airfield where a number of prominent Savannahians learned to fly, or to target shoot, or to improve their golf game.[35]

[35] Telephone interview with John Barnard Saffold, May 29, 2001.

The Gibson Family

Whitemarsh Island was the home of Robert Gibson, who immigrated to Georgia from Ireland in 1755. He petitioned the Trustees' council for land and was granted three hundred acres of land on Whitemarsh Island. He married Sarah Stewart and had three sons, Robert Stewart Gibson, Daniel Gibson, and William Gibson. Mr. Gibson established a home on a bluff beside Richardson Creek. At some point he planted a double row of live oaks leading from his home to the water, where he no doubt had a landing for boats coming up the creek, to bring needed supplies and to take away produce and cotton to the factors in Savannah. In addition to the cotton crop, the Gibson plantation produced such crops as cabbages, grapes and oranges. Hogs and poultry, as well as hides and butter, were marketed in Savannah as well.[36]

When Robert Gibson died, he left everything to his wife for use during her lifetime. At her death, the estate would be equally divided among his three sons. Mr. Gibson died in March of 1790, and was buried in a brick and tabby vault constructed on his property. The burial vault was enclosed by a brick wall and located just to the right of the long avenue of oaks leading to the water. His wife Sarah was eventually buried in the vault also, as were some of their children who died in infancy. In 1810, Gibson's sons commissioned a marble tablet, which was fastened to the side of the vault. The tablet was inscribed with the following information:

> Family
> Of
> Gibson
> Robert Gibson
> emigrated from Ireland in the year
> 1755
>
> Believing it to be a sacred duty his Sons
> have erected
> this Stone to his memory
> A. D. 1810[37]

For many years the Gibson vault remained undisturbed in its rather secluded location. In 1939, however, some children of Ernest R. Jones discovered that vandals had broken into the old burial vault, scattered the bones, and disturbed the contents of the vault. Chatham County Police were called to the scene and reported that the vault contained several skeletons and bullet-shaped iron coffins. They reported the body of a man occupied one of the coffins.[38] According to different sources, at least one of the coffins had been hermetically sealed and an iron plate covered a glass faceplate, through which could be seen the face of a perfectly preserved woman. She was described in various accounts of the discovery as wearing a white, high-necked dress with lace at the throat. A bunch of flowers, also preserved, rested on her bosom. Her auburn hair was parted in the middle.

Joy Waters stands beside the Gibson vault on Whitemarsh Island

Mrs. Leila Norton, a long-time resident of Savannah, was born in 1919, in Candler County, Georgia. Her father was one of the last of the mounted police in Savannah, and his beat included the Colonial Cemetery. Mrs. Norton is eighty-one years old, and remembers the incident involving the Gibson vault on Whitemarsh Island very well. Her recollection of what occurred is included here as follows:

> It was 1939, and I was dating the man who would later become my husband. On a Sunday afternoon he came to my house and said that he wanted to take us — my mother, my sister, and myself — for a ride to see something. He did not tell us where we were going or what it was we were to see. He drove us to Whitemarsh Island.
>
> There was a brick tomb which vandals had broken into, My mother would not go down into the tomb, but my sister and I did. There were some steps going down. Inside I saw some skulls and some bones scattered around as if someone had been raking them. There was the strangest bullet-shaped coffin. It had a cover of iron on top that had been pulled off and propped on the ground against the side of the coffin. It had once covered the glass face plate that was now

> exposed. Inside the glass I could see the face of a woman. She was wearing a light lavender dress with a high lace neck. Her grayish hair was still growing, and was lying over her right breast. Her mouth was open, and I could see that a front tooth was missing. She was very well preserved. I can still see all of that in my mind.
>
> Before I talked to you, I called my sister in Asheville, North Carolina. She is eighty-six. I asked her if she remembered this, as I wanted to make sure I was telling the story right. She told me that she certainly did remember it, and that she remembered saying, 'Oh, look, her hair is still growing.' [39]

Mrs. Norton went on to say that the county police sealed the vault a few days later.

Stories circulated that later vandals had broken the glass plates, thereby causing the disintegration of the human remains when they were exposed to air. Whatever the true version, in 1960 another examination of the contents of the now-open vault revealed empty iron coffins, and only bone fragments scattered nearby on the floor of the vault. The old vault has since been sealed once again, and reportedly, the bodies were removed. The current residents believe that the remains of several children still remain inside, however.[40]

Of the Gibson family, Robert Stewart Gibson married Sarah Turner who lived at Turner's Rock. They had three children, of whom a daughter, Louisa Catherine, married Dr. William A. Carruthers. An historical marker in Chippewa Square in Savannah notes that Dr. Carruthers was a novelist who died in 1848. He is buried in an unmarked grave in Marietta, Georgia.

Robert S. Gibson, who died about 1816, was quite successful as a planter. His estate consisted of a considerable amount of both real and personal property.[41] His land holdings alone added up to several thousand acres. George Herb was named as the executor for Gibson's estate. Another descendant, Robert T. Gibson, was one of the pioneers in growing melons for the northern markets in 1852. As was the case in so many other instances, the Civil War disrupted the old plantation system. The land was divided into parcels for the newly-freed slaves.

[36] Smith, J. F., *op. cit.*, p. 84.
[37] Tombstone on Gibson vault.
[38] "Thieves Scatter Bones To Loot A Burial Vault," *Savannah Morning News,* May 6, 1939. p. 12, c.2.
[39] Leila Norton, telephone interview September 27, 2000.
[40] Interview with Joy Waters, current resident on Gibson plantation, August 21, 1999.
[41] Smith, *op. cit.* p. 84.

Personal Reminiscences Regarding the Amorous and Goette Families

In talking with people who have lived on the islands for many years, I discovered that many of them had stories to tell and snippets of information to relate which seem to enrich the existing island lore. They were also willing to express their opinions on certain events that have occurred over the years, which often had a direct effect on island living. These human interest stories are important to understanding a way of life that had evolved over the years by people who were sometimes cut off from the mainland, either by geography, natural occurrences, or simply by choice. Interviews with these people was a way of stimulating their own memories and resurrecting stories, ideas, and information that had been tucked away in a forgotten corner of their minds. Old scandals were sometimes recounted with just a touch of humor which can only come with the passage of time and which only now has been allowed to surface.

One of these interviewees was Walter Schaaf who was born in Savannah and lived most of his life on Whitemarsh Island on property that had come down from his family. Mr. Schaaf is retired from the Savannah Corps of Engineeers. He graduated from Benedictine Military School in Savannah, and from the Citadel in Charleston.

Photographs taken of children at the Chatham County Recreational Dept. camp on Whitemarsh Island in the 1920's under the direction of Clarence Goette. Photos courtesy of Loretto Lominack

He has been a member of the Coastal Heritage Society for many years and makes his home on Whitemarsh Island.

In August of 1999, I interviewed Mr. Schaaf at his home on the island, on property that faces Richardson Creek. In the course of the conversation, he mentioned that Chatham County once operated a camp on Whitemarsh Island in the 1920's down near Battery Crescent. The county recreation department would take children by motor launch from Thunderbolt to the camp on Whitemarsh. Little houses and buildings had been built there to accommodate the children,

An old servant's cabin from the Depression Era still stands on the Schaaf property on Whitemarsh Island.

and when the camp finally broke up, Clarence Goette, who was in charge of the county recreation pro-gram, moved those buildings across Richardson Creek to a place known as Cotton Hammock.

Cotton Hammock is a little seventeen-acre island just across the creek from the end of Andrews Road. It was farmed after the Civil War with cotton. During the Depression, it was also under cultivation in order to keep the land occupied so as to meet certain real estate requirements. With this piece of property across Richardson Creek was a small lot on Whitemarsh Island where the Goettes kept their bateau. A man named Jeffreys had a truck farm over on Cotton Hammock, and when Mr. Schaaf was small, Mr. Goette would take Walter and his friends over there and give them cantaloupes and watermelons. The local residents started calling Cotton Hammock by the name Goette Island. What he remembers about Mr. Jeffreys was that he was a singer and sang in night clubs -- Johnny Harris' and other local clubs.

Schaaf went on to say that there was a black man by the name of Johnny Gray who lived near the marshes near the bridge to Oatland Island. Close by the blacks had a night club they called Dad's Place, and it was there they would go to drink the "Scrap Iron."

The red brick building on Oatland Island was built as a home for retired railroad conductors. When Walter was a boy, he said the old guys at the Conductors' Home would mend the boys' casting nets and fix their fishing rods. It later became a center where the government conducted research related to malaria during the Vietnam War. There were big screened cages filled with mosquitoes as part of the study. Someone went out there with a spray truck and sprayed all of the cages, killing all of the mosquitoes being raised there for research.

According to Walter, there were a number of Revolutionary War sites on Whitemarsh. During that period of history there were picket stations or outposts all along the marsh, placed there to watch for enemy troops coming up the river. This speculation is borne out by the discovery of Revolutionary period artifacts such as buttons from the tunics worn by the soldiers on picket lines. He mentioned that there were also such military sites here during the War Between the States. These fortifications ran all the way across the islands. There were earthworks and batteries all over the islands.

There was a lawsuit in the '30's between the people who lived on the island here and a Mr. Demere who owned a large area of the island, according to Schaaf. He thought that is probably the part called Camp Venture today. Mr. Demere had a quail preserve in there and wanted to close Bryan Wood Road. In order to prove to the judge that the road had been a public road for a long time, those opposing the road closing proved that there were Indian trails through there before white men ever came in; and, later, that the road was used extensively by Civil War troops. Mr. Demere put a lock on a gate across part of the road, and one day a year he locked the road to demonstrate his claim. On that day, the postman could not make his delivery.

Loretto Lominack, who lives in Savannah, related the following story regarding the Clarence Goette family's connection to Whitemarsh Island. It seems that Mr. Clarence owned a mule that achieved some degree of notoriety by enjoying boating on Richardson Creek. Paddy, as the mule was called, was equally at home on Whitemarsh and on Cotton Hammock, and on the larger islands which were also owned by the Goette family. Paddy was used for plowing on both islands, and the only way for Paddy to get to these

Paddy the Mule being rowed across Richardson Creek to Cotton Hammock by Mary Catherine Goette. Photo courtesy of Loretto Lominack

islands was by stepping into the Goette bateau and being rowed across Richardson Creek. Even when the crossing was rough, Paddy would stand calmly in the bateau and then just as calmly disembark when the landing was made. The children who visited the islands for the recreational department camp would often climb up on Paddy's back for a ride. In January of 1934, Paddy, the seagoing mule, made his last voyage.

He became ill, and Mr. Goette put Paddy in the bateau and rowed him across the creek for the last time. Upon reaching Whitemarsh Island, the mule was put in Mr. Goette's truck and taken to a veterinarian. It was too late, though. Before reaching the veterinarian's office, Paddy was dead at the ripe old age of twenty-six. The Savannah paper paid Paddy a final tribute.[42]

One interesting sidelight to the Goette lands concerns that tract of land which included Long Point on Whitemarsh Island. This tract was one which was part of a Confiscated Estate after the American Revolution. Lyman Hall, one of the Georgia Signers of the Declaration of Independence, received this land in recognition of his services to the American patriots.[43] In 1793, Mary and Jonathan Hall, administrators of Lyman Hall's estate conveyed this 380-acre tract to Joachim Hartstene. Over the following years property passed

Some of the Goette girls at Mr. Strobhar's house on Whitemarsh Island, probably in the area of Long Point, c. 1900. Photo courtesy of Mary Goette O'Malley.

Undated photo of "Tice," one of the freed slaves who lived at Long Point, Whitemarsh Island, on the Goette property. Photo courtesy of Mary Goette O'Malley

through the hands of various individuals and families, including Tobias V. Gray, Ann Margaret Harden, Mary Ann Hartstene, Henry Myer, Margaret Prendergast and her brother, George S. Gray, Patrick Martin, and finally to Mathias Amorous, and thus to Mary Amorous and her daughter Mary Catherine Goette. In the period following the War Between the States, the only inhabitants of the old Long Point Plantation were the ex-slaves who settled there.

Farming on the islands in the early 1900's.
Photo courtesy of the Lynes family.

In 1898, an injunction was filed in the courts of Chatham County pertaining to the Goette tract. It was concerned with the cutting of timber there by an unauthorized person, referred to in the injunction as "Desvergers."

Cassius Hunter, a colored man who had been born on Whitemarsh Island in 1820, was called upon to make a deposition in regard to this matter. He mentioned that when he was a boy, Tobias Gray owned the property. Gray planted cotton and also used the island for a cow pasture. Mr. Gray's property was sold to an Irishman named Patrick Martin. Martin's use of the land was also for growing cotton and for raising cows. Mathias Amorous then bought the property, the War Between the States broke out, and the property was sold to Mr. MacDonell who had cattle and used the land for pasture.

After the war, Mr. Amorous came back to the island, having reacquired it, and rented out a portion of the tract to some colored families who settled there. Cassius Hunter was one of these. When the property came into the hands of Mrs. Goette after the death of her father, Hunter continued to rent from her, acting as a sort of caretaker.

Cassius Hunter went on to state that he was seventy-eight years

Walter "Cork" Schaaf, Whitemarsh Island

old, and had lived on the Goette place for more than twenty-five years, farming a portion of it. He knew that the place was a part of Whitemarsh Island, but said that the black families on the island called the part of Long Point where he lived, "Fenk Island." It was possible to walk across to Fenk Island any time except during a spring tide. There were four acres on the "island," and he had put shell there, opened oysters there, and planted oysters in the creek. Mr. Ambos at Thunderbolt put a landing there in July of 1897, put up a dam, shelled it, and built a house and made a canal for a boat to come up almost to Hunter's door. An employee of Mr. Ambos', a man named Cribben Williams, had lived in the house there the previous winter. Cassius was hired by Mr. Ambos to keep an eye on the house. Cassius Hunter kept cattle near there, and built a fence to separate his cows from those of Mr. Goette. The fence confined them to Hunter's range, which included Fenk Island. Mr. Desvergers evidently moved into the house Mr. Ambos had built, and then moved in some tenants.

Another witness in the case was a man named Screven Williams, who stated that he had dug the canal mentioned by Mr. Hunter, hauled shell, and helped build the house. He, too, had been hired by Mr. Ambos. Williams had lived in the house for a while, but after his son drowned, he moved out. He had planted watermelons there, and Mr. Ambos had paid him to guard the oyster beds.

Mr. Desvergers continued to ignore statements from both Hunter and Williams, asserting that he did not have the right to cut wood on the property. Both men reported it to Mr. Ambos. Desvergers continued to cut wood every week, approximately five cords in all.[44]

Old slave cabin on Bradley Point, c. 1935.
Photo courtesy of Georgia Historical Society.

Finally, Mary Catherine Goette, who now owned the property, having inherited it from her mother, Mary Sowney Amorous, was forced to come back to Savannah from up north where she had gone some time after the War Between the States. She was informed that squatters had moved onto her property. Her return resulted in the court action, which was finally resolved in her favor.

Mary Goette O'Malley, who provided much of this information on the court case, told me that her mother spent the summers on an island looking toward Thunderbolt. Her aunt used to take food out to Long Point to an old black man who was living there. She also took food for his cow. This may have been Cassius Hunter, or perhaps, Tice, whose photograph appears in this book.

Chatham County Police Detective Billy Ray related to me how he was once called to investigate the desecration and vandalism of a grave on the Goette property at Long Point. The grave, which was located in a patch of woods, had been disturbed. The stone found bore the inscription of an Eliza Fogarty who died in 1915. Subsequent investigation by Detective Ray revealed that Eliza Fogarty was a black woman who once lived on Perry Lane in Savannah, but worked for a family named Walsh on Long Point. She died while on the island and was buried there.

Another example of a long-forgotten grave was that of Mollie Jenkins which, according to Frank Cullum, was discovered in the woods at Long Point when it first began to be developed for home sites. The grave had been dug up, and someone had tried to pry open the metal casket. Mr. Cullum recalls that a day or two later, after this gruesome discovery, he returned to find that the casket and its contents had vanished. The tombstone was found some distance away in the woods, and Mr. Cullum took it to his house in order to try to locate some interested family member, and to prevent it from disappearing as well. No one ever came forth to claim the stone, and it, too, has now vanished after years in the back of Mr. Cullum's garage.

[42] "Paddy, the Sea-going Mule, is Dead," *Savannah Evening Press*. January 10, 1934.

[43] Babits, Lawrence E. "Phase II Archaeological Investigation Long Point, Whitemarsh Island, Chatham Count, Georgia, October 10, 1983, p.1.

[44] "Goette vs. Desvergers - Injunction, Witnesses' Statements, July 27, 1898." Provided by Mary G. O'Malley.

FREE-RANGE LIVESTOCK AND FENCE LAWS

As the population in Georgia slowly increased after the war, the problem of roaming livestock prompted the General Assembly in 1872 to enact a bill regarding the fencing of livestock to protect crop lands.[45] Wire fencing was legalized in 1879, but few livestock owners used it because of the expense involved in fencing pasture lands. The purpose of this act was to protect croplands, the uncontrolled breeding of livestock, and to protect the scarce timberlands. This piece of legislation was not enforced, possibly because of the effort involved in putting up and maintaining fences, and as a result, many farmers allowed their livestock to roam freely.

In the mid-1880's, a number of complaints relating to the fencing of livestock on Whitemarsh and Wilmington islands were brought before the local county courts. Prior to 1885, livestock had been allowed to roam freely over the islands with little regard to property lines. Farmers fenced in their crops to protect them from the free-ranging livestock. Chatham County, along with much of the state of Georgia, permitted free roving of cattle and other livestock. The roaming cattle owned by the Negroes on the islands annoyed residents of Whitemarsh and Wilmington islands. In February of 1885, the white residents filed their intention of petitioning the next legislature for a strong fence law. Such a law, if enacted and enforced, would require livestock owners to fence in their cattle. [46]

Eventually such a law was passed, but there were frequently disputes and complaints about livestock owners who were not inclined to comply with the rules and regulations governing such matters.

[45] Flynn, Charles, *White Land, Black Labor, Caste and Class in Late Nineteenth Century Georgia*, Louisiana State University Press, Baton Rouge, 1983, p. 129.

[46] *Savannah Morning News*, February 27, 1885, p. 4, c. 3.

Turner's Rock

Turner's Rock, or Turner's Rocks as a Savannah newspaper from the 1800's refers to it, is a small island, approximately one hundred and eighty acres in area. It is located on the southeast sector of Whitemarsh Island. It is bounded by Bradley Creek on the east, Turner's Creek on the north and east, and the Wilmington River — or the Skidaway River as it was known in the Colonial period — on the south. Its history goes back to the 1700's when Lewis Turner received a Crown Grant to the property. At one time, Turner's Rock was known as Lacy's Island, named for Roger Hugh DeLacey who first owned the little island.

One of the earliest families to make a home on the island was that of Lewis Turner who received a grant of land on Whitemarsh, or Lacy's Island, in 1761. In 1765, Turner requested an additional 129 acres on the island. Cotton, corn, rice, and indigo were some of the early crops grown on the little island. Lewis Turner died between 1800 and 1803. His will mentions bequests to his sister, Elizabeth Whiting, and her children, Lewis Turner Whiting and Ann Lucy Whiting. He also made bequests to his brother, John Turner, and to the children of his brother, Richard Turner. Lewis Turner, the son of Richard, was included in this bequest as receiving a plantation on Wilmington Island. His executors were his brothers, John and Richard, and also Solomon Shad.[47]

Lewis Turner, the son of Richard Turner, died sometime between 1784 and 1786. His will mentions his wife, Jesten, three sons, Richard, John, and Lewis; and four daughters, Sarah Jenkins, Lucy Barnard, Ann Barnard, and Elizabeth Turner. In addition to his Whitemarsh plantation where he made his home, Lewis Turner also owned property in St. Mary's Parish, as well as a plantation on Wilmington Island.[48]

During the War Between the States, Turner's Rock played an important role in maintaining defense posts to guard the waterways by which enemy troops could reach the city of Savannah. Confederate fortifications, a powder magazine, gun emplacements, and earthworks remain today as mute testimony to that turbulent era in our history.

The Demere cemetery on Turner's Rock.

Today this small island is home to approximately ten or twelve families who have lived there from the 1930's, for the most part. Its history, however, predates the time when a few families bought property there and established their own little secure island hideaway.

Some of the present owners who call Turner's Rock home today are Harry King, Julian Space, and Raymond Demere. They maintain their own water supply, and have huge electrical generators as a guard against power outages from storms. The residents stock supplies of food and other items as well, making them quite self-sufficient in the event of natural disasters.

[47] Abstracts of Wills, Chatham County, Ga., Will Book D, p. 150.
[48] Abstracts of Wills, Chatham County, Ga., Will Book D, p. 148.

Confederate gun emplacements on Turner's Rock.

Confederate powder magazine on Turner's Rock.

WILMINGTON ISLAND

Situated between Tybee Island to the east, and Whitemarsh Island to the west, Wilmington Island is the largest of the islands that separate Savannah from the sea. Covering an area of approximately 7,918 acres, its name is of English origin, believed to have come from Spencer Compton, the Earl of Wilmington. Compton was prominent in English politics and had some interest in the colony of Georgia.

Although the island has undergone extensive development in more recent years, it was once the site of early plantations belonging to families such as Barnard, Shad, Oemler, Barstow, Tattnall, Bryan, and others. Little from those very early days remains. The old farms and plantations have long been subdivided, the small fishing camps are now upscale home sites, and the burial grounds have been razed and paved and built upon. Progress has linked Wilmington Island with Tybee on the east, and with Whitemarsh and Oatland Island on the west. Most of its grand old oak forests have disappeared, and cotton is no longer grown on the island. A few traces of its former rural past still linger — traces such as the old Oemler house, Green's Fish Camp, and a few of the older homes along the western bluff.

Today, homes cover much of the island, and the building trend continues to encroach on what little remains of the great old forests. Modern shopping centers occupy a swath of land that extends from the bridge at Turner's Creek to the Bull River Bridge and Highway 80, which continues eastward to Tybee Island. Life on the island has become much more frantic than when the island was a favorite summer haven at the turn of the century, when the living was easier and slower paced — that idyllic period when the Ambos family at Thunderbolt ran a regular ferry service to the island. It certainly would not be recognizable to those early settlers such as John Barnard,

Thomas Vincent, John Morel, and Henry Yonge, among others who first petitioned the Crown and were granted acreage there.

Harry King, of Turner's Rock, spent an afternoon reminiscing about early days on Wilmington Island. His recollections of growing up on the islands, and his opinions in regard to issues relating to the islands are recounted here in his own words:

> My dad had a very close friend named Herbert Green who lived at Wilmington Island. Herbert was always sort of a mystery man, but I never knew the entire story.
> Herbert Green was a famous New York artist under another name. He got into an altercation in New York and killed some guy over a woman and had to leave New York. He came down here and lived as a hermit and ran a fishing camp on Wilmington Island, over on the back side. That fishing camp stayed here forever. Herbert and my dad were very good friends. We used to come down all the time, and we would get to walk through Mr. Herbert's house. He had the most gorgeous paintings that he had done himself. I remember that he had a yard full of persimmon trees, and he raised quail.
>
> We used to keep a boat over at his fishing camp. Dad got a little bateau for us, and we would sneak off and cajole someone to take us to Thunderbolt. Later, when we were old enough, we would ride the streetcar to Thunderbolt where we would catch an outgoing tide and jump into the river there. We would swim down there and crawl ashore at the Oglethorpe Hotel, and then walk across and get in the boat on the Half Moon River and go down there and play around Butt Island. I spent my life in that damned river…sweating down mud flats, getting them slick, and diving into them, sliding down on them. Hell, if we had ever caught an oyster shell, it would have laid us open from one end to the other.[49]

Green's fishing camp on Wilmington Island, September 2000.

Mr. King's explanation of the artesian wells that once existed in abundance, and his opinions regarding deepening the river channel on the Savannah River were quite enlightening.

> Back in those days, we had artesian water all over this place. We had artesian water until 1936, and that was the predominant source of drinking water here. They used to have hydraulic rams. When you've got an abundant flow of water, you can have a ram, and you get the water flowing down a pipe until it reaches a certain point of inertia. There is a flapper valve, and the flapper valve then closes. Well, the inertia of the water behind it keeps pushing, and then it has a little relief tube which will knock open the valve and blow the water into a tank. You can put water almost thirty feet in the air with those rams. That way you can get pressure to distribute water around the island. There were hydraulic rams all over until '36 when they started drilling those big wells for Union Bag.
>
> The last flowing well on this island that I know of was just across the river in a field on the old Artley property. There were several wells there fifteen years ago still flowing, but the strongest artesian well was at Shellman's Bluff. The well there used to flow

thirty-two feet in the air. When they drilled those big twelve-inch wells at that pulp mill at Riceboro, our water level dropped so radically that we had to deepen our well. It was when they drilled that same well down there that just wiped out the artesian water. Back in those days if you wanted water on your property, you just took a big pipe and could drive it in the ground to the aquifer. The pressure on the aquifer was so intense that you didn't have to go more than ten or twelve feet before you hit water.

Now they're talking about deepening the channel in the Savannah River. I think it's too big a gamble. If they were to contaminate that aquifer, we would all have to get desalination kits to hook up to the house. There is an alternative. That is to make Union Bag and Scott Paper Mill, and all those people that have these massive wells, shut those wells off, then you could get the pressure back in the aquifer to keep the salt water intrusion out. The problem with the salt intrusion is the massive amounts of water taken out of the aquifer for industrial purposes, and they could just as well use the water out of the Savannah River. [50]

Harry went on to tell of a place off Daytona that used to be marked on the old nautical charts, a spot where sailing vessels used to pull up, where the fresh water was boiling up in the sea. The old sailors could fill their water casks right out of the ocean with fresh water. Harry said that he had drunk water out of that spot, and it was fresh water.

"It is located where there is a big crack in the aquifer, and the fresh water is churning up. From the air, you can see water bubbling out of it," he said.[51]

Harry King was not the only person I interviewed who remembered the artesian wells on the island and in the river. Marion E. Boyd, whose family lived on Wilmington Island before the bridge was built, mentioned the great pressure of the artesian wells before the aquifer was altered by the large wells sunk by the big industries.

He remembered how easy it was to get water in those days.[52]

The history of Wilmington Island centers on the people who created that history. It is best recalled by taking a look at some of these families who came to the island and made it their home. Originally this island was several land grants, but intermarriage among the families on the island, and purchases of the smaller parcels by some of these families, combined the various tracts into what was essentially one very large plantation.

These families increased their original holdings which, although delineated by property lines, still belonged to the same families. A few of these families are discussed in greater detail in the next section because they were important to the development of the island.

Some of the families who were known to have been living on the island during this period left few, if any, documents. These were families like the Tebeau family and the Treutlen family, whose names appear in documents as executors or as witnesses to wills and in a few property deeds. They intermarried with other island families and their history was thus joined to these other large landowners who left their mark.

[49] Interview with Harry King at Turner's Rock, July 14, 2000.
[50] *Ibid.*
[51] *Ibid.*
[52] Boyd, M.E. Telephone interview, June 11, 2001.

Harry King, Turner's Rock, Savannah

The Bryan and Screven Families

Jonathan Bryan, one of at least four children, was born in South Carolina in 1708, the son of Joseph Bryan and Janet Cochran, daughter of Hugh Cochran of South Carolina. Jonathan Bryan married Mary Williamson on October 13, 1737. His sister, Mary, married John Morel, and after his death, she married Richard Wylly in 1784. Another sister of Jonathan's, Hannah Bryan, married John Houstoun, son of Sir Patrick Houstoun.

Mary Williamson was the daughter of John Williamson of South Carolina, and Mary Bower, the daughter of William Bower and Martha Hext. Martha Hext was the daughter of Hugh Hext who, along with William Bower, had come from England to South Carolina.[53]

In 1752, Jonathan Bryan moved to Savannah with his wife and his six year-old son, Josiah. By 1764, Jonathan Bryan had acquired land on Wilmington Island from his brother-in-law, John Morel. The land had been a Crown land grant from King George III to John Morel in 1760. Bryan also acquired several other plantations in Chatham County, but his favorite was Brampton Plantation where he died and was buried in 1788.

The plantation on Wilmington Island, "Nonchalance" as it was later to be called, originally began as a land grant of five hundred acres from King George III to John Morel and his wife, Mary Bryan Morel. In January of 1764, this property was conveyed to Jonathan Bryan.

Jonathan's son, Josiah Bryan, was born in 1746. He married Elizabeth Pendarvis in 1770. Their son, Joseph Bryan, born August 18, 1773, married Delia Forman and came into possession of the Wilmington Island property. Nonchalance Plantation did not produce rice as did some of the others on the surrounding area. Instead, the major crop at that plantation was the well-known Sea Island cotton.[54] Joseph Bryan died in 1812, and was buried at Nonchalance. His will gave specific instructions as to his burial. A clause in his will explicitly stated:

> Having long entertained an antipathy to be buried under ground, I request and order my executors, that after my decease, a box of Cypress be made, two feet wide and six feet long, which shall contain My remains and be placed under a shed to the eastward of my home Until wooden building can be erected and when my executors can Conveniently attend, to erect a more solid building. I request that one Of tabby or brick be erected and that my remains be deposited there Above ground.[55]

Joseph Bryan's final wishes were honored, and a very large brick vault was built. It stands today on the property that was once called Nonchalance. When his wife Delia died, December 15, 1825, her body was also placed in the vault. Unfortunately, this vault has not been immune to vandalism. An article in the *Daily Georgian,* dated January 25, 1831, described how someone had broken into the vault twice in the past two years. The first forced entry to the vault occurred in January of 1830, but little damage was done to the coffins themselves. However, in January of 1831, not only did unknown persons enter the vault once again, but they also damaged the coffins and their contents. J. P. Screven and T. M. F. Bryan offered a reward of two hundred dollars for the identification, arrest, and conviction of the guilty parties.

The Bryan burial plot on the old Nonchalance plantation on what was then part of Wilmington Island, later called Screven's Island. Today it is known as Talahi Island.

The Nonchalance property was bought by H. L. Bowyer, Jr., around 1957. At the time of the purchase, Mr. Bowyer noted that the vault had been broken into, the caskets had deteriorated, and the bones were scattered on the floor of the vault. The marble name plaque was found in the woods near the vault. Mr. Bowyer hired a bricklayer to seal the vault, but before this could be done, the bones were stolen.[56]

It has since been brought to my attention that an unidentified individual removed the bones, ostensibly for the purpose of protecting and preserving the Bryan remains. There are indications that this individual is interested in returning the remains of the Bryans to the vault. Certainly this story provokes a number of questions that must wait for answers to be forthcoming. The current owners of the adjacent property, which was once part of Nonchalance, are committed to repairing the old vault properly and maintaining it.

Today, a marble obelisk surrounded by an iron rail fence stands beside the brick vault. This is the gravesite of Florida Bryan Forman, wife of Thomas M. Bryan Forman, who died December 23, 1847, in childbirth on Broughton's Island near Darien where the Formans were living at that time. Their son, George Troup Bryan, born November 26, 1835, and died September 19, 1838. Thomas Marsh Bryan Forman, born in 1809 on Wilmington Island, died September 27, 1875, in Brunswick and is buried in Oak Grove Cemetery in Brunswick, Georgia.

Since the Bryan and Screven families had intermarried, the title eventually passed to the Screven side of the family. The land, consisting by this time of 780 acres, five hundred acres of which were high ground, was bounded entirely by water, except at one point on its southeast boundary where its marshes touched the marshes of Wilmington Island. It was bounded on the north by the Bull or Tybee River, on the west by Turner's Creek, and on the south and east by Camoose Creek. It eventually became known as Screven's Island. The name "Nonchalance" was given to the Bryan plantation on Screven's Island.

In September of 1804, a hurricane struck Savannah. Hannah Proctor Screven, the wife of Major John Screven, and their one

Signpost at Nonchalance, Talahi Island, Georgia.

year-old son, John Screven, Jr., were killed when their house at Nonchalance on Wilmington Island collapsed.[57] It was during this same storm that the *Governor Tattnall*, carrying a cargo of coffee, was blown ashore near Nonchalance. It was refloated, and sailed into the port of Savannah a few days later.[58] Newspaper accounts of this hurricane reveal the devastation that took place in Chatham County. Numerous lives were lost as a result of the storm. Little damage, however, was reported from Wilmington and Whitemarsh islands, probably because communications from these islands to the city were difficult, and the islands were also less heavily populated at that time.

In 1831, Thomas Bryan Forman sold his property on Wilmington and Whitemarsh Islands to Dr. James P. Screven, and moved to Broughton Island down in Glynn County, Georgia. He had changed his name from Bryan to Forman in 1846 to comply with the terms of his grandfather Forman's will in order to inherit the Forman property there.[59]

The title to the property passed to James P. Screven. At the death of James P. Screven on July 2, 1859, this property was passed on to his three sons, John, Thomas F., and George P. Screven. When George P. Screven died, October 5, 1876, his estate, including his interest in Screven Island, passed on to John and Thomas Screven as the executors and trustees, in trust for his wife and children.

In 1905, the property was sold to R. H. Mayer for the sum of $1,398.33. The Mayer trustees then sold more than fifteen hundred acres on Wilmington Island, comprised of the Hunter, Burleigh, Bryan (or Screven), and Betz tracts to the Wilmington Island Land Company on June 26, 1922. The Screven Island tract was sold to Ernest J. Haar in November of 1928, who in turn sold the tract to Jamison Handy of Los Angeles in 1936. Mr. B. B. Comer bought the island from Mr. Handy in 1943, and finally in 1947, the property was purchased by Claude Falligant.[60] The land was then subdivided, improved, and sold in parcels to individual buyers.

Interestingly enough, a stipulation was included in the original sale which was honored throughout all of the other transactions that occurred throughout the years the property changed hands. This stipulation was one which excluded a one-acre lot containing the Bryan burial place. This act of preservation of the burial site stands in stark contrast to the wholesale destruction by land developers of other burial grounds which once were located on the islands. Of these, only an isolated photograph, a faded news clipping, the memory of older inhabitants, or occasionally, a single stone or small brick rubble pile remain to mark their sites.

[53] Heyward, James Barnwell. *The Genealogy of the Pendarvis-Bedon Families of South Carolina, 1670-1900*, Foote & Davis. Co. Atlanta., n.d., p.83

[54] Smith, J.F., *op. cit.*, p. 81.

[55] *Some Early Epitaphs in Georgia*, Georgia Chapter of Colonial Dames in America, 1924, p. 3.

[56] Letter from H. L. Bowyer, Jr. to a Mr. Kenneth H. Thomas of Decatur, Ga., March 4, 1983.

[57] *The Columbian Museum and Savannah Advertiser*, Sept. 15, 1804. p.3.

[58] *The Columbian Museum and Savannah Advertiser*, Sept. 19, 1804.

[59] Thomas, Kenneth H. *Georgia Family Lines*. Spring 1979, p. 38.

[60] "Falligant Buys Screven Island" *Savannah Evening Press*, September 20, 1947. No page number.

The Barnard Family

The first member of the Barnard family of whom there is any record in Georgia is Sir John Barnard who was prominent in the House of Commons in London. He was associated with James Edward Oglethorpe, and it is for him that Barnard Street in Savannah is named.[61] Sir John was born in 1685 in Reading, England, of Quaker ancestry. He converted to the Church of England, and throughout his life was a faithful follower of its principles.

At an early age, Barnard went to work in his father's counting house in London, and eventually, in 1721, entered public life as a member of the House of Commons where he served for thirty-two years. He gained the reputation of being a man of great integrity, and was known as "the man who could not be bought." [62] In 1737, Sir John was elected Lord Mayor of London. He died in 1764. It was Sir John's nephew, Colonel John Barnard, who came to Georgia, and who received a grant for five hundred acres of land on Wilmington Island.

Colonel John Barnard was born in England on January 29, 1720. He was married in London, December 13, 1742, to Jane Bradley, the daughter of William Bradley of Middlesex, England. Barnard was ordered to Savannah to command the Rangers. His brother Edward Barnard came to Georgia also, and acquired land near Augusta. Colonel Barnard and his wife Jane established a home on Wilmington Island on a five hundred acre Crown grant from King George II. It was there that the following children were born:

1. Mary Louisa Barnard, born 18 October, 1744
2. Timothy Barnard, born 3 November 1745
3. William Barnard, born 8 November 1747
4. John Barnard, born 12 November 1750
5. Elizabeth Barnard, born 14 July 1753
6. Jane Barnard, born 19 August 1755
7. Robert Barnard, born 10 January 1757[63]

John Barnard owned approximately eleven hundred acres on Wilmington Island. He was probably the largest single landowner on the island. Most of the property was located on the south end of the island, fronting the Wilmington River. The exact location of his home is not known, but he most certainly had a wharf for his trading vessels to dock and load. He died in 1786, and in his will appointed his wife Jane as executrix, and named her as the heir to his plantation. Jane Barnard died October 9, 1794, at her plantation on Wilmington Island. Both of the Barnards were buried in the family vault on the plantation. On January 9, 1861, John B. Barnard had most of the Barnard family remains moved from the Wilmington Island vault to a lot in Laurel Grove Cemetery in Savannah.[64]

Colonel John Barnard's oldest son, Timothy Barnard, married a Creek Indian girl, and became a member of her tribe. The couple had a number of children, many of whom moved west with the tribe when it was relocated by the government.

Barnard's second son, William Barnard, did not marry, but it is believed that he bought out his Indian cousins' interests in the Barnard family estate in Manchester, England.

John Barnard, the third son, was a major in the American army during the American Revolution. He married Lucy C. Turner. According to family tradition, he helped to raise the first Liberty Pole in Savannah. His command as major was primarily occupied in protecting the people on Wilmington Island from the British raiding parties. He once captured part of the crew of a British frigate that landed there on the island. As a result, a price was put on his head. Eventually, he was captured by the British and would have been hanged had not the American commander threatened to retaliate on British prisoners. Major Barnard was exchanged, and later participated in the Siege of Savannah in October of 1779.[65]

Major Barnard and his wife Lucy had at least six known children:

Timothy Barnard, born 1775
Lucy W. Barnard, born 1777
Mary E. Barnard, born 1780
John Washington Barnard, born 1783

James Barnard, born 1785
Henrietta Barnard, born 1789

    One of the Barnard family legends concerns John Washington Barnard, who married Ann Catherine Shad in 1814. John, or Jack, as he was called, was the son of Major John Barnard. Ann, or Catherine, as she was called, was the daughter of Colonel Solomon Sigismund Shad. They had two children, Catherine and Mary Ann Barnard. Evidently, though, the marriage soon developed problems, because Jack and his wife went their separate ways, although both of them continued to live on Wilmington Island, but in different residences.

    There are various accounts of the events that unfolded, but the most common version alleges that Catherine, who was staying with her father, Colonel Solomon Shad, on the other side of the island, desired to pay a visit to the city. Solomon Shad did not want his daughter to go down to wharf to board the boat for the city without an escort. Accordingly, he requested a close friend, William Patterson, to escort Catherine. William Patterson was engaged to Harriet Shad, a niece of Catherine Barnard's.

    On the way to the wharf, they met up with Jack Barnard who became angry at seeing his wife with Patterson. He called Patterson out and challenged him. Barnard had the reputation of being an excellent marksman, while Patterson was a New Englander and was not accustomed to the practice of settling differences under the "*code duello.*" However, according to custom, the two men rowed over to South Carolina to Screven's Ferry, just across the Savannah River from Fort Jackson.

    Whether Barnard became overconfident, or whether Patterson fired his pistol prematurely, or was just lucky, the outcome was the death of Jack Barnard. Those present accepted the duel as being conducted according to agreed-upon conditions, and the body of Jack Barnard was rowed back across the river. Family accounts state that, as the body was being rowed back to Wilmington Island, the Barnard slaves, alerted by the muffled oars, knew that Barnard was dead and began a weird moaning which could be heard all over the island. Jack

Barnard was buried in the family burial place on Wilmington Island.[66]

The will of Jack Barnard contained ample provisions for his wife, Ann Catherine, giving her a house and lot in Savannah, and also sixteen Negroes whom she had received as dowry from her father, Colonel Shad. Interestingly enough, the will also contained clauses which prohibited Ann Catherine from having custody of their two children. Jack's will further instructed that his children were not to live with their mother, nor were they to be under the control of their mother.[67] He appointed his brothers, Timothy and James, as guardians and custodians of his daughters. He also appointed Timothy and James Barnard, Lewis Turner, Matthew W. Stewart, Dr. James P. Screven, and Stephen B. Williams as the executors of his will which was probated February 11, 1827. John "Jack" Barnard's death occurred sometime between November 16, 1826, when he made his will, and February 11, 1827, when it was probated. The explicit instructions regarding the custody of the children seem to have been ignored. Harriet Shad, the niece who had been engaged to marry William Patterson, likely broke off the engagement, for she never married.

[61] Gamble, Thomas, "Barnard Street Named For the Man Who Could Not Be Bought." *Savannah Morning News*, March 17, 1918, p. 30.

[62] *Ibid.*

[63] Barnard Family. Genealogy File. Georgia Historical Society.

[64] *"Laurel Grove Cemetery, Savannah, Georgia, Vol. I, 12 Oct. 1852-1861*, compiled by the Genealogical Committee of Georgia Historical Society, Savannah, Georgia, 1993, p. 269.

[65] Barnard Genealogy File, Georgia Historical Society.

[66] Barnard Family Notes. Walter C. Hartridge Collection. Georgia Historical Society.

[67] *Ibid.*

The Shad Family

From the beginning of James Edward Oglethorpe's dream of a colony in Georgia until the American Revolution, there was an influx of German, French, and Swiss immigration to America. These colonists, who were Lutherans for the most part, were brought over by Jean Pierre de Pury who was hired by the English leaders to provide settlers who could contribute particular skills to the new province. One of these families was that of Hans Joachim Schaad.

The Schaad family originated in Wangen, Germany. Hans Joachim Schaad, Sr., a smith by trade, born in 1691, and his wife Eva, born in 1694, emigrated from Switzerland to Georgia in 1741. With them came their four children, Ana, Margareta, Hans Joachim Jr., and Solomon Hans Schaad Sr. Hans Schaad Sr. had received a grant of fifty acres of land near Hampstead in Chatham County. As the family became settled in the colony, the name Schaad evolved to Schad and then finally to Shad.

Margaret (Margareta) Schad, born in Switzerland in 1728, married Frederick Treutlen, who had a grant of fifty acres of land between Ebenezer and Savannah about 1752. Frederick Treutlen was the older brother of John Adam Treutlen who defeated Button Gwinnett in 1777 to become the first governor of Georgia after the signing of the Declaration of Independence. In 1757, Frederick Treutlen petitioned the Crown and was granted two hundred fifty acres of land on the north side of the Ogeechee River. In his petition he stated that he had a wife and three children at the time. His daughter Catherine married John Tebeau, the son of James Tebeau. Another daughter, Ann, married Peter Provost.[68]

Solomon Schad, born about 1723, married Catherine and had at least five children. One son, Solomon Shad Jr., married Mary A. Garbet. This Solomon and Mary Shad had seven children. These seven children are of special interest because they united, through marriage, a number of families who were early residents of Wilmington and Whitemarsh islands. Through intermarriage among the families of Shad, Barnard, Oemler, and a few others, a large portion of

Wilmington Island belonged to one very large family. These family connections are discussed more in depth throughout this work:
1. Ann Catherine Shad married John Barnard and had two daughters, Catherine L. Barnard, and Mary Ann Barnard who married Eben E. Barstow. Their children were John Washington Barstow, Elias Butts Barstow, and Eben E. Barstow, Jr.
2. Catherine E. Shad married Timothy Barnard and had four children. Some of these children and their offspring will be discussed later in more detail.
3. Margaret Shad married Isaac Norton and had four children. They were Isaac William Norton, Sarah Wilmington Norton, Thaddeus S. Norton, and John Robert Norton.
4. Sarah Shad had no children.
5. Mary Ann Shad married August Gottlieb Ocmler and had Armenius Oemler, who married Elizabeth P. Heyward, and Marianne Oemler, who had no children. Armenius Oemler and his wife, Elizabeth PritchardHeyward, had six children who married as follows:
    - August Oemler married Frieda Rauers.
    - Constantius Heyward Oemler married Sarah Pindar and had two children.
    - Elizabeth Latham Oemler married Fleming Yonge.
    - John Norton Oemler married Marie Conway and had two children. Their daughter Elizabeth H. Oemler married Villa Dale. Their son, Alan Norton Oemler married Mary Teasdale.
6. Solomon S. Shad III married first Susan F. Mongin and had twelve children. His second wife was Mary E. Henderson. The impact of all of these children will be discussed later in this narrative.
7. John Robert Shad married Eliza Butts and had three children: Lydia Shad, Harriet Shad, and Elias Shad.

Timothy Barnard and Catherine E. Shad Barnard's children and their marriages are as follows:
1. Martha Louisa Barnard married John T. Rowland and had three children.
2. Ann Matthews Barnard married William W. Wash and had three children.

3. John Bradley Barnard married first Martha J. Law and had three children. His second wife was Ann P. Law.
4. Timothy Guerard Barnard married Mary Ann Naylor Mongin and had four children.
5. Amelia Georgia Barnard married a Chisholm. Their only child was W. W. Chisholm.
6. Caroline Catherine Barnard married first William P. Rowland, and second John Clark Rowland, with whom she had three children.
7. Margaret Virginia Barnard married William R. Pritchard and had six children.
8. Solomon Shad Barnard married Ann Mary Walthour and had five children.

The twelve children of Solomon S. Shad III and Susan F. Mongin's children were as follows:
1. Mary Ann Shad married George A. McCleskey and had six children.
2. Daniel William Mongin Shad married Mary T. Hardee and had five children.
3. Savannah Schifelia Shad had no children.
4. Margaret A. Shad married first J. Francis Waver and had two sons, Francis and John Waver. William C. Frye was her second husband.
5. John Shad married Matilda Hudnall and had three children.
6. Frank Shad married Edith H. Lewis.
7. Robert E. Shad
8. Henry E. Shad had no children.
9. Solomon Franklin Shad married Caroline N. Bettilini and had six children.
10. Armenius Oemler Shad had no children.
11. Caroline Elizabeth Shad married Albert Holland and had one daughter.
12. Henry Charles Shad married Mamye L. Matthews and had two children.[69]

There are a number of interesting stories that involve Colonel Shad who fought against the British during the American Revolution.

Fae Oemler Smith recounted several of these stories in an unpublished paper she entitled, *A Sea Island Plantation, "China Grove," Wilmington Island*. The paper is undated, but seems to have been written around 1959.

One of these tales concerns a family legend of an incident that occurred during the Revolutionary period. Savannah had fallen to the British, and Solomon Shad, who was evidently well-known to the British troops and whose capture was greatly desired by the British, fled the city and sought refuge on Wilmington Island. Accordingly, British ships came up the river and fired their guns upon the Shad house, hitting the front door of the house. Colonel Shad, a staunch Patriot, supposedly swam the river, tramped his way through the marshes, and escaped. The general amnesty offered by the British to the Americans pointedly omitted the names of Colonel Shad and his brother-in-law, Frederick Treutlen, who had married Margareta Shad in 1752. Known for their intense hatred for British rule, Shad and Treutlen were exempted from pardon by the British. The bitterness of these two men had its origin in the murder of Frederick's brother, John Adam Treutlen, who, according to one version, was captured by the British and sentenced to be drawn and quartered in the presence of his own family.

Another family anecdote relates how Sarah Wilmington Norton, a granddaughter of Solomon Shad Jr., left Wilmington Island to attend a private finishing school in Baltimore. While at school, the young lady contracted one of the myriad illnesses that abounded in those days when medicine was still in its fledgling stages and died. Her family desired that she be buried on Wilmington Island. For this reason, her body was shipped home in a cask of wine and interred, still in the wine cask, in the Shad vault. During the War Between the States, some marauding Yankee soldiers entered the vault and discovered the cask which they then breached. Elated at the discovery of the wine, they proceeded to drink it.[70] Family legend does not mention whether or not they realized their mistake.[71]

In addition to his properties on Wilmington Island, Colonel Solomon Shad III was the owner of Elba Island in the Savannah River as well. James Whitfield received a Crown grant to Elba Island in 1762, the only known Crown grant to a marsh island. Subsequently, the island was acquired by Noble Jones, and came to Archibald Bulloch, who was a trustee for the descendants of Jones. Acting in this capacity, Bulloch conveyed the title of the island to Colonel Shad. Colonel Solomon Shad, who died in 1833, bequeathed Elba Island to his two sons, Solomon Sigismund Shad and John Robert Shad, and to their descendants.

In 1971, the Southern Natural Gas Company wanted to buy Elba Island to use as a base for Algerian liquefied natural gas. They planned to build a Savannah terminal for an extensive pipeline service. In trying to locate the heirs of Colonel Shad, genealogical researchers eventually discovered more than three hundred Shad descendants.[72] Interestingly enough, although the Shad families were prolific, there were no Shad descendants found by that name in Chatham County, nor were there any across the river in South Carolina where Mongin Shad had his home, and where he produced a large family. As for Colonel Shad, who died on Wilmington Island, he was likely buried in the Shad vault, but the exact location of that vault is unknown. There is no stone which marks his grave.

Recent examination of a piece of property on Wilmington Island that once belonged to the Shad family suggests the presence of an old brick vault. but there is no hard evidence at this writing that this is indeed the Shad vault, or any vault for that matter. The title search for the Shad heirs was described by the attorneys as the largest in the legal history of Chatham County, if not in Georgia. They rather humorously referred to the search as a "Shad fishing" expedition.[73]

[68] Shad, Terri Bray. *The Genealogy of the Shad Family*. Gateway Press, Inc. Baltimore. 1990.

[69] Shad Genealogy File. Georgia Historical Society.

[70] Smith. *Op. cit.*

[71] Shad Genealogy File. Georgia Historical Society.

[72] Sewell, Cliff. One Man's Family," *Savannah News-Press Magazine*, June 6, 1971.

[73] *Ibid.*

The Oemler Family

The Oemler family on Wilmington Island originated with the marriage of August Gottlieb Oemler, a native of Germany, and Mary Ann Shad on July 23, 1838. Armenius Oemler was their son.

Armenius Oemler was born in Savannah in September of 1826. A few years after his birth, his family took him to Germany where he lived for about twelve years. He was educated in Dresden, Germany. When he was still a very young man, he returned to Savannah and studied medicine. He went to New York where he graduated with a degree in medicine, and then returned to Savannah to practice. He married Elizabeth Pritchard Heyward, and soon left his medical practice to enter the rice planting industry. He established a rice plantation in South Carolina, about twenty miles from Savannah.

When the War Between the States broke out, Dr. Oemler enlisted as a private, but then he soon was placed in the Engineering Corps of the Confederate forces. His post in this capacity was the overseeing of the fortifications of Savannah. One of his engineering duties was that of creating a map of Chatham County.

The Oemlers had six children: Augustus Oemler, Elizabeth Latham Oemler, Mary Alexandra Oemler, Norton Oemler, Charlotte Hayward Oemler, and Constantius Heyward Oemler. Of these six, Constantius Oemler was the only one of Dr. Oemler's children to marry, and he remained on the family property on Wilmington Island.[74]

Dr. Armenius Oemler had acquired a reputation of being a prominent citizen and a respected scientist. He contributed articles to many of the agricultural journals of his day, and also to publications dealing with the subject of entomology. A book written by him on the subject of truck farming in the South was considered an authority for horticulturists.[75] He received recognition from the United States Department of Agriculture for his studies in entomology. A paper on this subject was presented by him at one of the monthly meetings of the Georgia Historical Society.

Dr. Oemler was interested also in the oyster culture, and was one of several men who secured the passage of the Georgia oyster law, which stipulated that oyster shells be dumped back into the marshes to provide a foundation for replenishing the oyster beds. He organized the Oemler Oyster Company on Wilmington Island, but it would be his son, Augustus Oemler, who would carry out his father's plans, for Dr. Oemler died August 8, 1897. His funeral service was held at St. John's Episcopal Church, and his body was then placed on the steamer *Doretta* which was docked at the foot of Whitaker Street. His remains were then taken to Wilmington Island and placed in the family burial ground there.[76]

It was Dr. Augustus Oemler, a son of Armenius Oemler, who actually started the oyster plant on Wilmington Island in 1890. This action apparently caused some concern at the time, because existing documents mention a piece of legislation in regard to oyster rights that disturbed some of the island residents during that period.[77] At the January 9, 1890, meeting of the Chatham County Commissioners, Augustus Oemler submitted an application for a lease of five hundred acres of oyster bottom. Constantius Oemler also submitted a similar application for two hundred acres adjacent to that of Augustus. Both of these requests for oyster leases were conditionally granted, subject to the approval of the State Attorney General under the new oyster law.[78]

In March of that same year, Augustus Oemler applied for a charter for the Oyster Company which already had seven hundred acres under lease between the west end of Wilmington Island and Joe's Cut. The company, which was to be organized at an early date, would carry on a general oyster business with Augustus Oemler as the superintendent of the company.

One of Dr. Oemler's proposals was to colonize Wilmington Island with white settlers from Wilkinson County, Georgia. This innovation would provide a labor force for the oyster company. He recruited sixty laborers who agreed to relocate from Wilkinson County to Wilmington Island. The company would furnish the settlers with houses, and each family would be given a plot of land to cultivate. The plan was to let the men raise vegetables for the markets in Savannah. The women and older children would be given jobs shucking and packing oysters. The company would provide steady employment for the women and children six months in the year. A regular village was to be established on the island.[79]

The following year, on January 11, 1892, the Oemler Oyster Company, as it was now called, announced that a Wilkinson County colony of workers would leave Gordon, Georgia, on January 12th, and would be arriving in Savannah on January 13th. The steamer *Camusi*, which was owned by the oyster company, would meet the workers at the Central Railroad wharves, and they and their baggage would be taken by steamer to Wilmington Island. [80]

This undated photograph shows one of the cabins built by the Oemler Oyster Company for its workers. Photo courtesy of the Lynes family.

The Oemler Oyster Company had built eleven cottages to house the workers, and more would be built as they were needed. Employment for entire families would be provided. In connection with the oyster canning factory, the company would also establish a vegetable cannery. This would offer a market for the vegetables grown on the island and elsewhere. The company hoped to produce ten thousand cans per day, and would also begin canning terrapin as well. Dr. Augustus Oemler himself was implementing this ambitious plan under the direction of Colonel John Screven.

The Oemler Oyster Company had applied for thirty-six oyster leases. The Vernon Oyster Company, which had been organized only three nights earlier and was the second oyster company to be established here, had applied for fifty-two leases. The lands which this company had staked out were on the Vernon, Burnsides, and

Gibbons rivers, an area of about 260 acres. A hearing was held on January 19, 1892, at the County Commission meeting to discuss arguments by various interests against the applications by the two companies. Opponents of the leases to both applicants, and also a large number of colored witnesses in attendance, were represented by R. R. Richards, Esq.[81]

Finally, on January 22, twenty-nine leases were granted to the Oemler Oyster Company by the county commissioners, effectively giving control of 837 acres of oyster lands, two hundred acres of which were breeding and propagating ground, to the Oemler Company. The Oemler Oyster Company at this time was producing between four and five thousand cans of oysters daily, but it planned to double this production within two weeks.[82]

At the time these events were unfolding, the Shad River was a large important river, able to accommodate large sailing vessels and wharves. There were wharves all along the bluff where the ships docked with oysters, and it was also from these wharves that ships carried the seafood, vegetables, and produce from the truck farms to market.

Harry King offered these firsthand observations about Mary and Alan Oemler, who were the last of the Oemler family to live in the old homeplace:

> Alan Oemler, who was Mary's husband, was a retired college professor. He was raised on the island. He was somewhat of an archaeologist and had all kinds of artifacts. The island used to be two major plantations. One was the Oemler plantation, and the other was the Walthour plantation. Down on the end where the Oemlers lived, that part was the port of call for all the sailing ships.
>
> The Shad River at that time was an enormous river. It has since filled in and is basically closed now, but Alan had pictures of these big sailing schooners pulled up along a wharf there on the Shad River where they would be loading vegetables that they grew down here on the island for the ships to take up north to sell. Then they also had a big oyster business. That old

oyster shack fell down several years ago, but some of the ruins are still there. The oyster shack was back up toward Oemler Loop Road, which used to be Walthour Road. That old oyster house had forty boats digging oysters from here to Little Tybee in that 'salt meadow.'

The old Oemler place on the Shad River on Wilmington Island. The oldest house still standing on the island, it was built about 1881. Photo courtesy of the Lynes family.

Harry King went on to relate the history of the term, "salt meadow," which is included here in his own words. It seems that Harry's father was the agent for J. D. Powell who owned the DeSoto Hotel and the Savannah Beach Club, as well as some other hotels. Mr. Powell got into a poker game with some cardsharks one day, and they wiped him clean. He was recounting this misfortune to Mr. King, and told him rather mournfully,

'Jeff, I've got to sell some property because I got to get some money together for these guys.'
'Who are they?' Mr. King wanted to know. 'Why don't you just trade something to them?'
'They're from up around Philadelphia or New Jersey or somewhere up there,' was the resigned reply.
Daddy said, 'Well, send them down and let me show them some property you can trade them.'

> Well, Daddy caught a real low tide and took these sharpies out in a boat and told them: 'Now gentlemen, Mr. Powell is willing to give you six thousand acres of this 'salt meadow'.'
>
> He laughed about it later. He said if it hadn't been for the boys down on Tybee who the Mafia were afraid of — actually they were scared to death of them because they were bigger bootleggers than Bugsy Seagram — he would have been in big trouble. When those card sharks found out the trick that had been played on them, Daddy had to the call the Haar boys at Tybee to keep the Mafia from coming down and getting him when they finally realized what he had done.[83]

Today, the Shad River has filled in and has virtually disappeared in places. Prior to 1930, the Shad River channel was sixty feet deep and approximately three hundred feet wide. [84] The small tidal stream that remains today is but a silent wraith of its former days as a very large, deep, and significant river. Many older homes along the river have remnants of boat docks that are no long usable. The disappearance of the Shad River occurred when canal and mosquito control channel work caused the river to silt up, thus rendering the channel nearly dry at low tide.

Possibly some of the silting was also due to natural processes. In 1974, owners and residents on Morningside Drive petitioned the U. S. Army Corps of Engineers to issue a permit for dredging part of the river to make it accessible to boat traffic. This was an attempt to restore the river to its former state. To date, little if anything, has been done to attempt such restoration of the river.

The old Oemler house, said to be the oldest house still standing on the island, sits neglected today in a clearing on a point of high land that rises above what was once the Shad River. The point was once known either as Sampson's Point, or Oemler's Point, depending on the period of time and the person to whom you are talking. An ancient gigantic live oak stands in front near the edge of the bluff. A more modern gazebo is about fifty yards to the right of the house.

Once a large navigable river, the Shad River is shown here. Ships docked near the Barstow home to load vegetables to take to northern markets. Courtesy of the Lynes family.

Access to the house and property is achieved by passing through an old farm gate, the fence of which is overgrown with rambling roses, in full bloom in the hot July sun. It is a pleasant setting, with a breathtaking view of marshes and tidal streams, and the outline of Little Tybee in the distance. The interior walls of the house are of old plaster that has withstood the ravages of time with only a few minor cracks. The floors are so solid one suspects they are the handiwork of a shipbuilder. According to the stories that abound in this isolated corner of the island, the house was built in 1881 with timbers washed up by a hurricane. Indeed, if one examines the beams and underpinnings of the house, it is not difficult to discern that the timbers used in the construction of the house are mismatched, and are of unusual thickness and length.

The house itself is a spacious frame house of simple design. The sharply-pitched, gabled roof is tin. A wide porch wraps around two sides of the house. Inside, a wide hallway leads straight through the house, broken only by the narrow, steep staircase that leads to the upper floor, where two rooms, each with a central chimney and fireplace, contain small dormers and odd crannies. It is a comfortable place, one that inspires a visitor to sit contentedly on the porch or in the gazebo and while away a summer afternoon.

A comment by a realtor suggested that a wealthy Northerner was interested in the property and had tentatively considered tearing the house down in order to build a much larger, estate-type dwelling there. The idea calls to mind efforts to raze the Davenport House in Savannah for a parking lot in the 1950's. Thankfully, the Northerner's plan had to be abandoned due to an unexpected shortage of funds for the project. Recently, I learned that the Oemler house had been sold. The new owner, an antique dealer, intends to restore the house. The historic significance and integrity of the house and property should be preserved. It is the oldest site of its kind left on the island and deserves restoration and preservation.

Not far from the house is a small burial plot. A single obelisk rises from the vines that curl around its base. Inscriptions on three sides memorialize Armenius Oemler, Constantius Oemler, and Thomas Wilson Heyward. Of the other Oemler family members, there is nothing to indicate that they are buried somewhere nearby, though it is quite likely that they, too, lie here. Presumably, their stones have vanished as have so many other gravestones in isolated locations.

[74] Shad, *loc. cit.*
[75] "Dr. Armenius Oemler Dead," *Savannah Morning News,* August 9, 1897, p. 8.
[76] *Ibid.*
[77] *Savannah Morning News*, January 9, 1890, p. 3, c.1&2.
[78] *Savannah Morning News*, March 2, 1890, p. 8 c.2.
[79] "To Colonize Wilmington," *Savannah Morning News*, December 24, 1891, p.8, c.3.
[80] *Morning News*, January 11, 1892, p. 8, c.4.
[81] *Morning News,* January 19, 1892, p. 8, c.1.
[82] *Morning News*, January 22, 1892, p. 8, c,4,
[83] King Interview, July 14, 2000.
[84] "Residents Seek Okay To Dredge In Shad River," *Savannah Morning News*, February 5, 1974, p. 12B.

The Oemler cemetery on Wilmington Island.

Mr. Barstow's Family and the Cuban Filibustering Attempt

In 1840, approximately forty-five percent of the population of Cuba was slave. Wealthy *criollas* and *peninsulares*, the white Cuban elite, were not anxious to free themselves of Spanish rule.[85] Cuba was a thriving nation which supplied nearly a third of the civilized world with sugar. Tobacco and coffee were also major sources of revenue for the little country. Each of these crops depended on the large slave population. The British had abolished slavery in their colonies in 1832 after a slave revolt in Jamaica; Spain had not.

Leonidas Polk was President of the United States in 1848. The nation was busy dealing with a variety of issues, not the least of which was the question of American imperialism abroad. The issue closest to home, however, focused on Cuba, a small Spanish-controlled island nation ninety miles south of Florida. Several Presidents had wanted the United States to buy Cuba from Spain, or failing that, to take Cuba by force. The principal actor in the filibustering drama, Narciso Lopez, was heavily involved in a conspiracy to annex Cuba to the United States. Lopez's motives were questionable. After the failure of the 1850 expedition from New Orleans to Cuba, which consisted of about six hundred soldiers, mostly veterans of the war with Mexico, Lopez sought exile in the United States, where he was active in recruiting a new army for another attempt to free Cuba from Spanish rule.

Between 1849 and 1851, three expeditions were launched against the Spanish government in Cuba. These expeditions were led by the Venezuelan-born General Narciso Lopez, who had previously fought to free South America from the Spanish. The first attempt, which included American soldiers, failed when American federal authorities intervened. In 1850, a second attempt was launched under the leadership of General Narciso Lopez and General Ambrosio Jose Gonzales with private backing from sympathetic Americans and with many Southern volunteers. The forces landed at Cardenas where they were once again defeated by the Spanish.

In the spring of 1851, Lopez sent General Gonzales to Savannah to raise money and men from sympathetic Georgians for a third invasion of the island nation. Lopez had managed to purchase a steamer, the *Cleopatra*, which he sent from Wilmington Island to New Orleans to await troops to sail to Cuba.[86] In the meantime, Gonzales had been in touch with Mirabeau Lamar in Macon, brother to Charles Augustus Lamar of Savannah, and was attempting to gather Southern support and men for the filibustering expedition. The federal authorities tried to thwart this attempt by declaring Lopez and Gonzales outlaws and issuing orders for their arrest. Sympathetic Southerners gave the men refuge and hid them from the authorities. Mr. Elias Barstow was a Whig, and was thus not a Cuban sympathizer, but as a Southerner he offered them his hospitality and the sanctuary of his home. According to family tradition, Gonzales and Lopez were hidden in the Barstow burial vault, and the Negroes on the place brought them food.

The men eventually made their way to New Orleans, and it was from there that the third invasion of Cuba debarked. The troops, with a contingent of Savannah volunteers, landed at Havana in 1851. The Spanish captured General Lopez, and he and fifty-one American soldiers were hanged at Havana in August of 1851. General Gonzales made his way back to the United States and settled in Charleston, South Carolina, where he married a member of the prominent Elliott family.

In 1884, General Ambrosio Jose Gonzales, who was then living in the United States, wrote an account of the 1851 expedition. This account was published in the *Times Democrat* in New Orleans. According to this account, General Gonzales was ordered to Savannah by General Lopez in order to assemble troops and war materials, and to raise money for the expedition. In the spring of 1851, Gonzales was successful in establishing several volunteer companies and raised thousands of dollars for the Cuban cause. The money contributed by Southern sympathizers was used to purchase the steamer *Cleopatra* to transport the troops to Cuba. Armaments from the 1850 expedition were moved from the Gulf of Mexico to Savannah. From Savannah, the steamer was sent in secret to a point just below Darien on the Satilla River. There, at David Bailey's plantation, the vessel was hidden.

General Gonzales then sent a telegram to General Lopez who was waiting in New Orleans, informing him that everything was ready for transporting to Cuba. Lopez, with his staff, traveled to Macon, Georgia, where he met with Gonzales and the companies of Georgia volunteer troops that Gonzales had recruited. In a lengthy explanation published in the April 6, 1884, edition of the *Times Democrat* in New Orleans, Gonzales described the chain of events that then unfolded.

> I received a telegram from our Savannah friends stating that the collector and United States marshal would be at the depot in Savannah to arrest us on our arrival there. I telegraphed back to send a carriage to Station No. 1 on the Georgia Central (ten miles from Savannah). The expedition (about 400 men) was put on the train, and when we reached Station No. 2 (twenty miles from Savannah), was landed and sent under sealed orders to the Satilla River. Gen. Lopez and staff went down to the next station, where we found the carriage, and entered Savannah by country roads in the evening. Of course the collector and marshal inquired for us at the depot but could get so satisfaction from the conductor.
>
> At midnight we were driven by Mr. George McCleskey to Thunderbolt, some five miles from Savannah. There we took a rowboat and went about as many miles down Augustine River and landed on Wilmington Island, at the plantation of Mr. Elias Barstow, a Northern man, married to a Georgia lady. Mr. McCleskey rapped and Mr. Barstow came to the door, wondering what could be the matter at such an unusual hour. Mr. McCleskey stated who we were. 'I

am a Whig,' said Mr. Barstow, 'and opposed to the expedition, but as my guests you are welcome, and my house is yours.'

On the next day a dispatch was received from Mr. O'Sullivan announcing that President Fillmore had seized the *Cleopatra* in New York, and there was an end of the expedition...Orders were given by the government for my arrest. I determined to go for greater safety to Sapelo Island, on the Georgia coast, the property of my friend Mr. Randolph Spaulding. When the steamer *Magnolia* by Capt. McNulty, passed down the river I hailed it; a boat was lowered to take me on board, but as soon as it came within hearing the boatswain roared out to me: 'Go back, go back! The collector and the marshal are on board to arrest you.' I went back, and was sent to the woods where I remained all day, in a continuous rain, with a Negro guide, who sat by me, and brought me my meals.

Meanwhile, the United States officers, who had witnessed their discomfiture from the steamer, caused the captain to land them, and the latter steamed away and left them. They came up to the house and asked for me. Said Mrs. Barstow: 'Do you see that lunch on the table? Well, that is what he has been partaking of.' To which Mr. Barstow added: 'Have you, pray, a search warrant?'
'We do not,'" replied the officers.
'That's satisfactory, ' said Mr. Barstow, 'make yourselves at home.'
Baffled in their endeavor, and having no means to get away, they had to beg Mr. Barstow to send them back to Savannah, which he did after exacting a promise that they would not inquire for me until they got to town.

General Gonzales goes on to say that Mr. Barstow took him by boat to Screven's Ferry in South Carolina. There he met Mr. S. Prioleau Hamilton, the son of General James Hamilton who had once been the Governor of South Carolina. Mr. Hamilton then took Gonzales down the Savannah River. He continues,

> As we were going down we passed the custom-house boat with the collector on board, who had gone to look for me on Dawfawsky (sic) Island, Mr. Mongin's place. Mr. Hamilton, who knew him and his craft, made me lie flat on the bottom of the boat, covered me with an overcoat, and we went unnoticed.

He then mentions arriving at dusk at a landing near the mouth of the river. From this location the small party continued their long journey on horseback to Mr. Hamilton's plantation arriving there at midnight.

Gonzales continues his narrative by telling of his stay in this location:

> In a lonely pine land, in a small wooden house, one mile from the rice fields, I remained secreted for one month in charge of the overseer, an old bachelor. Desirous of inspecting my armament on the Satilla River, and the excitement having subsided, I went down to St Mary's, Ga., on the Florida boundary, for Mr. Bailey's place was only accessible from there by land. I hired a buggy and a Negro guide. It was a long journey through a wilderness of pine woods. At mid-day we were caught in a furious rain and thunder storm and drenched, and what was worse, our horse gave out.

The guide for Gonzales' party recommended that they take a road that led to a cotton plantation. They soon arrived at a cotton field and eventually spotted a mansion with a wide piazza, "raised from the ground in the Southern style."[87]

Gonzales noticed a man standing on the piazza, and approaching it, introduced himself. The gentleman happened to be John Hardee Dilworth, the collector for St. Mary's. Mr. Dilworth informed

Gonzales that although he had a warrant for Gonzales' arrest, he was at home rather than at St. Mary's, and thus he welcomed Gonzales to his house because he sympathized with the Cuban cause.

Gonzales reflects that Mr. Dilworth was "A true type of the Southern gentleman. *Noblesse oblige*. It was a singular accident that I should have come so fortuitously upon the only man south of Savannah who had the authority to hold me."[88]

The newspapers of the day gave false impressions regarding the victories of this ill-fated attempt to overthrow the Spanish in Cuba. General Lopez, inspired by the false talks of victory, left New Orleans with five hundred men. Eventually the troops engaged with the Spanish troops unsuccessfully, and Lopez, along with others, taken prisoner. General Narciso Lopez was executed. General Ambrosio Jose Gonzales sought exile in the United States, and went to Charleston, where he met and married Harriet Rutledge Elliott.[89]

In 1850, various members of the Oemler and Shad families, relatives of Mr. E. B. Barstow, booked passage to New York on the steamer *Isaac Mead*. Mr. Barstow supplied the group with fifty melons that had been grown on his property on Wilmington Island. This number was much too great for the party to consume, so they gave the excess melons to the captain of the ship. Captain Brown of the *Isaac Mead* made the comment that if he had wished to sell the melons, he could have more than paid for the Oemler-Shad party's passage on the ship.[90] This comment would eventually reach Mr. Barstow and he would begin serious consideration of growing melons for the northern market. But tragedy struck the Wilmington Island families in October of 1850.

On October 4th of that year, the *Isaac Mead*, on its voyage from New York to Savannah, was struck by the steamer *Southerner* out of Charleston bound for New York. The *Isaac Mead* sank, taking with it twenty-eight passengers. Among those on board, all of whom were lost, were Miss Catherine L. Barnard, Master John Barstow, Mrs. C. Barnard, all of Wilmington Island, and also Savannah's Dr. E. S. McGinnis, along with his wife and child.[91]

[85] Suchlicki, Jaime, *Cuba From Columbus To Castro and Beyond*, 4th Edition, Brassey's, Washington & London, pp. 55, 62.

[86] Gonzales, Jose A. "The Cuban Crusade, A Full History of the Georgian and Lopez Expeditions," *The Times Democrat*, April 1884, p. 9.
[87] *Ibid.*
[88] *Ibid.*
[89] "Elliott and Gonzales Family Papers," Manuscript # 1009, *Southern Historical Collection*, University of North Carolina, Chapel Hill, N.C.
[90] "Dr. Oemler," *Morning News*, 15 August 1889, p. 8, c. 3.
[91] *Daily Morning News*, 7 October 1850, p.2, c. 1.

Citrus Fruits and Melons

Many of the planters experimented with various crops that might flourish on the islands. Surprisingly enough, citrus fruits seemed to do rather well. Oranges and grapefruits were widely grown and shipped to northern markets, as well as sold locally. In January and February of 1851, William P. Rowland, who operated a store at Number 80 Bay Street, advertised in the *Daily Morning News* that he had received a shipment of 125,000 oranges, "freshly picked from the orange groves on Wilmington island."[92] This contrasts vividly with the news-making event today if a citrus tree in a local resident's yard yields a few edible fruits. Eventually, Wilmington Island would acquire the title "Grapefruit Capital of the World" in recognition of its numerous citrus groves. The groves no longer exist, the once proud title forgotten, but the memory of them lives on in the old news-clippings and advertisements of long-gone newspapers.

In 1853, Mr. Barstow sent his first shipment of melons to the North. This venture was so successful that after two or three years, other planters on the island, such as R. T. Gibson of Whitemarsh, and W. R. Pritchard of Skidaway Island, also began growing and shipping melons.[93] It was not long before the planters in and around Charleston, South Carolina, and other planters in the inland counties of Georgia also began to devote more of their time to the melon industry.

When the War Between the States broke out, interrupted communications made these planters unable to market their crops in the North, and they were forced to take a loss on that year's crop. It was only after the war ended that farmers in these areas were once again able to resume shipping melons to the north. By the 1880's, melons were a major cash crop, but the market suffered in 1889 when there was a glut of melons on the market. In July of that year, more than six hundred carloads of melons were shipped from Savannah in a two-day period alone.[94]

[92] Advertisement. *Daily Morning News*, 15 January 1851, p.3, c.4.
[93] "Dr. Oemler," *Morning News*, August 15, 1889, p. 8.
[94] *Ibid.*

Vandalism

Vandalism of old graveyards and tombs is not a recent phenomenon. Since ancient times there have been those who disturb, destroy, and plunder burial sites for reasons of curiosity, in the name of science, in hopes of recovering various artifacts or treasure, or perhaps that most disheartening reason of all, so-called "progress." Modern society has not been immune to this practice by any means. There is something about an old tomb or crypt, particularly when it is located in a remote area, that attracts those who would desecrate the site for some sort of personal satisfaction or gain. Curiosity seekers compound the problem.

The *Savannah Morning News* carried the story of one such incident that occurred in 1904 at the old Barstow burial place.[95] It seems that a hunting party on Wilmington Island decided to visit the Elias Barstow vault, which was located in an isolated, overgrown area about three miles from the wharf. When they were unable to find the vault, they enlisted the services of an old Negro man who knew its location and agreed to lead the hunting party there.

One member of the party, Mr. Charles Sipple, described the tomb as being constructed of brick, above ground. Unlike other similar vaults in the area, this vault had a wooden door. The door was badly charred by forest fires to the extent that it was no longer hanging properly, and the men could see that the caskets and skeletons had been scattered on the floor. It was obvious that at least two of the coffins were extremely old, being made of cast iron. The others in the vault were modern metallic caskets. It appeared that someone had used a sledgehammer to break open all four of the coffins, and the contents were scattered about. Evidence that a search of the coffins, perhaps for some valuable item that may have been buried with the dead, was obvious to the observers.

Elias B. "Bud" Barstow, who died in late October or early November of 1898, was the last member of the Barstow family to be interred in the vault. He had been found dead in his house on Wilmington Island, and when found, it was apparent that he had been dead for some days, causing his death to be described in the records as "mysterious."[96] The notice in the *Savannah Morning News* for November 3, 1898, invited relatives and friends to attend his funeral on Wilmington Island. The steamer *Mermaid*, leaving from Thunderbolt at 3:00 p.m., would transport those who wished to attend the funeral. The notice went on to say that Mr. Barstow, age 50, was unmarried, and had lived on Wilmington Island most of his life. His mother had died some years before. Elias Barstow was described as a man who had once been possessed of considerable wealth, but in his later years, much of his wealth had disappeared.

The undertaker who had originally interred Bud Barstow in the vault was Albert Goette. Accordingly, the Goette Funeral Home in Savannah was notified of the tomb break-in and vandalism, and they brought new caskets out, placed the Barstow remains in them, and also repaired and replaced the original wooden door. The comment made by some of the parties present during this sequence of events was that Bud Barstow, being the last immediate member of the family, left a large estate which created "considerable litigation" by hopeful heirs to the estate.

Presumably, this vault is the same one referred to in the account of the Cuban incident where General Gonzales and General Lopez were forced to hide from the U. S. Marshals for some length of time. The location of this old burial vault has been lost. Quite likely it was leveled in order to build upon the land on which it stood. It may have been located across Wilmington Island Road from the old Walthour place. If this is the case, then it was razed and paved over by Mr. Walthour who wanted to build a golf course on that site.

Bud Barstow may have been Elias (or Eben) Barstow, Jr., the son of Mary Ann Barnard Barstow and Elias Barstow. Mary Ann Barnard, the daughter of John W. Barnard, married Elias Barstow Sr. in 1834.

[95] "Ghouls Robbed Barstow Grave," *Savannah Morning News*, December 22, 1904. n.p.

[96] Barstow Obituary & Funeral Notice. *Savannah Morning News*, November 3, 1898, p. 6.

ISLAND LEGENDS

Due to the transient nature of living human beings, it is not unexpected that dead ones also wander. Many of the graves that were once on Whitemarsh and Wilmington islands have long vanished, destroyed by natural forces, construction workers, and by blatant vandalism. In talking to older residents of these islands, the stories regarding these old graves and graveyards abound. A few old photographs survive to tantalize the researcher. Sometimes graves were moved, but too often, they were not. Sometimes the dead protest in the only way available to them—by returning!

Tina Pope, a long time resident of Wilmington Island, encountered one of these long-forgotten residents when she moved into her new home on Wilmington Island Road. Shortly after moving into the house, she awakened in the early hours of the morning with the feeling that something was amiss. She recalls waking for some inexplicable reason and seeing a large shadowy figure standing in the door of her bedroom. Being a rational individual, her first reaction was that she was dreaming. After blinking her eyes several times, pinching herself and her sleeping husband, she concluded that she was not asleep and that there was someone standing in the doorway. As her eyes adjusted to the darkened room, she noticed that the dark shape was that of a large man wearing some sort of cloak and a hat. She realized that there actually was someone standing there. Her next thought was that an intruder had entered the house, and that if she remained still and quiet, he would take whatever he was after and leave without knowing that he was being observed. She lay there, terrified and unmoving, watching the figure which just continued to stand there.

At length, as the gray hours of dawn lightened the room, she saw the figure moving away down the hall, and she heard him stop beside a small bathroom down the hallway. When it finally got light, she got up, believing that the intruder had left, and went to check on the house. As she walked through the house, she noticed that the exterior doors were still locked and that the windows were all closed and locked. Nothing seemed to have been disturbed. She then checked the small bathroom, which she and her husband seldom used, and near which she had heard the intruder pause. The small room was extremely cold, more so than other rooms in the house. In relating the story to her husband, he dismissed the episode as a vivid dream, but Tina knew that she had been awake. This was the only time Tina actually saw this unnerving presence.

Several years passed, and the strange episode faded with time, but the eerie feeling persisted that she had not dreamed this occurrence. Tina did notice that this bathroom was always cold, even when the heat was turned on, and that the family dogs absolutely refused to go in that room. She tried not think about it too much, until the day a friend she worked with talked her into joining her into a visit to a psychic, Mrs. Otto Trammer, who lived on Walthour Road. The visit was supposed to be merely a lark, because they had heard about this woman and were curious as to what she would tell them.

Mrs. Trammer used ordinary playing cards to help her focus, and as she laid them out for a reading of Tina's friend, she related the sort of observations that they had expected — family problems which would be resolved, financial matters that needed to be taken care of — the ordinary things commonly heard from people such as Mrs. Trammer.

When the psychic began to "read" Tina's cards, however, Mrs. Trammer's whole demeanor changed, and she told Tina, "You live in a house on property where nothing has ever been built before." Tina nodded, and then Mrs. Trammer continued, "Your house has a long hall, and on the right is a small room. There is a presence in your house. This presence needs help to move on."

Tina was shaken. She had vanquished the old episode from her mind several years past, and had tried not to think about it too much. Mrs. Trammer told her that this presence was a hunter who had been killed or buried on Tina's property. He needed help to cross over. The psychic told Tina that she needed to take a Bible and bury it outside her house near the room where the presence was the strongest, and then to say a prayer for the hunter.

Tina returned home and thought about what she had been told. Finally, feeling slightly ridiculous, she followed Mrs. Trammer's instructions and buried a Bible just outside below the window of the bathroom, saying a prayer for the spirit as she did so. Amazingly, the ritual seemed to work. The tiny bathroom no longer harbors the chill it once did, and the family pets regularly go in and out of the room with no ill effects or reactions.

Several possible explanations offered here present themselves for serious consideration. In researching material for this book, I discovered that a Hunter family once lived on the island. Could this be the name of the presence rather than a descriptive term? Tina has no way of knowing if Mrs. Trammer's statement about a "hunter" may have really referred to "a Hunter." [97]

It was interesting to learn later that a neighbor a few houses away recently had several rather frightening experiences with a tall, dark figure wearing a hat. This spectre appeared in the neighbor's house several times, looming over the bed where she and her husband were sleeping. When this lady mentioned this to her husband, he admitted seeing the same figure sitting in a rocking chair in the their bedroom. This couple, who also have some small children, were terrified enough by this occurrence to ask the Catholic Church for help dispelling this figure. Accordingly, a well-known local priest visited the house in late summer, and with the whole family present, went from room to room, blessing the house. The efficacy of this rather drastic measure has yet to be determined.

John Gammert, son of Fred Gammert and Margie Merken, has lived on the island all of his life. In fact, his father, Fred Gammert, drowned in Wassaw Sound in 1959. Johnny, as he is called, is a member of the Wilmington Island Fire Department, and when interviewed, he offered the following comments regarding old graveyards and tombs:

> There are gravesites all over Wilmington Island. The Hunter Cemetery was on the corner of Todd Street and Wilmington Island Road, and it used to have five or six stones that dated from 1803. The writing was mostly illegible. There were also graves at Twenty-seven Oaks. They were marked with flat stones. The Epting house, next to the old Walthour house and across from the Hunters', was haunted. There were five or six people buried under the house. That house has since been torn down. Over where Grady Hext lives on Walthour Road, at the creek end of Todd Street, there used to be horse stables. There was an old "wishing well" on the property, and there were bones scattered on the ground around the well. There were lots of graves around here at one time. [98]

Another person who was interviewed was Sam Roberts, a long-time resident on the island. In the course of the conversation, Sam mentioned that at one time there were a number of private cemeteries on Wilmington Island. The property at the corner of Todd Street and Wilmington Island Road once belonged to a family named Hunter. There used to be several above-ground tabby vaults there, but when Mr. Walthour built a golf course on that property, he had the vaults knocked down and cemented over. Col. Walthour owned the property from Todd Street north, and later it was sold to Stillwell and Compton. The old horse barns are still there, but the Walthour house, which was shingled, has been altered many times. Another house, one down on the point, was over a hundred years old, and had once belonged to the Weeks family. It was renovated by Don and Judy Martin in the 1970's.[99]

On Morningside Drive there were some more above-ground tabby vaults. They had caved in, and five torpedo-shaped metal coffins could be seen. There was some attempt at archaeological work, and then the coffins were placed in the ground. There were also some old tabby ruins nearby.

The removal or destruction of tombs and graves on the island seems to have been a common practice, particularly when the land was desirable for development. Fortunately, Georgia has recognized the need for laws protecting old gravesites. The Georgia Code is one of the strictest in the nation. It is now illegal to destroy or to disturb a human gravesite, or to remove anything from a gravesite. Penalties for such activities are quite severe and expensive. Regrettably, this law is often ignored, even today. A classic case in point is the vandalism and removal of human remains from the Bryan vault on Talahi Island.

[97] Interview with Tina Pope.
[98] Interview with Johnny Gammert
[99] Interview with Sam Roberts, July 20, 1999.

The Turn of the Century

The 1880's and 1890's saw many changes on the islands. Following the aftermath of the War Between the States and the Reconstruction era, businesses were established, or re-established, fortunes were made by some, and many new people arrived to establish homes on the islands, although only a few were year-round residents at first.

The turn of the century saw summer places being built on Wilmington, Whitemarsh, and Tybee islands, as well as other islands in the southern part of the county. These were occupied mostly by Savannah residents who sought to escape the humid temperatures of the city and to enjoy a leisurely existence on "the salts" during the summer months. A number of Savannah residents spent their summers on Wilmington Island, traveling back and forth to the mainland by steamers which generally ran between Thunderbolt and Wilmington Island. Adam Kessel built a pavilion on the south end of Wilmington Island, and this facility was the scene of picnics and dances and parties. A summer spent on "the salts" was *de rigueur* for many. Several steamers made the trip from Thunderbolt regularly, ferrying passengers to summer homes, parties, picnics, and other social events.

Wild game has been abundant on all of the islands from the earliest times. The woods harbored wild boars, turkeys, deer, and fur-bearing animals in significant numbers. It is reasonable to expect that it was not long before hunters and trappers were using the islands with great regularity for sport and for profit. Indeed, the fur business in Savannah must have been a thriving one by the early 1900's.

The *Savannah Morning News* of November, 1913, commented on the recently opened fur trapping season. Observing that store owners who dealt in hunting and trapping supplies had reported unusually heavy sales of traps in recent weeks, the newspaper suggested that the trapping season promised to be a lucrative one this year. The article mentioned that both black and white trappers had reported a plentiful number of raccoons and brown sea otters in the marshes and swamps of the Savannah River, Ossabaw, Skidaway, and the other islands. It also reported that large quantities of pelts had already been delivered to the fur dealers in Savannah. Raccoon skins were bringing a price of between twenty-five cents to one dollar per hide, depending upon the size of the pelt and the condition of the fur. Some trappers customarily set a hundred or more traps, the cost of which came to twenty-five cents per trap. Good freshwater otter pelts commanded anywhere from ten to sixteen dollars apiece when they were coal black in color. The brown saltwater otter fur brought prices of six to ten dollars, or even twelve dollars each when the skins were in perfect condition and not ruined by improper skinning. Experienced trappers could make enough money in one trapping season to support their families for the rest of the year.[100]

[100] "Trappers Ready For Fur Season," *Savannah Morning News*, November 23, 1913, p.9.

Land Development

In the late 1880's, a group of local investors formed a land company known as the Wilmington Island Pleasure and Improvement Company. The company bought large tracts of land, which they subdivided into smaller tracts and laid out lots which were then sold. The company advertised the sale of lots, and various people and groups purchased many. The Eureka Club, composed of Mr. Claghorn, Mr. Hull, and others, bought one of the lots and built a clubhouse there in March of 1891. Other groups and organizations also considered locating on Wilmington Island. One of the enticements offered by the board of directors of the Wilmington Island Pleasure and Improvement Company was a boat which would make regularly-scheduled runs between Thunderbolt and Wilmington Island. Maps produced by the company showed the layout of streets, a public wharf, a park, and other amenities, including a pavilion on the southern end of the island.

In 1892, Adam Kessel and his associates gave property to Chatham County for use as a park on Wilmington Island. This park, which is shown on early maps, had not been named. It was located directly behind the Kessel house and is today the lot occupied by 1813 Wilmington Island Road. The Kessel group also gave a tract for the public pavilion and the public wharf.[101]

Obviously all was not well with the new developments on Wilmington Island, for in 1895 a lawsuit was initiated in Superior Court by Charles Jemdal against the Wilmington Island Pleasure and Improvement Company, Horace Rivers and Charles H. Dixon.[102] As reported in the *Morning News*, July 31, 1895, this lawsuit was described as "a three-cornered one, being a dispute with regard to the boundaries of some property on the island."[103]

The *Morning News* of August 1, and also August 4, 1895, reported that a verdict was rendered in favor of the defendants in the case of Charles Jemdal and others against the Wilmington Island Pleasure and Improvement Company, Horace Rivers, and Charles

H. Dixon. The final decree was "in accordance with the verdict of the jury which was in favor of the defendants, allowing them to keep the fences across a certain promenade which was laid out according to a plan of a number of lots on Wilmington Island, several of which were sold to the plaintiffs."[104] Strangely, the court dockets for this case, along with the judgments rendered, are missing from the county court files as well as the Georgia Historical Society, where some of the old records were sent, so I was unable to discover the original cause that led to this lawsuit.

One of the early purchasers of a lot on Wilmington Island was Mr. Charles Henry Sipple Sr. He built a summer home at the southern end of the island and named it "Liberty Hall." This house was a large two-story home with large porches on both floors that circled the house. An interview with Mrs. Leonora Sipple Kuhn, who was born in Savannah in 1919, revealed that she was the granddaughter of Mr. Sipple. Her grandfather owned a livery stable on West Broad Street in Savannah. He also operated a mortuary on Hull and Barnard streets and owned a horse-drawn hearse.

Mrs. Kuhn's description of the house called Liberty Hall is as follows:

> There was a large living room, a hallway, and two large bedrooms, each with its own bath, on the first floor. Beyond this, was a dining room, a butler's pantry, another full bath, and two huge kitchens. Each of the kitchens had its own wood stove and huge icebox. An outside shower was used by the family after swimming in the river, and before entering the house. The back upstairs porches were used for additional sleeping, as were the upstairs bedrooms. A large bell in the yard called the family to dinner.[105]

Mrs. Kuhn said that Liberty Hall was quite a gathering place, and a very festive place in the summer time. Located on the property next to the house was a private pavilion where the young people played the piano, danced, drank lemonade, had watermelon cuttings, and oyster roasts. Mr. Sipple had a yacht, the *Ina Louise*, which was used to bring young people from Thunderbolt to Liberty Hall. At that time, Liberty Hall had the only dock on the island and the road to Tybee was still only a dream. The only road from Savannah ended at Thunderbolt.

Because the Sipples were never sure exactly how many young people would be coming to Liberty Hall for the weekend, Mr. Sipple's favorite expression when a large number stepped off the *Ina Louise* was, "Water the tea, and slice the bread thin."[106]

By the late 1800's, as people began to rediscover the islands, particularly those that were suitable for resort areas, it became fashionable to build summer homes on Wilmington Island in order to escape the heat and the bustle of the city, and to enjoy the healthful sea breezes and leisure life upon "the salts," as the marsh islands were called. Some of the summer residents referred to themselves in this idyllic setting on the island as "marooners." There being no road or bridge to the island, it is probable that this fact gave the more imaginative residents a sense of actually being marooned on the island. Steamers sailing out of Thunderbolt (or Warsaw, as this small village had been previously called) made regularly scheduled trips back and forth across the Wilmington River. Many families who owned these summer homes spent the entire summer on the island, while the male heads of the families made daily trips across the river to work at their businesses by day, returning to their families in the evenings.

Miss Mildred Gartelmann, in talking about her family, told me that a large group of Germans came to Savannah in 1890. They all came from the same little place in Germany, and were all related. Her father came to this country in 1880 when but a teenager. Her mother came in 1890. Both of them went to Ascension Church where they met and were later married. Mrs. Gartelmann and Mrs. John Stahmer were sisters. Mildred Katrina Louisa Gartelmann was born in 1899 in Savannah. Mr. Gartelmann, her father, owned a summer home at Vernonburg, but Mildred often visited her Stahmer cousins on Wilmington Island in the summer.[107]

Churches have traditionally played a vital role in the settlement of early communities in this country. This concept applied not only to the cities, but to rural areas as well. It is a concept which survives in modern times as well. Wherever there was an influx of people establishing homes, churches began to be organized and built.

Many of these summer island residents were German Lutherans who were firm believers in religious training for the young. Thus, in the 1890's a Sunday Bible School was organized to educate the residents' children in religious matters. Many of these residents were members of Ascension Church in Savannah. A significant number of Negro families had lived on the islands since the end of the Civil War. Miss Lottie Lang and other members of the ladies' church circle taught the Sunday school for the white children in the morning, and

Mildred Gartelmann, right, and Margie Merken pose on one of the island steamers that made regular trips between Savannah and Wilmington Island. Ca. 1910. Photo courtesy of Lisa E. Murdock.

then again for the Negro children in the afternoon. Miss Lang was the prime force behind the movement to build a church, and by enlisting the aid of some of the other ladies, funds were raised to build a church, which could be used by all denominations, and also by the Union Mission Sunday School. The Wilmington Island Pleasure and Improvement Company donated the land for the church. The plans for the structure were drawn by Mr. J. H. H. Osborne.[108] Accounts from various residents state that summer services were rather informal and flexible. A description of the church indicates that it was made of wood and was a rather rough structure, raised about five feet above the ground. There were shutters at the windows rather than glass. In the summer time pigs often sought shelter from the sun and heat, and their grunts were often audible during the services. Family pets sometimes attended the Sunday School along with their young masters and mistresses.[109]

Some of the other ladies who were instrumental in the fundraising efforts to build the church were Lottie Lang, Louise Carter, Martha

This photograph, taken on Wilmington Island in the early 1900's, shows two unidentified little boys with Millie and Tillie Stahmer.. This may be part of the early Sunday School established on the island. Photo courtesy of Lisa E. Murdock.

Ruwe, Annie Kessel, Josie Lang, Etta Judkins, May Ruwe, and Minnie Schaeffer.[110]

On August 5, 1899, the cornerstone for the Union Mission Church of Wilmington Island was laid. This momentous occasion was celebrated with a large ceremony which included music by the choir of the Lutheran Church of the Ascension in Savannah. A special steamer was engaged to ferry the people from Thunderbolt to Wilmington Island, and then back again in the afternoon.[111]

In 1918, Miss Lottie Lang and others organized a Bible School for the Negro children. Socials, games, and activities for the children were held regularly. However, in 1920, the church closed due to illness in Miss Lang's family which necessitated her leaving the island. Although several people tried to keep the church going, it was not a successful effort as attendance declined. Finally, in 1922, the Bible School for the Negro children resumed, and by 1923, Miss Louise Sipple was conducting a daily Vacation Bible School for the Negro children. Records from 1924 indicated the total attendance was 102 children. Dr. G. Hermann Lang and Mr. Elmo Weeks were Trustees during this period. Miss Lottie Lang received the deeds to the church property on Wilmington Island from Mrs. Anna Chisholm.

Miss Mildred Gartelmann, age 101, in August 2000.

By 1936, there were no longer any Negro children and few adults on the south end of the island. Therefore, the services for the Negroes, which had begun in 1918, came to an end. The Wilmington Island Union Mission Church on Skidaway Road was located there on the mainland when its black congregation relocated there.[112]

Eventually from these early efforts, the Lutheran Church of the Redeemer was formed in 1948 to accommodate the growing number of families who had become permanent or year-round residents on the island.

During the late 1880's, the Wilmington Island Pleasure and Improvement Company bought large tracts of land on the island and subdivided large portions. Maps from this period show lots and streets laid out, and special features such as a park, a public wharf, and a pavilion.

Many various organizations and social groups took full advantage of the recreation offered on Wilmington. It became a popular destination for numerous outings. The German Club of Wilmington Island permitted the Episcopal Home for Girls to use its clubhouse so that the girls from the home could spend part of the summer "on the salts."

Eventually the German Club relocated to Bona Bella. Activities taking place on the islands were deemed newsworthy and received mention rather frequently in the Savannah paper.

One item in the *Morning News* of July 24, 1895, described the Ancient Order of Hibernians' picnic on Wilmington Island. Part of the entertainment for this event consisted of a number of athletic activities, including the 100-yard dash, putting the shot, and throwing the hammer. The running high jump on that occasion was tied between Jerry F. O'Connor and B. L. Spindle, and a toss-up was necessary to determine that O'Connor was the winner of that event. The 100-yard dash also ended in a dead heat between Joe Counihan and R. A. Brady. A run-off was necessary to proclaim Counihan the winner. A few days later the *Morning News* made mention of a group of ladies of Wilmington Island who presented Captain J. J. Judkins, the owner and master of the steamer *Flora,* with a marine clock in appreciation for his courteous and obliging conduct of the steamer and his efforts to insure the comfort of the passengers who traveled back and forth to Wilmington Island on his vessel. Dr. George H. Stone made the formal presentation on this occasion.[113]

According to Marion Boyd, there were several black families who lived on the island and had been there for quite a long time. Two of them he recalled were the Solomons and the Isaac Youngs. He described these families as hard-working, God-fearing people who made their living mostly by oystering, fishing, and shrimping. The Isaac Young family had a small farm across from where the Methodist Church is now. Mr. Young sold the vegetables from his farm in a truck. He went from door to door. He also had a pavilion and a kind of night club which hosted parties from the mainland. That is now the location of the Young's marina.

Mr. Boyd's grandfather was Barton R. Rhines, a farmer from

Pennsylvania who came to the island to plant not crops, but flowers. Mr. Rhines established a large bulb farm and shipped irises and gladioli up North. He built not only a two-story dwelling for his family, but also packing houses and houses for his workers. This farm and business was located on property where a kind of mini-mall sits today. There was a two story log cabin there, the ground floor of which was a small grocery, while the upper floor was a sort of dance hall. There was one gas pump in front.

By the spring of 1922, the construction of a primitive road and bridge was completed, thus making the island accessible to the general public by automobile. This early road was made of oyster shell. As a result of this improvement, extensive development of the island was initiated. Permanent homes, as well as summer cottages, were built. The *Savannah Morning News,* dated May 24, 1922, in a rather lengthy article, described some of the new homes being constructed on the island, as well as those older summer residences which were being renovated. Of particular note was the new home of Henry S. Walthour which had just been completed and boasted six bedrooms, a library, living room, breakfast rooms, pantries, and a kitchen. The kitchen contained the most modern cooking facilities, and it came equipped with such wondrous conveniences as electric light, speaking tubes, electric bells, and a huge garage with spaces for "machines," as automobiles were then called. There were also quarters for the maids, chauffeurs and other servants.

Dr. Hermann Lang purchased the Osborne house. He had the house renovated and improved by installing running water, showers, and servants' quarters and garages. Next door his neighbor, Henry C. Greene, improved his own house by adding a sun parlor where Miss Helen Greene planned to open a tea room which she intended to name "The Green Door Tea Room." Other island residents who immersed themselves in the home improvement and home building frenzy were Mr. and Mrs. Nicholas Lang, Charles H. Sipple, William H. Artley, Armand Chapeau, Mrs. John Buckman, Mrs. Harriet Rossignol, and Dr. J. O. Baker.[114] Some of these homes were intended as summer homes, while others would become permanent residences.

Unidentified scene on Wilmington Island, photo dated 1911.
Photo courtesy of Georgia Historical Society.

An early, undated advertisement by the Dexter Realty Company of Savannah, describes the house known as Twenty Seven Oaks which was owned by the late Colonel Bratton. It was considered a "commodious year 'round home in a choice location." The advertisement went on to describe the three large porches which ran the full width or length of the house, one screened, one open, and one glassed in. The most notable feature of the house was the English basement which contained a large kitchen with a fireplace, as well as numerous large rooms, all designed for luxurious living. The sale of this property also included a number of modern appliances such as a television antenna, electric dishwasher, Venetian blinds, and many other items necessary to maintain a luxurious life style.

[101] *Morning News*, March 7, 1891, p.8, c. 6.
[102] *Morning News*, July 31, 1895, p.5, c.4.
[103] *Ibid.*
[104] *Morning News,* August 1, 1895, p.8, c.4.
[105] Telephone interview with Mrs. Leonora Sipple Kuhn, January 25, 2000.
[106] *Ibid.*
[107] Interview with Miss Mildred Gartelmann.
[108] Gartelmann, Mildred, *Early History of the Lutheran Church of the Ascension, Savannah, Georgia,* n.d., p. 34.

[109] *Ibid.*
[110] "Exercises at Wilmington," *Savannah Press*, August 5, 1899, p.1.
[111] *Ibid.*
[112] Gartelmann, *op. cit.*, p.34.
[113] "Wilmington Island Scene of Activity," *Morning News*, July 26, 1895, p.8, c.4.
[114] *Ibid.*

Two early 1900's homes on the Wilmington River. Both were part of the building boom that followed construction of a bridge to the island. The older house facing the water is the Walthour house; the other is known as Oakley.

Wilmington Island Tragedies

In the natural order of things, misfortune has a way of intruding into the most idyllic settings and situations. Although the island was only rather sparsely populated until well into the 1960's, Wilmington Island has had an unusual number of tragedies throughout its recorded history. Many of them are related to its status as an island, and therefore, its proximity to large bodies of water and the dangers, occupations and pursuits found in such areas. As is often the case, many of these tragedies seem to involve young people. The story of Carl and Johnny Stahmer in 1922 is one such tragedy.

In order to establish a little background on these young men, it is necessary to go back to the year 1917. In July of that year, John Stahmer Sr. died at age fifty-eight. He had been born in Schoenebeck, Germany, but was evidently one of the German immigrants who came to the United States around the turn of the century. He married Catherine Gartelmann and had two sons, John William and Carl F. Stahmer, and two daughters, Matilda and Millie Stahmer. Mr. Stahmer was one of the regular summer residents of Wilmington Island, and it is quite probable that he instilled a love of hunting in his young sons.

According to his niece, Miss Mildred Gartelmann, John Stahmer Sr., had a large boat somewhat like a regular steamer that would hold at least eight people. Miss Gartelmann told me that they used to have to take a streetcar from Savannah to Thunderbolt. At least one of those times, the Stahmer boys took her and other cousins across the river to Wilmington in their canoes one night. They went down the wrong creek and got lost.[115]

Certainly, from later accounts and old photographs, both boys were blessed with a good-natured sense of humor and a fun-loving personality. Evidence of these traits are reflected in a newspaper article in the *Savannah Morning News*, dated November 1921, the headlines of which read, *Nimrods Haled To Court Say Were Accompanied On Chase By Diana Duo*, tells of an incident in which Johnny, and a friend, L. T. Jones, were charged with hunting on posted property on Wilmington Island. Mr. Henry G. Green who owned the property in question had brought the case to the police court. On Thanksgiving afternoon, the young men were ordered off the property by Mr. Green, and an argument ensued. At the court hearing, the two young men testified that they were not the only guilty parties, but that two young ladies dressed as males in soldiers' uniforms had accompanied them on the hunting expedition. The names of the two young ladies were not mentioned for the sake of propriety. The disposition of this case was not reported, but presumably amends were made to the satisfaction of all involved with no lasting hard feelings between the involved parties. Johnny eventually went to work at the Citizens and Southern Bank, as did his cousin Dennis Harvey.

Carl and Johnny Stahmer, and Dennis Harvey. Photo was taken at the south end of Wilmington Island during the summer of 1921. Photo courtesy of Mildred Gartelman.

The following year, events unfolded that resulted in a double tragedy. The Stahmers were then living on Wilmington Island. On Sunday morning, December 10, 1922, young Carl Stahmer, who was then fourteen years old and his older brother Johnny, who was twenty-four at the time, decided to go duck hunting. With them was their twenty-one year-old cousin, Dennis Harvey. John had procured a canoe for the hunting trip. Both John and Dennis wore high boots and carried two pump guns loaded with Number 4 shot. Mrs. Stahmer said that whenever John went hunting, he never, never put bullets in the gun ahead of time. Instead, he always waited to load the gun until he reached the hunting site. He wore a belt that held the bullets until they were needed. The morning the boys were killed, a neighbor came across the road and handed Johnny two or three bullets which he had previously borrowed. Since Johnny's belt was already full of bullets, he put the returned bullets in his gun.

When the three started out that fateful Sunday morning, the tide was low, and they had to push the canoe out of the marsh into the water. Since Carl Stahmer was not equipped with boots, Johnny lifted his younger brother into his arms to wade out to the canoe.

John placed Carl in the stern of the canoe and handed him the two guns they were carrying. Carl placed the two guns against one of the cross braces with both of the barrels pointed toward the stern.

Carl knelt in the canoe, and both John and Dennis pushed the canoe away from the marshy shore. As the boys shoved the canoe into the water, one of the guns dropped and discharged. The recoil caused the other gun to fire as well, striking the first gun. Charges struck all three boys. Carl received the full force of the blast which penetrated his chest, killing him instantly. John Stahmer was hit in the leg above his boots, and Dennis Harvey received eleven small shots in his legs. The injuries sustained by Dennis were not serious, and he was sent home to recover from his wounds.

Johnny, who was able to give the details of the accident to the Chatham County Police, was taken to St. Joseph's Hospital in Savannah. Miss Gartelmann told me that the accident occurred on a Sunday, and that young Carl Stahmer was buried on Monday from the Gartelmann house on Fortieth Street. She said, " Johnny got what people called 'gas bacillus' on Tuesday, and his leg was amputated on Wednesday. Thursday, Johnny died. He was buried from our house on Friday."[116]

The Stahmer accident was not the only hunting accident to occur on Wilmington Island. In 1886, the *Savannah Morning News* carried the following item:

> August 19, 1886. Shortly before Tuesday midnight, Mr. O. L. Tilton was brought to the city from Wilmington Island suffering from a gunshot wound inflicted by his young son, Octavius, who had been playing with a shotgun. Drs. Purse and Duncan were summoned and treated the patient. Yesterday the wounded man was doing as well as could be expected, but his condition is very critical.

Other tragedies, many of which were directly related to the surrounding waters, also occurred on the islands. There are many accounts of drowning, lightning strikes, fires, and boating accidents.

The *Morning News* reported an account of one of these tragedies that happened on March 1, 1891. This story concerned E.J. Dawson, a farmer whose age was given as between sixty-five and seventy years old. Mr. Dawson had gone out in his boat which ran aground on a mud-bar between Fort Oglethorpe and Mackey's Point. His body was discovered by a range light keeper named Daniel Z. Duncan. The body was examined by the coroner for Chatham County who ruled that the old man's death had occurred from exposure to the cold while on his way from Savannah to Wilmington Island. Since it was not necessary to hold an inquest, the coroner, who also happened to have an undertaking establishment, took Dawson's body to his mortuary to await instructions from Dawson's sons who lived in Augusta.

This article went on to say that Mr. Dawson was a Confederate veteran who had once been a wealthy businessman in Charleston where he had owned a large stationery business before the war. He was quite well-known in Savannah. His wife was related to Dr. Oemler, and they had lived on Wilmington Island for a long time, apparently engaged in farming, as this was given in the report as his occupation.

Accidents and tragedies such as these were repeatedly written up in the newspapers. A more modern example was that of James A. Duncan, a teacher who had once taught mathematics at Savannah High School. Mr. Duncan had retired in 1932, and lived on Wilmington Island. His friends on Wilmington Island knew Mr. Duncan as being an avid fisherman. In October of 1953, Mr. Duncan set out in his boat on a fishing trip. On the morning of October 30th, Sammy Tattnall, a Negro fisherman, discovered Duncan's body on a mud bank along the Half Moon River. It was believed that Mr. Duncan, who was seventy-seven years old, had a heart attack and had fallen out of his boat.[117]

Mildred Gartelmann's description of Wilmington Island during the early 1900's reiterates accounts by other people I interviewed. She remembers that the only road on Wilmington Island went from the south point to the houses at the other end. There was a very high bluff that sloped down and flattened at one end. She emphasized that she was not referring to the northern end of the island, but what she, as a child, perceived to be the end of the island. From a child's point of view, the island consisted of the part which extended from the public wharf north along the only road which ended only a short distance away. She said they used to walk from the high bluff through the woods to what was called the "shell rake." This was an area that was full of oyster shells, and someone had built a small shack there and sold oysters. The only transportation to the islands in those days was by steamer, and there were many steamers that made regular trips from Savannah and Thunderbolt to the various islands.

One of these steamers was the *Clivedon*, which Mr. Boyd said made regular daily runs from Savannah to Beaufort. It carried supplies as well as passengers. The *Clivedon* stopped at all of the islands in between, including Beaufort and Daufuskie Island. "Sometimes you could see the *Clivedon* just stopped in Calibogue Sound. In a short while you would see a little boat row out and a person would board the waiting steamer." He recalled that sometimes there would be a funeral, and the relatives and friends of the deceased would take the body home on the *Clivedon*. He said it was easy to know when this occurred, because the sound of the mourners singing or chanting would carry across the water.

In the 1950's, Wilmington Island caught the attention of land developers who were looking for investments in large homesites. This echoed a vision first proposed by Henry C. Walthour who had dreamed of an exclusive residential community in the early 1900's. A group, composed of Maxwell W. Lippitt, Sarah Walthour Stillwell, Helen Walthour Clark, Virginia Walthour Moss, and others joined with William Lattimore to develop such a community. The original acreage for this new development, a total of six hundred acres, came primarily from the Walthour and Lippitt families. Wilmington Park, as the venture was named, was to be a planned community made up of one thousand large homesites on which would be constructed higher priced homes. Included in the plan were a number of improvements such as paving and curbing, landscaping with winding streets, schools, churches, and recreational facilities. The Wilmington Park Home Association would levy annual dues for security, maintenance, lighting, and other amenities.[118]

In 1957, the Board of Education accepted a deed for the gift of a ten-acre tract for an elementary school. Additional acreage was also acquired for a junior high school should the anticipated increase in population warrant an additional school. The first phase of this planned community opened in 1958. A number of homes were constructed, and a new era of suburban living was launched.

Today, building construction covers much of the island to such a great extent that long-time residents fear overcrowding. Sections of forested land are being cleared at a rapid rate, and the face of the land itself is being altered to such a degree that in recent weeks a moratorium has been temporarily enacted on new construction in order to assess what is occurring on the island, and to determine necessary procedures and guidelines for future responsible development so as to address environmental and ecological concerns.

A long time resident on Wilmington Island, Sam Roberts, consented to talk about his recollections of earlier days on the island. Sam stated that he had been coming to Wilmington Island since the 1920's, and he and his wife, Addie, who is eighty, have lived on the island since the 1930's. At the time of the interview, July of 1999, Sam was eighty-nine years old. He died six months after the interview, on January 17, 2000.

Mr. Roberts began by talking about a black couple, Uncle Jack and Lizzie Tattnall who lived on Walthour Road and were the caretakers at Half Moon River. "Uncle Jack" kept a boat at the Roberts' bluff way before the Roberts moved to Wilmington Island. Tattnall and his wife made their living by working the river — fishing, oystering, and by hiring themselves out for odd jobs. Uncle Jack lived to be way up in his hundreds. As an elderly man, he still rowed into Thunderbolt daily. When questioned about his longevity, Tattnall attributed his long life to his daily practice of drinking the phosphorous rich water from Wassaw Sound as a cure-all. [119]

Older black residents of Wilmington Island were interviewed in the 1940's when the Georgia Writers' Project of the W.P.A. collected and published a study of the coastal Negroes entitled *Drums and Shadows*. The people who were interviewed at that time were those like Jack Tattnall who made a living by shrimping, crabbing and fishing in the Wilmington River. Tattnall was born on the island and spent his entire life there. A son of Jack's, Gene Tattnall, also lived on Wilmington Island. Robert Pinckney, a slave, came to Wilmington Island from Clinch County, Georgia, with his new owner in the late 1850's. After the War Between the States, he remained on the island. Others who lived on Wilmington Island during the period surveyed by the W.P.A. were Lonnie Green, Jack Pinckney, Celia Small, and Peter McQueen.[120]

Uncle Jack Tattnall's name was one which cropped up more than once when talking to some of the older people who consented to interviews. Marion Boyd remembered Uncle Jack and his twin sons, Sam and David Tattnall. They all made their living from the river. Boyd made the comment that these Tattnalls all made their own boats and oars. Uncle Jack used a sand firebox and a piece of old canvas in his boat to keep warm in the winter evenings when he would be rowing back to the island. Boyd said that many times on winter evenings his family would be returning by boat to Wilmington Island from Thunderbolt and would come upon Uncle Jack. They would take him in tow and bring him home to the island.

Some of these older residents were buried on the island near the old Indian mounds. A few of the descendants of these old families still live on Wilmington Island and on Whitemarsh Island, near Turner's Creek, but most have moved on to other homes elsewhere. The old river men no longer make their living from the waters of Wassaw Sound and the tidal creeks that surround the island. The old truck farms are gone as well.

[151] Gartelmann Interview August 30, 2000.

[116] Interview with M. Gartelmann

[117] "James A. Duncan Drowns While On Fishing Trip," *Savannah Evening Press*, October 30, 1953.

[118] "Wilmington Island Park, Pattern For Suburban Living," *Savannah News*, February 16, 1958, p. 8C.

[119] Roberts Interview, July 20, 1999.

[120] Georgia Writers' Project, W.P.A., *Drums and Shadows,* University of Georgia Press. Athens, 1940, pp. 103-108.

The General Oglethorpe Hotel

It was the early 1920's when a group of investors led by Thomas P. Saffold formed a company known as The General Oglethorpe Hotel Corporation. Henry C. Walthour, who was vice-president of the corporation, donated land overlooking the Wilmington River for the new hotel. Stock was sold, and the resulting Spanish style structure was built at a cost of $1.9 million dollars.

The General Oglethorpe Hotel opened its doors to guests in 1927. It was touted as the grandest hotel in the area, complete with its own golf course designed by Donald Ross, the renowned architect of fine golf courses. Guests could choose to play the very private Walthour course, as well as the Ross course. A stable with thoroughbred horses and a swimming pool, filled by an artesian spring, and an elaborate diving tower were also part of the numerous attractions offered to guests.

Sand-clay tennis courts were available for the pleasure of hotel guests, and fishing was possible either from the hotel's private dock, or by motorboat on the river. Two hundred guest rooms, several dining rooms, and a huge lounge were prominent features of the new hotel, as were the tiled plaza and the pavilion near the pool where tea was served.

An early undated brochure publicizing the hotel listed the hotel rates in several categories of accommodations as follows:

> Single room with bath, $11.00 to $13.00 per day
> Double room, with bath, $18.00 to $22.00 per day
> Other rooms, $6.00 to $8.00 per day
> Greens fees were $10.00 per week

Horseback riding was one of the many activities available at the General Oglethorpe. This 1900's postcard shows some hotel guests enjoying a morning ride. Postcard courtesy of V & J Duncan Antique Maps, Prints & Books, Savannah, GA.

The General Oglethorpe became the scene for numerous social events and attracted guests from all over the country. Well-known jazz bands played in the ballrooms.

The hotel operated for several seasons under the leadership General J. Leslie Kincaid, president of the American Hotels Corporations. Mr. J. Melvin Derr was the manager. One of its outstanding features during this period was the large trunk room or closet in each of the bedrooms. A large variety of activities and entertainment was planned for guest and visitors, with weekly programs being printed in the newspaper. In addition to the golfing, swimming, and dancing, there were formal banquets, trap shooting, motoring, and speed boat trips.[121]

In 1933, the hotel was purchased by Mr. and Mrs. B. B. Cain, Jr. of Washington. They made elaborate plans to reopen the resort after renovating the hotel to include a heating and cooling system. At a cost of $50,000, the entire hotel would be cooled by refrigerated air during the summer. This innovation would be a great advantage over other comparable hotels. No other hotel would have such a system.[122] The resort also planned to have a live orchestra playing at dinner dances every evening which would include a five-course

An image from a brochure advertising the new General Oglethorpe Hotel in a pastoral setting pictured farming methods used on the islands as late as 1930. Photo courtesy V & J Duncan Antique Maps, Prints & Books, Savannah, GA.

dinner for the price of one dollar, and there would be no cover charge. The hotel was to be designed to provide the best of everything for the people of Georgia, although, according to a newspaper article, people from places outside of Georgia would be welcome also. The luxury hotel was planned to open in May of 1933.[123]

The best-laid plans, however, have a way of not always coming to fruition. In 1935, the hotel was sold once again. This time when it reopened, it would be one of the DeWitt Hotels, a well-known chain at that time. Theodore DeWitt, president of the Cleveland, Ohio, company announced that he planned to spend a sizable sum on renovations and improvements to the facility. The General Oglethorpe Hotel would be open year-round.[124]

A bankruptcy action filed in Ohio in 1937 resulted in yet another reorganization of the Oglethorpe. The Oglethorpe Company conveyed all of the hotel property, under a debt deed, to a group of trustees which included Mr. L. H. Smith and Mr. H. M. Bissell, among others.[125]

Three years later, the Hotel General Oglethorpe was sold yet again at public auction at the Chatham County Courthouse. This

A view of the General Oglethorpe Hotel as seen from the Wilmington River. Photo courtesy V & J Duncan Antique Maps, Prints & Books.

sale was undertaken to perfect the title before being transferred to new owners. These new owners, the J. B. Pound Hotels, were said to be experienced in hotel operations, and planned to reopen the hotel in June of 1940.

The old hotel was the site for the International Monetary Conference in March of 1946. Two hundred fifty delegates from forty-five nations, along with more than a hundred financial writers, photographers, and newspaper reporters, attended this conference. The purpose of the conference was to promote foreign trade and to organize a World Fund and Bank. One of the delegates to the conference was Lady Nancy Astor. She amused the delegates with her witty quips and remarks, one of which attained widespread attention. She referred to Savannah as "a lovely lady with a dirty face."[126]

The hotel's popularity notwithstanding, the General Oglethorpe was once again placed on the market. This time, Sidney L. Albert of Akron, Ohio, a financier with a controlling interest in the Bellanca Aircraft Corporation and a total of seventy other companies, including the Waltham Watch Company, bought the hotel in 1956. Once more, the structure was to undergo massive renovation and improvement.

Included in the plans of the new owner was the addition of a 400-foot white sand beach on the Wilmington River, and a sprinkler system to be installed on the golf course. The newspapers mentioned that the new owner would construct a barbershop, beauty parlor, and exclusive clothing shops for men and women. There would also be a large auditorium capable of seating fifteen hundred people. A future consideration would be the construction of a villa-type building with fifty additional rooms. The well-known Crystal Ballroom was scheduled to be enlarged as well. Mr. Lloyd Bumpas would be the new manager.[127]

These ambitious plans followed the same pattern as previous ones. The hotel seemed ill fated. In 1961, the Teamsters' Union Pension Fund acquired the General Oglethorpe properties in foreclosure proceedings. Jimmy Hoffa, who was then president of the Teamsters' Union, announced that the hotel company had defaulted on a $2.4 million loan made in 1959. A hotel consultant from Miami made the bid for $1.9 million at public auction at the Chatham County Courthouse for properties which included the DeSoto Beach Hotel and the Savannah Motor Lodge, as well as the General Oglethorpe Hotel.[128]

An interesting note to the history of the hotel was the announcement in 1963 by a man named Leighton Nieman of St. Louis, that the Oglethorpe had been sold once again, and would be reopened as a retirement center. Mr. Nieman stated that he was the executive director of the General Oglethorpe Retirement Center, Inc., and that he would come to Savannah in April to direct this new venture. When the current hotel management was questioned about this transaction, the personnel stated that they were unaware of such a sale. Representatives of the Teamsters' Union also denied knowing anything about this alleged sale. Mr. Nieman was contacted for a comment, and again he confirmed his original statement regarding the retirement center, which he said would cater to senior citizens and provide an active retirement in luxurious surroundings. An open house was planned February of 1963.[129] As with so many others, these plans also failed to materialize.

Between 1961 and 1982, the hotel attracted the attention of unsavory groups from the northeast because of its seclusion. Some of the rather notorious names associated with organized crime were often registered as guests. Their young girlfriends accompanied them and were frequently photographed enjoying the amenities of the secluded hotel, along with their companions of dubious reputation. One of these frequent guests was Anthony Provenzano, a known member of the Mafia. Another name associated with the Chicago mob was Lou Rosanova, who was the executive director of the hotel in the 1970's.

During this period, the Teamsters' Union, which was under investigation by a United States Senate Committee, bought and sold the hotel twice. One of the more persistent rumors circulating about the General Oglethorpe occurred in 1975 when the infamous Jimmy Hoffa disappeared in Michigan. This happened to be the same time it was decided by the owners of the hotel that a helicopter pad was an immediate necessity, and a rush job was arranged in order to have the concrete for the pad poured during the night.

This gave rise to the story that Hoffa's body had been buried under the concrete of the helicopter pad. This particular rumor has never been laid to rest and is yet another piece of Wilmington Island lore.

The luxury hotel was purchased by the Sheraton group and was renamed the Sheraton Savannah Resort. It was operated under this management until 1994 when the doors of the hotel closed once more. It was used as the venue for the Olympic Yachting events in the 1996 Olympics.

A Macon developer, Bill Foster, bought the grand old hotel which had been vacant since 1994. The selling price was $6.5 million. Foster is currently renovating the hotel and also constructing condominiums on the site. This time, the old hotel will serve as a clubhouse and will house amenities for the planned condominiums.

[121] "General Oglethorpe, South's Newest Hotel, Will Open on Monday," *Morning News*, October 16, 1927.

[122] "Wilmington Island Resort to Have New Features," Morning News, February 18, 1933.

[123] *Ibid.*

[124] "Wilmington Island Hotel Sold, DeWitt Acquires Property Today," *Savannah Press*, August 6, 1935.

[125] "Reorganization of Oglethorpe Hotel," *Savannah Press*, February 2, 1937.

[126] "Scene of World Monetary Conference," *Savannah Morning News,* January 8, 1946.

[127] "Associates in Bellanca Buy Gen. Oglethorpe," *Savannah Evening Press*, March 13, 1956.

[128] "Teamsters Union Buys Savannah Inn," *Savannah Evening Press*, February 3, 1970.

[129] "Hotel Sale By Union Reported," *Savannah Morning News*, January 18, 1963.

SKIDAWAY ISLAND

Skidaway Island, located about nine miles south of Savannah, and approximately eight miles long and three miles wide, was the site of one of the early colonial settlements in 1734. It covers an area of approximately eight thousand acres of land once considered excellent land, suitable for the cultivation of Sea Island cotton. It, along with the Tybee settlement and the settlement at Thunderbolt, served as one of the guardians of the water passages leading into Savannah. The northern end of the island was the site of a small fort near the site of the present Skidaway Institute of Oceanography.

The original inhabitants of Skidaway Island, like those of the other marsh and sea islands, were native Americans who hunted and fished. The woods were full of various nuts, acorns, and berries which provided additional sustenance. The cultivation of corn came later, and it was during this time that a more complex society developed and created a set of religious ceremonial practices. The archaeological surveys conducted at different times on the island indicate that fifty-six significant sites have been located. Of these, the ceremonial shell rings, which according to the archaeologists date to 1750 B.C., are most significant.[130] The rings are located at three different sites on the island, and are of particular interest due to the fact that there are only about fifteen such shell rings known to exist, and these are all along the southeastern coast of the United States, with the exception of one in Ecuador.[131] Two of the rings on Skidaway Island are located on the shoreline on the eastern side of the island. V. E. Kelly says in his history of Skidaway Island that the larger one is about five feet high and two hundred feet in diameter. It is located on what is now private property. A smaller shell ring is located about one hundred feet out in the marsh, and may be fully visible only at low tide. It, too, is about five feet in height. The third ring is located on the southeastern shore near Adams Creek, and is referred to as "Indian Fort." It stands about six hundred feet out in the marsh.[132]

The early settlement, established by General Oglethorpe, consisted of five families and six single men who had arrived on the *James* in January of 1734 from England. In the process of selecting colonists to settle on Skidaway Island, a critical error was made. Not one of the people chosen by Oglethorpe to live on Skidaway Island was a farmer. There was a wigmaker, a shoemaker, and a ropemaker. There was also a bookbinder, a former soldier, and a victualler.[133] The plan of the Trustees was for the colonists to provide for themselves by raising food crops and livestock such as cows, pigs, and chickens. Given the makeup of the group sent there, it is not surprising that they were unable to establish a successful settlement on the island.

While the Trustees initially issued supplementary rations to help the colonists establish themselves, the poor quality of the soil and their lack of agricultural experience doomed this settlement to failure. Within the first year or two, most of these early settlers had succumbed to the various fevers and diseases that prevailed throughout the coastal region. Although the military reasons behind the selection of this site on the island were legitimate ones, that particular location was not one suited to agriculture, and as a result, only one of the original families remained on the island in 1740, the others having either died or left the island.[134]

During the period between 1754 and 1771, approximately twenty-two people received grants of lands on Skidaway Island. Although no fortifications were built on the island in Revolutionary times, there were lookout points. Colonel Lachlan McIntosh sent a detachment of men to Skidaway in August of 1776. British marines landed on Skidaway in 1782 after Savannah was evacuated by the British. This group of British were driven off by a group of American forces. This was probably the only action to occur on the island during the American Revolution.

One of the early families on Skidaway Island was that of Thomas Mouse. After death of Thomas, his wife, Lucy Mouse, gave their tract of land to her grandson, William Norton. The daughter of Thomas and Lucy Mouse, also named Lucy, married a man by the name of Peter Tondee and moved into Savannah to live. Lucy Mouse Tondee would be remembered for providing her tavern as a meeting place for the Liberty Boys in Revolutionary Savannah, after the death of her husband Peter Tondee in 1775.

Another early family which settled on Skidaway was that of Thomas and Frances Smith. Soon after establishing a home on the island, Frances gave birth to a daughter. The child was given the name Anne Skidaway Smith.

Early newspapers carried many items of interest that relate to the islands. One such newspaper item from *The Columbian Museum and Savannah Advertiser* on October 15, 1799, told of the cotton planting being done on the island around Savannah. It mentioned that in 1767, John Earle of Skidaway Island had planted a crop of what would later be referred to as Sea Island cotton. Earle had previously owned the plantation which now belong to Colonel Wylly. In 1791, a man by the name of Gray, who had been a tobacco grower and who worked for the East India Company, obtained some black seed cotton. He managed to ship ten thousand pounds of the cotton to England.[135] Other planters on the island who also planted the cotton were the Deveauxs. This crop was to become a staple crop during the period between the Revolution and the War Between the States.

Although early settlements were made on the island, and some owners of land there in the 1800's had property titles dating to 1749, Skidaway Island's natural inaccessibility made it comparatively unpopulated in its early history. It was not as easily reached from the mainland as some of the other islands. Its eight thousand acres of good arable land made it an extremely valuable sea island.

The first large plantation on the island was that of John Milledge. His son, also named John, became the governor of Georgia, and later was United States Senator for two terms of office. John Milledge Sr. died in 1781 on his way to Savannah from Augusta. The Milledge plantation was located on the northern tip of the island.

Other early 18th century landowners on Skidaway Island were

Henry Yonge Sr.; Francis Robe; James Deveaux, who owned Springfield Plantation in 1785; John Jarvis and Nicholas Buchenau, both of whom had land on the island in 1796; and Philip Delegal.

Throughout its history, Skidaway Island property has changed hands many times, and property lines have changed radically over the years. One of the plantations that covered most of Skidaway in the early 1800's was Modena Plantation, which is at the north end of the island. It is one of the oldest plantations in Georgia and was originally granted to Richard Palmer, and then later sold to James Deveaux. John Milledge acquired Modena and enlarged it through the purchase of several smaller grants of land. Cotton seemed to be the principal crop, but sheep and oranges were also exported from Modena.

John Milledge was born in Savannah in 1757. He became quite prominent in the affairs of Savannah, particularly on the eve of the Revolution, and was numbered among the party that arrested the royal governor, Sir James Wright. Milledge was nearly hanged as a spy when he was captured by a small contingent of Americans in South Carolina where he had gone when Savannah was taken by the British. By 1779, he was fighting with the Americans at the ill-fated Siege of Savannah. He was also a participant in numerous other battles during the Revolution.

John Milledge was elected Governor of Georgia in 1802, an office which he held for two terms. Perhaps his most noted achievement was his role as the principal founder of the University of Georgia. He had owned a tract of land near Athens, and he donated this land for the purpose of establishing a university on that site. John Milledge died in 1818, but he was honored for his contributions to Georgia by having the capital of the state named for him. Milledgeville, Georgia, served as the capital of Georgia from 1807 until 1867, when the seat of government was moved to what is now Atlanta.

Henry Yonge owned land at the northern end on the Wilmington River. His land was part of what is today The Landings residential development. Dr. William Waring, and then later some of his descendants, owned a large tract of land called Wakefield in the central part of the island. This plantation was located along Romerly Marsh and is now part of The Landings. Wakefield was once the property of George Haist who died in 1801. Haist left the plantation to his son, George Haist Jr. Haist's will, which was probated in December of 1801, also mentions his daughter, Elizabeth Haist.

Orangedale, or Cedar Grove Plantation, which once belonged to Henry Yonge, eventually became part of Hampton Place, owned by Hampton Dupon in the mid-1800's.[136] This land would become the location of a Benedictine monastery and school. Robert Delegal owned property on the southwestern section of Skidaway and his plantation was called Bloomsbury. Other early owners were Michael Reitter and John Davis. Hibernia Plantation was purchased by Union Camp Corporation in 1977, and today that tract encompasses Skidaway Island Plantation.

Other owners who were on Skidaway Island throughout the 1899's were Mary Wylly, Matthew McAllister, Adrian Mayer, David Adams, and William C. Campbell. There were a number of absentee landowners as well. Lachlan McIntosh, Hampton Lillibridge, and John McNish were some of these.

The plantation awarded to General Lachlan McIntosh in appreciation of his service during the American Revolution was passed on to his son, George McIntosh, who farmed the land until his death on the island in May of 1808.

[130] Kelly, V. E., *A Short History of Skidaway Island*, p. 6.
[131] *Ibid.*
[132] *Ibid.*
[133] Kelly, p. 14.
[134] *Ibid.*
[135] *Columbian Museum and Savannah Advertiser*, October 15, 1799, p.41.
[136] Kelly, p. 32.

The Waters Family

One of these early planters to establish a plantation on Skidaway Island was a Scotsman named John B. Waters. He not only operated a plantation in the vicinity of what is now part of Oakridge Golf Course, but also maintained a home on Broughton Street in Savannah. He married a young lady named Alicia. A son, John B. Waters Jr., was born about 1802. This child died in 1804 at the young age of fourteen months. He was buried on the Skidaway plantation. It is probable that John Waters and his wife lived in Savannah most of the time. The 1806 Tax Digest for Chatham County lists John Waters as being assessed at a rate of seven-and-a-half mills, one of the higher rates in the digest. This indicates that he owned a considerable amount of property. They were living in the house on Broughton Street in 1808, for it is there that Alicia died in childbirth on March 17, 1808, at the age of twenty. Her body was taken to Skidaway Island for burial beside the couple's son, John Jr. The small cemetery on the golf course on Skidaway Island is enclosed by a low tabby wall.

Only the graves of Alicia -- her name is spelled "Elecy" on her tombstone -- and her son John are marked. If there are other graves in the small plot, the stones which once marked them have long since disappeared.

Marriage records for Chatham County show John Waters marrying a widow, Sarah Tiot, on November 30, 1815. Notice of another marriage, that of Amanda C. Bryan and Charles L. Dell of Alachua County, Florida, on October 3, 1845, makes mention of the fact that the bride is the granddaughter of John Waters. John Waters died in Savannah of "bilious fever" on September 17, 1835 at the age of sixty-six.[137] He was originally buried in Colonial Cemetery, possibly in the Tiot vault, but his remains, along with those of some other family members, were moved to Laurel Grove Cemetery in Savannah in September of 1859.

[137] *Register of Deaths in Savannah, Georgia, Vol. V, 1833-1847*, comp. by The Genealogical Committee, Georgia Historical Society, 1989, p. 36.

THE DELEGAL FAMILY

The Delegal family came to the Georgia colony in 1733. Philip Delegal and his son, also named Philip Delegal, went first to St. Simons Island. The younger Philip attained the rank of Lieutenant in Oglethorpe's Rangers and saw action at the Battle of Bloody Marsh in 1742.[138] In 1767, Philip Delegal had acquired some land on Skidaway Island. He continued to add to his property, and by 1775, he had become the owner of a considerable plantation on the island and was prominent in various civic offices and affairs. He married first a woman named Jane and had several children, one of whom was a daughter, also named Jane. This Jane married Henry Preston at Skidaway Island in 1744.[139]

After the death of his first wife, Philip Delegal married Margaret Curtis. Margaret Curtis was the owner of property on Skidaway Island and also on Little Wassaw Island, which added a considerable amount of acreage to Delegal's holdings. By 1780, Philip Delegal owned nearly four thousand acres on Skidaway Island. His loyalty to

Burial site of Philip Delegal on Skidaway Island

England in the American Revolution resulted in the loss of not only his home, but also his property which was confiscated after the Revolution. In fact, the last skirmish in the Revolution in Georgia was said to have occurred at the Delegal plantation at the southern end of the island.[140]

Burial sites of Alicia Waters, who died in 1808, and also her son, John Waters, Jr. on Skidaway Island, on the old Waters plantation.

Philip Delegal died in 1781 and was buried on his property. Margaret, his wife, took their two children and moved to Florida where she eventually remarried. Today, a small tabby enclosure on the thirteenth hole of the Palmetto Golf Course is the visible evidence of his burial place. A modern marker outside the enclosure reads, "Philip Delegal, Georgia Citizen. Died October 19, 1781." The name Delegal survives as the name of a tidal creek and a road on Skidaway Island. Some of his descendants still living in Chatham County also still bear the name.

[381] Laist, Shari, "Delegals of Skidaway: Is Philip Alone on 13th Hole Palmetto?" TWATL, Vol. XVIII, No. 28, pp. 28-32.

[139] *Marriages of Chatham County, Georgia, Vol. I, 1748-1852*, comp. by the Genealogical Committee of Georgia Historical Society, Savannah, Georgia, 1993, p. 14.

[140] Johnston, Elisabeth Lichtenstein, *op cit*, p. 21.

Delegal tabby cemetery enclosure

The Lightenstone/ Lichtenstein Family

The information on the Lightenstone or Lichtenstein family came from a book written in 1836 by Elizabeth Lichtenstein Johnston.[141] Both spellings of the name are used, but it is probable that the name was spelled Lightenstone in Georgia; when Elizabeth moved to Canada, she reverted to the original German version of the name, likely as a protest to what she, as a Loyalist, may have considered proper.

Catherine Delegal, a daughter of Philip Delegal, married Captain John Lightenstone (or Lichtenstein) in 1774. John Lightenstone was born in Cronstadt, Russia, the son of Beatrice Elizabeth and Gustavus Philip Lightenstone. His father, Gustavus Philip Lightenstone, who was born in England, had established an academy in Cronstadt and taught there. He was also the Protestant minister at Cronstadt. The Lightenstone family had originated in Germany, and the German version of the family name, Lichtenstein, became anglicized during the years when the family lived in England.

Elizabeth Lightenstone (or Lichtenstein), the only daughter of

Captain John Lightenstone and his wife Catherine Delegal Lightenstone, was born at Little Ogeechee May 28, 1764. The Lightenstone family moved from Little Ogeechee to Yamacraw on the outskirts of Savannah. Captain Lightenstone served the Crown in a position as commander of the scout boat which took the Royal Governor, Sir James Wright, as well as other officers of the Crown to surrounding places such as Charleston to political functions. He also had occasion to visit Cockspur Island to impose quarantines on ships coming into Savannah.

It was on one of these visits to Cockspur Island that Lightenstone purchased the plantation on Skidaway Island. His daughter Elizabeth was to later describe the Skidaway plantation in rather glowing terms, commenting on the numerous fruits that grew in abundance there, as well as the cultivation of indigo, Indian corn, and sweet potatoes.

When the Revolution broke out, John Lightenstone, remaining loyal to the King, was forced to flee his home on Skidaway Island in 1776 when a party of Patriots, led by John Milledge, a Lightenstone neighbor, arrived with a group of soldiers to arrest him. Lightenstone managed to escape to Tybee Island where he boarded the British ship *Scarborough,* and sailed to Halifax, Nova Scotia. Elizabeth, twelve years old at the time, was then living with an aunt on her plantation near Savannah. Philip Delegal, Elizabeth's grandfather, filed a petition asking that Lightenstone's property be given to Elizabeth. This action prevented the Lightenstone property from being confiscated and sold.

At the age of fifteen and a half, Elizabeth Lightenstone married Captain William Martin Johnston, a physician, on November 21, 1779, in Savannah. She would later author the book, *Recollections of a Georgia Loyalist,* which she wrote in 1836 and from which much of the foregoing information is taken. In her book, Elizabeth told of her life in Revolutionary Savannah. Elizabeth Lightenstone Johnston died in 1848 in Halifax, Nova Scotia. Her husband, William Martin Johnston died in Kingston, Jamaica, in 1807.

[141] Johnston, Elisabeth Lichtenstein, *Recollections of a Georgia Loyalist, written in 1836,* The De La More Press, 52 Holborn, London.

The Odingsells Family

Charles Odingsells, who was born in South Carolina in 1754, lived on his plantation of Skidaway Island in the early 1800's. He had inherited the plantation on Skidaway Island from his father, Benjamin Odingsells. His mother, Mary Odingsells, had inherited the other plantation at Little Ogeechee in 1785 when her husband, Benjamin Odingsells, died. She married Isaac Young in 1787.

Charles Odingsells served in the Georgia Militia during the American Revolution, and was considered a meritorious officer by his peers, attaining the rank of major. Odingsells, in addition to his membership in various societies, served as a state legislator, and was also a member of the Union Society.

In 1806, Odingsells married Sarah Spencer, the daughter of Joseph Spencer. Four years later, in 1810, Charles died on his Skidaway plantation, leaving a rather large plantation to his widow and children. He was honored with a full military funeral performed by Wall's Corps of Artillery, and was laid to rest in Colonial Cemetery in Savannah. Sarah, his widow, married David E. Adams in 1812. Unfortunately, Odingsells' two children, Charles Spencer Odingsells and Mary Susannah Odingsells, both died of fever on Skidaway Island in October and November of 1817. They were also buried in the Odingsells' tomb in Colonial Cemetery.

Old Bones and Other Things

The year 1822 heralded an important scientific discovery on Skidaway Island. Ebenezer Stark, a plantation owner on the western side of Skidaway Island, following up on a report of the discovery of some bones by several of his slaves, located the site and notified a friend, Dr. Joseph Clay Habersham, to come over and take a look at the discovery.

On a trip to the island, Dr. Habersham tied his boat to what he first thought to be a post of some sort, but which he soon realized was actually a large bone. Returning to the site later at low tide, he discovered that more bones were exposed by the receding tide. Dr. Habersham, after examining the bones, which Mr. Stark gave him, determined that they were the bones of a woolly mammoth, the first one discovered in Georgia. An account of the discovery appeared in the April 1823 issue of *The Georgian*. Other scientists and paleontologists, who had been notified of the find by Dr. Habersham, came to Savannah, and after more intensive examination, arrived at the conclusion that the bones in question were actually those of the *Eremotherium*, commonly called the Giant Ground Sloth, a prehistoric creature that lived more than two million years ago.[142]

In 1842, the bones of another sloth were found there also. Additional discoveries included the remains of a prehistoric elephant, the mastodon. Some of these fossils are on display in the museum at Skidaway Island State Park.

In 1857, a bridge connecting the mainland and Skidaway Island was completed at an expense of four thousand dollars, making the island more conveniently accessible. The bridge was eleven hundred feet in length, and included a causeway and another smaller one hundred-foot bridge. It was built by W. R. Symons and some of the other residents on the island. This bridge extended from a part of Wormsloe at Isle of Hope and crossed the Skidaway Narrows to Skidaway Island. The completion of this bridge was an occasion observed by the islanders with a picnic and public celebration.[143]

During the War Between the States, the Chatham Artillery established earthen fortifications on the island which guarded the sea route, and comprised one of Savannah's main defenses. These were built near Priest's Landing, and at several other locations on the island, including the area where Skidaway Island State Park is today. Remains of some of these old earthworks still exist. The Fourth Georgia Battery was posted on Skidaway Island, and the Twentieth-fifth Regiment of the Georgia Infantry trained on the island. Skidaway Island was abandoned by Confederate troops in 1862.[144] The fortifications built by the Southern troops were left to

Negroes fired on passing fishermen in 1868 from these old Confederate earthworks.. Today, trees have overgrown the site, and the river's course has been diverted.

become overgrown. The naval blockade by Federal gunboats made the fortifications on Skidaway Island no longer necessary. The bridge was burned by departing Confederate troops to prevent its use by the Federal troops.

The enactment of the Emancipation Proclamation in 1863 produced a huge number of refugees and freedmen from the plantations, and this situation posed many problems for the Union Army. A "field order" declared that the abandoned rice fields along the rivers were reserved and set apart for the settlement of the newly freed Negroes.[145]

According to the records of the Freedmen's Bureau of 1865, approximately seven hundred fifty acres of the William R. Waring plantation was broken up into tracts, ranging in size from fifteen acres to forty acres, and given to about twenty-five freedmen and their families. This property would eventually be restored to the Waring family. The White, Ziegler and Jones plantations on Skidaway Island were likewise divided as well. Some of these acres would also eventually be restored to their original owners.

The Bureau of Refugees, Freedmen, and Abandoned Lands was created in 1865. The bureau's primary purpose to assist the newly-freed slaves. From the beginning, the agency was rife with corruption, inefficiency and the misappropriation of funds. It was used to help the Republicans maintain control of the states occupied by Federal troops. It created an intolerable situation for many former planters.

After the war, the labor force was gone, cotton prices had dropped, and the Freedmen's Bureau had sent some of the recently freed slaves to establish farms and raise crops on the island. This combination of events conspired to create new problems in a state that was now faced with rebuilding homes, farms, and a new economy.

In 1868, a group of Negroes took possession of the old fort on the island and used it as a vantage point from which they could fire on fishing boats passing by the island. Their targets were white men only. This unruly group made public their intention of not allowing any white man to fish in the waters of the Thunderbolt River off Skidaway. The *Savannah Mornings News*, dated December 21, 1868, reported that two well-known fishermen in the area, Charles E. Ross and Archibald Griffin, had sworn out an affidavit before the Justice of the Peace for Chatham County in which they had lodged a complaint stating that they were fired upon by this unruly mob of Negroes on Skidaway Island.

According to their published complaint, which was duly turned over to the Sheriff, they were peacefully pursuing their livelihood on December 16, 1868, and were on their way to Little Tybee Creek about fourteen miles below Thunderbolt. In order to reach their destination, they had to pass Skidaway Island. When they were opposite the old Confederate fort on the island, a large group of Negroes opened fire on them with intent to kill. The Negroes informed the fishermen that they "ruled the waters, in defiance of the law, and did not, and would not respect the law."[146] Other editorial comments and letters appeared in the newspapers, decrying the lawlessness and insisting that action be taken against the murderous group. One of the articles indicated that a group of Northern radicals may have encouraged the mob, but the writer suggested that the time had come for the two races to learn to live together.[147]

The Freedmen's Bureau had hoped for a massive redistribution of confiscated Confederate lands. However, President Andrew Johnson restored the abandoned lands and pardoned the Southerners. The

A solitary tabby-and-brick chimney stands amid the silent forests on part of the old Springfield Plantation on Skidaway Island. Photo courtesy of Eda S. Kenncy, Skidaway Island State Park.

Freedmen's Bureau was disbanded by an Act of Congress in 1872.

[142] Womack, Todd, "Plentifully Charges With Fossils: The 1822 Discovery of the Eremotherium at Skidaway," *Fossil News, Journal of Avocational Paleontology, Vol. 6,* July 2000, pp. 14-15.

[143] *Daily Morning News,* July 10, 1857, p. 2, c.2.

[144] "Historic Facts Guide," Skidaway Island State Park.

[145] Duncan, Russell, *Freedoms' Shore: Tunis Campbell and the Georgia Freedmen.*

[146] "The Skidaway Trouble," *Savannah Morning News,* December 21, 1868.

[147] "Trouble on Skidaway Island—Negroes Firing on Fishing Boats," *Savannah Morning News,* December 22, 1868.

The Benedictines

In 1859, the Right Reverend John Barry, Bishop of Savannah, had purchased Hampton Plantation from William Wade for the sum of nine thousand dollars. At that time a large house, described as a "stately mansion, four stories high and crowned with a cupola,"[148] stood on the site. This mansion's value was said to exceed the value of the entire plantation. Bishop Barry's plans for the property had been to establish a Negro male orphan asylum there. Unfortunately, the mansion was totally destroyed by Federal troops during the War Between the States.

In 1874, at the request of the Reverend William H. Gross, Bishop of Savannah, two Benedictine fathers, the Reverend Gabriel Bergier and the Reverend Raphael Wissel, arrived in Savannah with the intention of serving the colored population.[149] Several young men in Savannah expressed an interest in becoming candidates for admission into the Benedictine Order at that time. Stephen Dupon of Isle of Hope, a physician whose family had owned land on Skidaway Island, donated land at Isle of Hope for the Benedictines

Benedictine Church and Monastery, Skidaway Island. Photo courtesy of the Catholic Diocese of Savannah archives.

Benedictine School for Negro Boys, Skidaway Island
Photo courtesy Catholic Diocese of Savannah archives.

to establish a novitiate and a chapel there.[150] These structures were constructed on the property, but in less than a year, the yellow fever epidemic of 1876 that raged in Savannah claimed the lives of several of the Benedictines.

Bishop Gross transferred the seven hundred and seventeen acres known as the Hampton place on Skidaway Island to the Benedictine Order in Georgia in 1877. Father Oswald and other Benedictines moved to the island to resume their work with the black population. Since the original mansion on the property had been destroyed during the war, the Benedictines set about building a monastery and also an industrial school for young black boys. The school was dedicated January 16, 1878. The Benedictines lived at the monastery on Skidaway, but came to the chapel at Isle of Hope on Sundays. Negro families lived on the monastery grounds, and farmed the land with the help and guidance of the Benedictines there. They also buried their dead near the monastery.

A tragedy at the monastery occurred October 31, 1883. One of the priests there, Father Daniel Heftl, a native of Switzerland, sought to rid the area of some stray dogs that had been annoying the residents there and causing sleepless nights to those at the monastery.[151] Thus it was, that Father Heftl took a gun with the idea of frightening the dogs away. Whether or not he intended to kill them is uncertain.

He had an encounter with the dogs and did have a clear shot at them, but Father Daniel decided to try to hit the dogs with the butt of his rifle. Instead of hitting the dogs, Father Daniel struck a log. This action caused the gun to discharge a bullet which lodged in Father Daniel's intestines, inflicting a mortal wound. He lingered almost a month, but a notice in the *Savannah Morning News*, dated December 7, 1883, invited those who wished to attend his funeral at the monastery. He was buried in the small cemetery located near the monastery. When the monastery property on Skidaway Island was sold, Father Heftl's remains were removed and reinterred at Belmont Abbey, North Carolina.[152]

Regrettably, the industrial school for Negroes was not a successful venture due to its isolation, and also because the Negroes on the island were less than enthusiastic about pursuing manual training. A number of setbacks culminated in 1889 when a hurricane swept across the island, submerging it and contaminating the drinking water there. Fire destroyed some of the buildings in 1889 as well. The school closed its doors in 1889, and the monastery was eventually abandoned as impractical. Some of the black families continued to live on the property, and they provided palm branches for Palm Sunday to the Catholic churches in Savannah.[153] These people later moved into the country in Bryan County. The Union Camp Corporation, which had purchased the property, determined that the old monastery ruins had become a safety hazard, and they were razed in 1946. An old cemetery near the site of the monastery is all that remains of this period.

[148] Gamble, "First Benedictines Came to Savannah Isle 62 Years Ago." *Georgia Miscellany, Vol. 4.*
[149] *Ibid.*
[150] *Ibid.*
[151] DeLorme, Rita H., "Skidaway Island Footnote: A Tragic Halloween Misadventure," *The Southern Cross,* p. 3, November 2, 2000.
[152] *Ibid.*
[153] Letter written by Joseph D. Mitchell of Brunswick, Ga. to Thomas Gamble, February 2, 1938, *Ga. Misc. Vol. 4,* pp. 79-80.

Modern History

Cotton market prices had fallen to seven cents a bale by 1890, and Skidaway Island ceased to be a major area of large farms or cotton plantations. The planters and farmers were deeply in debt and some of them were forced to sell their land. Investors from the North bought up large tracts of land which they planned to hold as long range investments.

Modena Plantation was acquired by Ralph Isham in 1927. Robert Roebling bought the plantation from Isham in the 1930's and developed the property as an important cattle-breeding center.[154] Roebling eventually closed down the cattle operation in the early 1950's. He offered a large portion of Modena to the University of Georgia. A proposal was proffered for an oceanographic center to be established there. The Skidaway Institute of Oceanography was established in 1967, and operates as an important research facility today.

Union Camp Corporation acquired extensive acreage on Skidaway in the 1940's. Its logging operations there ceased in 1953. In 1964, Union Camp offered five hundred acres at the northern tip of the island for use as a state park.[155] This offer was contingent upon the construction of a permanent bridge and road to the island. The site for the bridge was once a portion of the old Springfield Plantation which was originally allotted to Richard Palmer. The property was originally bordered by the lands of John Milledge and Henry Yonge during the 1700's and 1800's. A bond referendum was passed in 1967, enabling the construction of a modern bridge and road to the island.

The Skidaway Institute of Oceanography, a part of the university system of Georgia, was located on a six hundred and eighty acre tract that was once a portion of two colonial plantations, Modena and Springfield. The property was donated for this purpose by Mrs. Dorothy Roebling and Union Camp Corporation. An aquarium was constructed in 1972. The purpose of this facility was to provide exhibits of marine life, and also for the study of aquaculture, marine biology, marine ecology, and the various facets of marine technology.[156]

The Marine Resource Center was formerly dedicated by President Richard M. Nixon on October 9, 1970. Bill Carpenter, a staff writer with the *Savannah Evening Press* who covered this event along with other reporters, told me of an amusing incident that had occurred a few days prior to the dedication ceremony. He wrote an account of the incident, and the story appeared in the newspaper on October 9, 1970.

It seems that prior to President Nixon's visit to Skidaway for the ceremony, a number of Republicans, including the chairman of the State Republican Party, made a trip to Skidaway Island to make preparations for Mr. Nixon's visit. When darkness approached, most of the group decided to leave the island by helicopter, leaving behind Georgia State Senator Oliver Bateman of Macon, Georgia. Senator Bateman was to drive Chairman Wiley Wasden's car back over the Skidaway Narrows Bridge.

When Mr. Bateman drove to the bridge to cross back to the mainland that evening, he found the drawbridge raised and the gatekeeper on the other side of the river. Senator Bateman blinked the car lights several times, and finally he got the gatekeeper to notice his dilemma. The problem, however, was that the gatekeeper was on his way home and was not inclined to stop and lower the bridge. A shouted discussion then took place which ended in a sort of compromise. The gatekeeper would shout the instructions for lowering the bridge, but in order to accomplish this, Mr. Bateman would have to slide down an embankment where the bridge mechanism was located.

Having accomplished this act, Senator Bateman attempted to follow the directions for turning the gears to lower the bridge. "Turn the gears, this way," the gatekeeper motioned, demonstrating with his hands. Senator Bateman took "this way" to mean clockwise, but the gears did not seem to work. After several attempts at turning the mechanism clockwise, with no success, Bateman finally in desperation, tried a counterclockwise turn of the gears. This time, he was successful, and the bridge lowered. Senator Bateman then got back in Wasden's car, which he had left running while he climbed down the embankment, and drove across the bridge. Just as he reached the other side, the car ran out of gas and stopped. Thus, while his companions were enjoying their supper, Senator Bateman was forced to walk through the woods to Ferguson Avenue before he could get someone to help him. His comment on the matter was that getting on the island was easy, but getting off was the real problem.[157]

Development of additional residential areas on the island was thwarted in 1972 when the State Coastal Marshland Protection Agency rejected a proposal to endorse a one million dollar causeway to be built between Skidaway Island and Green Island.

Island Investments, Incorporated, under the leadership of Albert Lufburrow, proposed to develop Green Island for residential purposes. The plans were first announced in 1968, and called for a bridge and road to link the area at the southwest end of Skidaway to Green Island. Green Island had previously been owned by the heirs of Judge Peter W. Meldrim who sold the island in 1958 to the investment company for a reported sum of fifty thousand dollars. Objections to this plan surfaced when the Savannah District of United States Engineers received an application for a dredging permit. The Marshland Protection Agency questioned the ownership of the involved marshlands. This agency was resistant to marshland development regardless of who the owners might be. The Corps of Engineers and the State of Georgia tightened its requirements concerning altering the marshlands and the waterways.

[154] Giese, Kay, "Very Few Things on Skidaway Remain Unchanged," *Savannah News-Press*, January 28, 1973, p. 17.
[155] *Ibid.*
[156] Dlugozima, Barbara, "Skidaway Potential Lab Site," *Savannah Morning News-Evening Press*, March 5, 1967, p. 1B.
[157] Carpenter, Bill, "Senator's Problem: Leaving the Island," *Savannah Evening Press*, October 9, 1970, p.23.

TYBEE ISLAND, COCKSPUR ISLAND, AND LITTLE TYBEE ISLAND

Chatham County's northernmost true barrier island lies at the mouth of the Savannah River. Its strategic location has made it militarily important from its earliest days of recorded history. Indeed, five different flags have been hoisted over the small sandy island lying approximately eighteen miles east of Savannah. These five flags -- Spanish, French, English, Confederate States of America, and the United State of America -- represent the island's importance to the various nations that claimed it.

Before the Europeans arrived, however, Tybee Island was inhabited by native Indian tribes who went there to gather the two resources which were of most interest to them; namely, salt and sassafras. The name "Tybee" itself comes from an Euchee Indian word meaning "salt." This commodity has always been of value to nomadic peoples who used it for preserving food supplies and for medicinal purposes.

The sassafras, which grew wild in and around the pine forest that once covered the island, had medicinal value as well. This particular plant was prized by Europeans, and the Indians were not slow in developing a thriving business trading with French ships which boldly defied Spain's claim to the coastal area known as "La Florida" or "Spanish Guale." The island itself was labeled on Spanish charts as "Los Bajos," meaning the Bay of Shoals. The Savannah River was called "Rio Dulce," which translated into English as "Sweet River," referring to the fresh water of the river.[158]

In 1605, the first known naval battle in the New World occurred when a French ship, seeking to trade with the Indians for the important sassafras for the European market, was surprised by the appearance of a Spanish vessel under the command of Captain

Francisco de Ecija. The Spanish defeated the French, capturing the ship, the captain and crew and taking them to St. Augustine as prisoners.[159]

General James Edward Oglethorpe recognized the military advantage of securing the island to guard the entrance to the Savannah River against England's old enemy, Spain, which occupied the territory to the south, called Florida. He also was aware that it was imperative that ships arriving from England with supplies and more settlers have a well-marked entrance to the Savannah River. With this in mind, Oglethorpe had a lighthouse constructed in 1736. The tower was ninety feet tall and was made of wood. It was maintained by the English settlers on the island. A small fort was also constructed on the island. Erosion forced the construction of a second lighthouse, but this one was destroyed in a storm in 1741 before it was completed. The following year a tower, reaching one hundred twenty-four feet into the air and constructed of stone and wood, was erected.[160]

This new tower, however, was also situated too close to the water. In 1768, a new site, which was much further back from the ocean, was selected for a new structure that was built of brick with wooden stairs inside. After 1790, this lighthouse was operated and maintained by the newly formed Federal government.

The ensuing years would see many changes and alterations made to this lighthouse. During the War Between the States, Confederate soldiers would try to burn the stairs in order to render it useless to the arriving Union troops. The Union troops, however, were able to repair the damage and used the lighthouse to view the Confederate troops at Fort Pulaski.

The present lighthouse was built in 1866 of brick and cast iron on the foundations of the previous one. It sits on a five-acre tract of land on which is located the old lighthouse keeper's cottage as well as other support buildings. It stands one hundred fifty-four feet tall, and its light is visible twenty miles at sea. The Tybee Lighthouse is considered to be the oldest and the most complete structure of its kind still standing in the United States.[161]

During the Revolutionary War period, Tybee Island was the scene of much activity. In July of 1776, a British ship loaded with gunpowder and destined for the British forces in Savannah was captured by an American schooner. The gunpowder was diverted to the American forces.

When Royal Governor Sir James Wright escaped from Savannah after his arrest by a party of Liberty Boys, he sought refuge aboard the British man-o-war *Scarborough* which was anchored off Cockspur Island near Tybee. Learning that the British officers were enjoying respites on Tybee with some of the Loyalists living there, Archibald Bulloch took a group of Patriots in small boats from Savannah to Tybee and burned all of the houses there except one for giving shelter to the British. But in 1778, the British Navy arrived to anchor off Tybee just prior to capturing Savannah and re-establishing the royal government there.[162]

It was at Tybee Island that Charles Henri, Comte D'Estaing, commander of the French fleet, consisting of thirty-seven ships, anchored and landed five thousand men to aid the American fight for liberty in 1779. Although this attempt to defeat the British who occupied Savannah was unsuccessful, it served to underline the strategic importance of Tybee Island.

Some of the early property owners on Tybee Island, in the years between 1758 and 1767, were those whose names are almost synonymous with Savannah. Names such as Josiah Tattnall, who owned two lots, a total of three hundred thirty-eight acres; Mary Tattnall, one hundred acres; Catherine Mulryne, one hundred acres; Isaac Young, one hundrd acres; Patrick Mackay, three hundred sixty acres; and Mary Farley, two hundred acres.[163] Other owners of property on the island during the early years of the colony were names such as Bryan, Bolton, Habersham, Screven, and Milledge, whose names are found on the old property records. Many of these, however, seemed to ignore their holdings there, for the most part. In 1808, a woman by the name of Martha Higgins died in Savannah. Her death notice in the mortuary records describes her as being the principal owner of Tybee Island at that time. At this period of time, the island was sparsely populated, and it is likely that the principal activities there involved fishing, and perhaps, small farm lots.

The map of Chatham County, which was compiled by Charles Platen in 1875, shows tracts of land on Tybee with the owners listed. Some of these names are better known than others. Most of these landowners likely owned the properties several decades before Platen's map was drawn. Beginning near the Tybee lighthouse and going southeast, these tracts were identified on the map as belonging to Catherine Mulryne, Mary Tattnall, and Josiah Tattnall. The location of these particular tracts encompasses most of the modern commercial area of Savannah Beach. On the southwestern portion of the island were the lands of Mary Torlay. An area just opposite Cockspur was that of Eden Somerville. Another tract was marked as belonging to J. Younge.

At the turn of the century, in the 1870's, the sleepy island of Tybee began to see an influx of visitors from the mainland who traveled by steamer to enjoy the sea breezes and bathing in the warm Atlantic Ocean. Screven's heirs began to sell off lots from his property, and people started to build summer cottages there. Hotels sprung up as the steamers from Savannah began to bring more summer visitors to Tybee. Hotels, such as the Ocean House and the Bolton Hotel, both of which were located near the lighthouse began to draw more and more visitors.

In 1887, the construction of the railroad to Tybee Island was completed, and the island became a popular destination, for those who wished to spend their summertime "on the salts." Hotels such as the Graham House and the Tybee Hotel and others flourished, as the construction of pavilions, amusements, clubs, and other amenities began to attract more and more people.

The railroad ceased operation in 1933, its business having markedly declined by the construction of the Tybee Road which stretched from Savannah across miles of islands, marshes and hammocks to bring automobiles to Tybee, thus giving birth to a new generation of beach goers. The road was also instrumental in the development and settlement of the islands, which it crossed on its route to Tybee. Big name bands and other entertainment and a fine restaurant at Tybrisa Pavilion, helped to lure visitors to the island.

Today, Tybee Island is a popular seaside resort. Although the popular Tybrisa Pavilion, built and operated by the Central of Georgia

Brick ruins on Little Tybee which may be an old burial vault or a kiln.
Photo taken by Tommy Solomon, July 2001.

Railroad, the largest of the pavilions built on the island and the most elegant, burned on May 17, 1967, a new pavilion was built on the site and opened in August of 1996, just in time for the 1996 Olympics which used Savannah and Wilmington Island for the yachting venue. The old Tybrisa hosted well-known musicians and entertainers, and was extremely popular.

To the south of Tybee Island lies another island known today as Little Tybee. This island, bordered by both the Atlantic Ocean and Wassaw Sound, once contained an area which was shown on the Platen map labeled "Arkwright's Village." A number of roads or streets were neatly laid out. One of these roads extended west to the Tybee River and showed a small tract that was labeled "Arkwright."

This simple notation on the Platen map has excited the curiosity of a number of individuals. There are those who insist that there were never any structures on Little Tybee or Beach Hammock. Another small contingent of Tybee locals, however, tell a different story. Some adventuresome residents at Tybee who have seen the map have done some intensive exploration of Little Tybee and Beach Hammock, which was also referred to as "Arkwright's Island" at the turn of the century. Tommy Solomon told me that he had found ruins on the island which appear to be foundations of buildings. Rusty Fleetwood mentioned that he had seen the brick ruins which are obviously foundations for buildings. He further added that there are also the

Old brick ruins on Little Tybee. Possibly part of Arkwright's Village.
Photo taken by Tommy Solomon, July 2001.

remains of a causeway leading to a dock. Fleetwood was of the opinion that perhaps Arkwright's Village was a manufacturing village of some type. Such villages were relatively common at the turn of the century, as is witnessed by Dr. Oemler's company village on Wilmington Island, or the one that was to be established on Ossabaw Island. They were established to provide housing for the workmen engaged in various industries. Sometimes they were only made up of houses, but often there were also commissaries where various staples could be purchased by the workmen.

The idea behind such settlements was to enable the workmen to live near their place of employment. While this may have been the reason for Arkwright's Village, there is a more plausible explanation. The few available records indicate that this may have been a summer resort. Certainly, such a resort was planned by Thomas Arkwright, but as to whether it was ever built is a matter for speculation. If this were the case, then it is likely that Arkwright's Village fell prey to one of a number of the killer hurricanes that swept the coastal area in the late 1800's. A brief look at the man who gave his name to this venture is vital in the understanding of what was occurring in the area in the 1870's.

[158] Godley, Margaret, *Historic Tybee Island, Savannah Beach, Georgia*, Savannah Beach Chamber of Commerce, 1958, pp. 2-3.
[159] Godley, p. 6.
[160] "Tybee Island Historical Society, *The Historic Tybee Island Light Station*, n.d., n. pag.
[161] *Ibid.*
[162] Godley, p. 7.
[163] Colonial Plat Book C.

Thomas Arkwright

Thomas Arkwright was born in northern England in 1821. Some sources state that he was born in Preston in Lincolnshire. At the age of eighteen he came to this country to Savannah, sometime about 1839, and entered the foundry business with a cousin, Robert Lachlison. He later became a member of this firm. Thomas Arkwright married his cousin Lydia Lachlison. Lydia died in 1855. Their eldest daughter, Ellen died in 1860.[164]

During the War Between the States, Thomas Arkwright, who was by that time a co-partner with William Rose in a foundry, manufactured munitions for the Confederate Army. After the war, Rose and Arkwright dissolved their partnership, and Arkwright established the Planters' Rice Mill at the foot of East Broad Street in Savannah. In 1866, he married Martha S. Stanley of Philadelphia and the couple had five children. Arkwright continued to invest in businesses that caught his attention. He bought the Savannah Theatre for the sum of sixteen thousand dollars. He also established a cotton manufacturing business in 1870 and purchased a cotton gin in 1874, when he advertised his business as the Arkwright Cotton Manufacturing Company. This cotton manufacturing venture was the first of its kind in Savannah.[165]

The year 1874 was a time of rapid growth and interest in resort or summer homes on "the salts." Thomas Arkwright acquired a portion of Beach Hammock, which is located south of Tybee Island on what is now Little Tybee. Arkwright had the property surveyed and drew plans for a resort village. This plan was marked on maps as "Arkwright's Village. Beach Hammock soon became known as Arkwright Island. A number of lots were apparently sold, and Arkwright planned a number of houses which he intended to construct there. These houses consisted of a kitchen, a hall, two piazzas on the front and the rear, and three additional rooms for sleeping and sitting. These were neatly built houses and were rather plain in appearance. Six lot owners signed an agreement to buy these houses, which would cost three hundred and fifty dollars each. The notice concerning these houses stated that as soon as twelve houses were purchased, construction could begin.[166]

Mr. Arkwright, in an effort to make Arkwright's Island accessible to the public and to prospective buyers, purchased a steamer to make daily trips to the island. The New York Yacht Club accepted the donation of a lot on Arkwright's Island and planned to build a winter resort there.[167]

A news item in 1875 praised Mr. Arkwright for offering the use of his steamer, the *Mary Draper,* to transport the orphan boys under the care of the Sisters of St. Joseph on an excursion to the resort he had created.[168]

Thomas Arkwright died in Savannah on July 16, 1881, of anthrax at the age of fifty-nine. His vision of a summer resort on Beach Hammock, or Arkwright's Island as it had come to be called, never really became a popular spot at which to spend the summer. Exactly how many houses, if any, were actually built there is not known.

Numerous items in the newspapers report various groups going on excursions by steamer to Beach Hammock, or Arkwright's Island. It seemed to be one of the many resort areas that steamer companies visited on a regularly scheduled basis. A number of civic and social organizations made trips to this resort. One article suggested that it would become as popular a resort as Tybee. The last article I found regarding excursions to Arkwright's Island was dated July 19, 1883.

[164] "*Laurel Grove Cemetery, Vol. I,* 12 Oct. 1852-30 Nov, 1861, pp. 86, 185.

[165] Simpson, John,"Thomas Arkwright," a paper dated November 12, 1986, from the biography files of the Georgia Historical Society.

[166] "Houses For Beach Hammock," *Savannah Morning News*, March 10, 1875, p. 3, c.2.

[167] *Savannah Morning News*, March 20, 1874, p. 3, c.3.

[168] *Savannah Morning News*, July 10, 1875, p. 3, c.3.

MILITARY HISTORY

Cockspur Island lies to the north of Wilmington Island. Though not a large island, its strategic location made it desirable for military fortifications. Its name is believed to be derived from its spur-like shape. It was here on Cockspur on February 6, 1736, that John Wesley set foot on what would eventually become American soil.

Fort Greene was the first fortification erected on Cockspur Island. Built in 1794, this fort was ill fated, lasting only nine years before being totally destroyed by the great hurricane of 1804. A large number of the soldiers who were garrisoned there lost their lives in the gigantic waves that inundated the island from one end to the other.[169] When the storm finally abated, no visible trace of Fort Greene remained.

During the War of 1812, Cockspur Island was used as an outpost to provide warning of a sea attack by the British. It was during this period that the Martello Tower was built. Its purpose was to guard the Savannah River. A lazaretto, or pest house, was built on the western side of the island. This facility was used to quarantine sick and possibly contagious passengers arriving by boat, particularly slaves brought in to Savannah. Those who died there were either consigned to the waters surrounding the island or to unmarked graves on Tybee itself.

One interesting structure that stands on Cockspur Island is the lonely little beacon that occupies a precarious perch on the southeastern tip of the island. Completely surrounded by water at high tide, it seems too small to be of any significant value to shipping, yet this small light beacon, rebuilt after a hurricane in 1854, has stood as sentinel on the South Channel of the Savannah River. It was first constructed in the 1840's, having been designed by John Norris of New York who is better known for the homes in Savannah which he designed. As commerce increased in the port of Savannah, and larger freighters were built which required a greater draft, the use of the shallow South Channel declined, until by the end of the nineteenth century, nearly all of the vessels coming into the port of Savannah were using the deeper North Channel. The little beacon was finally retired from active duty in 1909 after nearly eighty years of guiding ships into port.

In 1821, Cockspur Island was surveyed by Captain John LeConte with the idea of erecting a new fort. However, it was 1829 before work on the new fort, to be called Fort Pulaski, was actually begun. In 1829, a young West Point cadet, Robert Edward Lee, was appointed to his first military post at Cockspur, and his first task was to survey, build a system of dikes and drainage ditches, and to select a suitable site for the new fort. Throughout the construction of this fort there were many delays due to diseases such as malaria and yellow fever, typhoid fever, and all of the various other illnesses prevalent in the low country. Despite all of the most advanced techniques, this fort, believed to be invincible, would fall to the Union Army in April of 1862. It was decimated by the use of the new rifled guns and by mortars fired from Tybee by the Union troops.

Although the fort saw little use in the post-war period, there was some military activity there during the Spanish-American War. Margaret Godley says that some efforts were made in 1915 to preserve Fort Pulaski, but it was not until 1933 that the National Park Service began serious preservation work on the old fort.[170]

[169] Lattimore, Ralston B., *Fort Pulaski National Monument, Georgia*. National Park Service Historical Handbook Series No. 18, Washington, D.C., 1954, p.3.

[170] Godley, p. 33.

"The Immortal Six Hundred"

One of the most heinous atrocities of the War Between the States occurred in late October of 1864. Union General J. G. Foster retaliated in response to a stratagem used by Confederate General Samuel Jones in a desperate attempt to end the bombardment of Charleston. Jones sent a dispatch to Union General J. G. Foster saying that six hundred officers of the Union Army had been quartered in a residential area of Charleston which had been under constant bombardment by Union guns.

In a brutal act of retaliation, General Foster reacted by having six hundred Confederate officers sent from Fort Delaware to the stockade on Morris Island in Charleston harbor. General Jones then sent the Union prisoners to Columbia and Florence. General Foster's response was to send his Confederate prisoners out of Charleston to Fort Pulaski. When the men arrived at Fort Pulaski, they were ill-clothed, suffering from myriad diseases of which the most debilitating was diarrhea. Although Colonel Philip P. Brown, Union commander of Fort Pulaski, was a humane man and requisitioned blankets, clothing, and rations of food, these requisitions were ignored, and Brown was ordered to place the prisoners on a daily starvation diet consisting of one-quarter pound of bread, ten ounces of corn meal, and one-half pint of pickles. Every five days the unfortunate men would receive one ounce of salt.[171] The ragged, starving men grew weaker as the onset of winter produced freezing temperatures.

Finally, on January 21, 1865, Fort Pulaski came under the command of Brevet Major General Cuvier Grover, and, after an inspection by his medical staff, the prisoners were put back on full rations.[172] This act saved many lives, but out of the original six hundred, only four hundred and sixty-five Confederate officers survived to be sent back to Fort Delaware. The dead were buried in unmarked graves outside the southwest walls of the fort. Lee's surrender

Monument commemorating the landing of John Wesley on Cockspur Island in 1736.

Grave of Lt. Robert Rowan of N.C. He served in the U. S Artillery & Engineers during construction of Fort Pulaski. He died there in 1800.

Walls of Ft. Pulaski showing some of the damage done by Union cannons in 1862. Photo by author, June 2001.

on April 29, 1865, did not end Fort Pulaski's use to house prisoners. It was here that the leaders of the Confederacy were brought as prisoners, and many of them would remain imprisoned there for months.

Although Fort Pulaski was modernized and strengthened after the war, there was little activity there, and after 1872, there was no active military use of the fort. The hurricane of August 1881 swept away all of the houses on Cockspur Island, except for one that was the Ordnance Sergeant's residence. Captain Poland, who was the lighthouse keeper, and several other residents there took shelter in the circular stairways leading to the old parapet on the walls.[173]

This 1936 photograph was taken at Ft. Screven on Tybee Island. The Skoda 100mm Model 14 cannon was made in Austrian about 1913, probably a memorial piece brought here after WWI, according to Leon Lovett of Wrightsboro, GA. The child sitting on the cannon is John Piechocinski, age 3 years.

In 1883, a new fort on the north point of Tybee Island was begun for the purpose of preventing hostile ships from taking control of Tybee Roads. It was also meant to defend the channels which approached the Savannah River. The land for this purpose had been acquired in 1875 by the government. This new fort was first named Fort Tybee, but this name was later changed to Fort Graham. In the late 1890's the name was changed once again to Fort Screven.[174] Three jetties to aid in the preservation of the site and to deter erosion were erected, and in 1883, the height of these jetties was increased. The northeastern point of Tybee was subject to continuing substantial erosion, and the jetties were used to combat this problem. Fort Screven formed a part of the American Coastal Defense system, and troops trained there during the Spanish American War in 1898, as well as troops during World War I and World War II. In 1947, the fort was closed. The government sold the property to the town of Tybee.

There were few year-round residents on Tybee in the 1870's. It was difficult to reach, being accessible only by water. By the 1890's however, there were more than four hundred beach cottages for summer residents, who were now able to reach the island by the railway which had been built in 1887.

[171] Lattimore, R., pp. 38-39.
[172] *Ibid.,* p. 40
[173] "Terrific Tempest, The Fiercest Gale Ever Known", *The Morning News*, August 29, 1881.
[174] Adams, James Mack, *A History of Fort Screven Georgia* , JMA2 Publications, Tybee Island, 1998, pp. 19-20.

The Hurricane of 1881

On August 27, 1881, a hurricane hit the coastal areas of Chatham with devastating results. It was described in the newspapers as the "fiercest gale ever known".[175] Tybee Island was hard hit, with many homes and lives lost. For two days there was no communication with the island. Wind speed was measured at seventy-five miles per hour, and the brunt of the gale arrived at six o'clock in the morning. The most substantial house on the island, that of Henry Solomon, located on the ocean front, was blown down and then caught fire. Some colored men saw the destruction of the house and helped get the occupants out to safety. Neighbors H. P. Smart, D. R. Kennedy, and A. E. Abbott braved the raging storm to rescue Mrs. Solomon and her son, Nathaniel, from the burning house. Several members of the Wolf and Falk families died in the flames that engulfed some of the other buildings. Some of the known dead were Mrs. Georgianna Wolf, the wife of Joseph Wolf, their daughter Halle Wolf, and Joshua Falk, a brother of Mrs. Wolf. When the storm finally subsided, the survivors of the storm, along with bodies of those who perished were brought into Savannah on the steamer *Forest City*.

Many of the residents who lived sought shelter in the woods and hammocks, while others went to the Ocean House Hotel. The ground floor of the hotel was soon flooded. A. T. Sanders braved the rising waters to light the Tybee beacon light which had been moved sixteen feet from its original position. He also climbed to the top of the lighthouse to wind up the clockwork gears which provided oil for the lamp there.[176]

The effect of the 1893 hurricane that struck Tybee is perhaps best recounted in a letter written by M. S. Workman on Taylor Street in Savannah to her uncle, Mr. Hough. Mrs. Edward Workman, her husband, and two daughters, Marjorie and Dorothy, were staying at Tybee. Sometime after the storm occurred, she wrote the letter to her uncle, in which she tells the sequence of events that took place that fateful Sunday in August of 1893. Mrs. Workman refers to her husband as "Teddie" in the letter. Her infant son, Frank, had died in July. Teddie Workman had been with a Mr. Comer in Savannah and did not arrive at Tybee until early Sunday morning on the train.

According to Mrs. Workman, the winds and rains began about ten o'clock that morning. Sometime after dinner that day, Mr. Graham, who was staying with the family, called them to come and look at the big waves that were forming. A neighbor in the cottage next door to the Workmans, Mrs. Ulmer, came running in, telling them to leave the house immediately. Mr. Ulmer had gone over to his island earlier, and, seeing that his cattle were in danger, had stayed there to see what he could do about getting them to a safe place. They decided to go to the Naylor house which was much higher, but upon arriving there, discovered the house locked up.

Mrs. Workman then began preparations to leave their cottage, gathering thick cloaks for the children, blankets, and other supplies. She also moved as many things as possible from lower shelves and placed them on the beds, tables and chairs. Mrs. Ulmer, Mr. Graham, the servants, and the children went with the Chief of Police, and Mrs. Workman thought that they had all gone to the police barracks which was considered to be a very strong building.

Having placed most of their possession on tables and other high pieces of furniture, the Workmans locked the dining room door which by this time had water rushing up to it. They waded to the Ryan cottage, whose occupants called them in. They then learned that the police barracks had fallen, and the horses there had been crushed to death. By this time, the water was rushing between the Ulmer house and the Workman house, and was quickly surrounding the Ryan house. Plunging into water that was by now up to their knees, they observed people rushing into the woods to get to safety in the trees. When they reached the police barracks, which had collapsed, they learned that Mrs. Ulmer and the children were not there, but had gone to the Blun house near the new hotel, a little over a mile away.

As the Workmans trudged their way to the Blun house, they saw more people fleeing into the woods. Looking back, they saw a house burning, but did not know whose it was. Upon reaching the Blun house, they were reunited with their children and the servants. The little party sat huddled together in a house which they were not certain could withstand the high winds. A plan was formulated that each man in their party would take one woman or child when the house fell, and would swim out if possible, the house by that time being surrounded by eight feet of water. One person held a small lantern, their only source of light, so that if the house collapsed, they would not have to deal with fire as well.

The Blun house lived up to its claim of being the strongest house on the island. The next morning, when the rains had stopped and the winds had abated somewhat, an assessment of damage revealed the chimney had cracked from top to bottom and the wall of a room upstairs, above where the Workmans spent the long night bulged out more than one foot. The brick pillars under the house had begun to give way.

The scene on Tybee Island revealed complete devastation, with articles of furniture, clothing, timber, and other debris everywhere. The beach from the railroad track down to the ocean had been scoured clean. From the condition of the railroad track, it was evident that it would be weeks before they could return to Savannah by train. The Naylor house was down, and under some of the wreckage were the remains of four Negroes who had drowned. Ships had been blown ashore. The party made their way to what remained of the bridge, and there they found a tug waiting to bring them back to town. The Quarantine Station was a complete wreck, and many vessels were piled up. Another tug signaled them to allow a boarding party, and the Mayor and Mrs. Ulmer's brother came on board their tug. The Mayor went up to Mrs. Ulmer and rather abruptly said, "I am sorry to tell you that your husband was drowned last night — sad, but true." He then turned and walked away.

Mrs. Workman concluded her letter by stating that she was happy that her aunt's visit to Tybee had ended before the storm, and she was thankful that her infant son was not with her, having died the previous month.[177]

[175] Gamble, Thomas, "Memories of Savannah's Greatest Hurricane Fifty Years Ago Recalled," August 22, 1942, *Georgia Misc. vol. 4*, pp. 32-33.

[176] Ibid.

[177] Letter written by M.S. Workman of Savannah to her uncle, not named. 1893. From pamphlet collection, Savannah Public Library.

THE FRESH AIR HOME

In 1898, the Fresh Air Home was organized and operated by the Froebel Circle. It was first visualized by Nina Anderson Pape, who was well known in Savannah as an educator. Being concerned with the welfare of children, Miss Pape, with the help of contributions from private individuals as well as a number of large business groups, began with a rented cottage and a group of fifty children from the city who spent the summer of 1898 at Tybee. By 1918, the Fresh Air Home had expanded, and contributions continued. The Central of Georgia Railway provided free transportation for the children and for supplies for the Home. Members of the Froebel Circle did the bulk of work themselves. The will of Percival Randolph Cohen, and also the will of John Devine Carswell, included bequests to the Fresh Air Home which amounted to fifty thousand dollars. This money, combined with a lot donated by Mrs. C. F. Graham, made possible the construction of newer and larger buildings. The purpose of the home was to provide a happy, healthy environment with nourishing food and character-building activities for young children from the city.[178]

During the latter part of the nineteenth century and well into the twentieth, Tybee experienced growth as more and more people came there to summer, or even in quite a few cases, to establish permanent residency. A building boom gave rise to resort hotels, pavilions such as Tybrisa, which was the largest, piers, and entertainment. The railroad provided easy access to the island, followed by the construction of the Tybee Road in 1923. This road promoted the development and the settlement of the islands between Savannah and Tybee.

While Tybee Island has been known for more than a century as being a beach resort, few residents and visitors today are aware that Tybee, like its neighbors, Wilmington, Whitemarsh, and the other islands, was also known for oranges. An article in the November 11, 1913, *Savannah Morning News* mentions that some oranges were grown at Lovell Station by Charles Lane. It noted that Mr. Lane was able to keep his orange tree from suffering from the cold weather by building fires around the tree during the cold periods. The village of Lovell Station was located on the north end of the island. It no longer exists as it was washed away, as were the trees and dunes that were also there.

Another article appeared in the *Savannah Evening Press* on November 21, 1932. This time the number of oranges was estimated at several hundred. This may have been the same tree which made the news in 1913, as it was located in front of the telephone exchange at the north end of the island near Fort Screven. The manager of the telephone exchange, Mrs. B. F. Cook, picked a number of them from the lower branches, and they were described as being very juicy and sweet. This tree attracted a great deal of attention both from the local residents, and from the visitors. There was speculation that when the population increased, a number of people would establish small vegetable farms on the island. It had already been observed that some of the banana trees on Tybee had produced ripe fruit.

In 1932, unusually strong tides in November, which cut away twenty-five feet of the beach beyond the high water mark and leveled large sand dunes, created a mystery that was considered newsworthy. The skeleton of a whale, which had been buried under the beach sands, was uncovered. It was discovered by Savannah Beach Police Chief Dennis Lysaught and Lieutenant Hildreth, who had been patrolling the beach. What created the mystery, however, was the remnant of a harpoon embedded in the skull of the huge sea mammal. None of those older residents who were questioned about whaling could ever recall a time when whales were hunted off the coast of Georgia. Whaling was usually conducted in the colder northern waters. Some suggested that perhaps the creature had been harpooned in northern waters, but had been carried by strong tides and currents to wash ashore at Savannah Beach, and there to be covered by the sand. There was no clue to indicate how long the skeleton had been buried there. A more immediate concern was how to dispose of the skeleton so that bathers the following summer would not be tripping over the bones.[179]

Over the years, Tybee Island has evolved from a place where mostly local people rode the train to enjoy a brief sojourn on the beach and at Tybrisa with their families, and as a place where a goodly number of Savannahians either owned or rented a summer place, to an island that is filled with year-round residents. The old railroad that brought crowds of eager vacationers has long since vanished. The road that leads to the island was in essence the death of the train.

World War II saw Tybee threatened by German submarines. Some of the older people remember when U-boats sank ships not very far from Tybee. An old watchtower still remains in place on Back River, rusting in the salty air; a sentinel that once guarded the island's shores.

Today, condominiums and spacious homes occupy most available space. In between are the more modest cottages, some of which have withstood both storms and progress. The island is no longer that sleepy little place at the mouth of the Savannah River where people went to while away the summer. Some areas seem to remain frozen in time, but most are testimonials to progress and to modern hurried life. The waves still crash upon the sands and storms still spur a rapid exodus. The island still continues its slow, but inexorable journey to the southwest to join the mainland. Jetties and seawalls may temporarily interrupt its journey, but in the end, the natural events that shape our world will win.

[178] Godley, p.44
[179] "Harpoon in Skull of Whale Dug Up At Savannah Beach," *Savannah Press*, December 10, 1932.

WASSAW ISLAND AND GEORGE PARSONS

Wassaw Island, a young barrier sea island, is separated from the mainland by more than nine thousand acres of salt marshes. Its name, Wassaw, comes from a Creek Indian word meaning "a cow."[180] Located to the southeast of Savannah, between Wassaw Sound and Ossabaw Island, it is more than ten thousand acres in size. It lies between Skidaway Island and the Atlantic Ocean, and is five miles long and about a half mile wide. Wassaw is the most natural, unspoiled island of the well-known sea islands which extend along the coast of Georgia. Its most notable features are the miles of pristine beach and a huge virgin forest. Its untouched natural environment owes its existence to the Parsons family who owned the island for more than 103 years before it was finally conveyed to the United States Fish and Wildlife Service by the family to be preserved as a wildlife refuge. The island's remoteness from civilization has been a key factor in retaining its wild nature, the only transportation to the island being by boat. Two other small islands, Little Wassaw Island and Pine Island, at the south end on Ossabaw Sound, complete what is today the Wassaw National Wildlife Refuge.

The first mention of Wassaw Island in the colonial records in Georgia is in regard to a Crown grant of a portion of the island to James Deveaux in 1756.[181] Others who were early owners of land on the island were Peter Deveaux, Josiah Tatnall, William Wall, Robert Watts, Samuel Wall, Nicholas Turnbull, and Joseph R. Gibbons. No evidence of any of these men ever living or farming on the island exists today. There are a few references to an artesian well and old dock at the south end where early sailing ships would sometimes stop to replenish their drinking water.

Girl Scout troop from Mickve Israel waiting to go camping on Wassaw Island, July 1913. Photo courtesy Juliette Low Birthplace.

Girl Scouts on their way to Thunderbolt to board a steamer for Wassaw Island. Photo courtesy Juliette Low Birthplace.

The modern history of Wassaw begins in 1847 with George Parsons who moved to Savannah and opened an office on Factors' Walk next to the old Cotton Exchange. His various business endeavors involved the first railroad to Isle of Hope, as well as a lucrative cotton brokerage business.

In 1866, Mr. Parsons bought Wassaw Island at public auction for the sum of $2,500. The ownership of the island would remain in the Parsons family for the next one hundred and three years. In the late 1880's, when it became fashionable to take steamers to the various islands around Savannah for pleasure and recreation, the Parsons family built a pavilion on the south end of the island in 1890, and many Savannahians took excursions by steamer to Wassaw. In fact, it was possible for those pleasure-seekers of the 1890's to rent bathing suits at the pavilion there in order to enjoy dips in the ocean. Music and dancing were also provided at the pavilion.

The steamers *Doretta* and *Alpha* made regularly scheduled trips from Thunderbolt to Wassaw every day except Mondays in the summertime, leaving from the wharf at the foot of Whitaker Street and then on to Thunderbolt, Wilmington Island, and Wassaw Island. Tickets for these excursions cost thirty-five cents, except on Sundays when the fare was forty-five cents, which included streetcar fare to and from Thunderbolt to the city.[182] The pavilion on Wassaw was the island's only commercial venture, and it only lasted about seventeen years before it was abandoned and pulled down.

Activities and events which occurred on the islands were often deemed newsworthy. *The Savannah Morning News* on July 15, 1905, allotted a lengthy column recounting a "big fish" story. It seems that a group of Methodist ministers and their families camped out on Wassaw Island for ten days. They lived in the pavilion and spent a good bit of their time enjoying the pleasures of boating, bathing, and fishing. The Reverend J. A. Smith of Savannah was said to be the only member of the group who was not successful at fishing, but he did return home with what was described as a "pet," or boil, on his cheek from the sulfur water on the island.

Two of the other ministers, the Reverend Bascom Anthony of Macon, and the Reverend J. W. McDonald of Valdosta, tried their luck at shark fishing. They were able to hook a shark, which circled their boat and then rapidly headed out to sea, towing the boat and fishermen along behind it. After running about a half mile, the shark turned and headed back toward shore. The ministers described the shark as a monster which looked like a whale when they finally beached

1913 photo of Girl Scouts on Wassaw Island.
Photo courtesy of Juliette Low Birthplace.

it. It took nearly an hour to land the shark, which measured eight feet in length.

Girl Scout troops from Savannah made a number of encampments on Wassaw Island during the years that such camping was permitted. They called such trips "Maroon Trips." In July of 1913, a large group of girls, not all Jewish, from a Mickve Israel troop in Savannah loaded up their gear for an encampment on the island. An old truck was their transportation to Isle of Hope to board a steamer to carry them to the island, where they pitched their tents. A steamer later brought them back to Savannah. There were a number of such camping trips to the island by the Girl Scouts.[183]

Although originally the Parsons family permitted Girl Scouts, Boy Scouts, Y.M.C.A. campers, and other groups to camp on the island, other irresponsible visitors came uninvited, violated laws against night hunting, and set fires in the woods. The family finally forbade all visitors to the island.[184]

[180] Charles Wessels

[181] Notes on Crown Grant to James DeVeaux, Walter C. Hartridge Collection # 1349, Box 23, Folder 344, Georgia Historical Society

[182] "Wassaw and Wilmington Island," *Savannah Morning News*, June 21, 1897, p.2.

[183] Information provided by Katherine Keena, Juliette Gordon Low Birthplace, Savannah, Ga.

[184] Whitfield, Archie, "Wassaw Owners Enjoy George Parsons Legacy," n.d.

"The Recluse of Wassaw"

One of the more interesting characters who came to live on the island was a man named William Lenoir Copp, known to many as Cap'n Lenoir. How he happened to come to Wassaw Island and the primitive shanty where he lived as a hermit is not known, but in the 1920's, he was somewhat of a legend. How much of his life as he related it for reporters and visitors to the island is actually true is open to doubt, but there is no question that he was an intriguing individual.

According to Cap'n Lenoir, he was born March 20, 1854, in Charleston, South Carolina, at his parents' home on Society and Washington streets. During the War Between the States, the Yankee guns being fired in Charleston drove him and his mother from their home. They went to Ridgeland where he went to school for a time. His father died in 1862, and eventually he and his mother returned to Charleston. When Cap'n Lenoir's mother died, a man by the name of Charles E. Webster adopted him and brought him to Savannah to live at Isle of Hope. He and Mrs. Webster made a good living by fishing. After Mr. Webster died, Lenoir went to sea as a commercial fisherman, going as far north as Nova Scotia.[185]

Cap'n Lenoir came to Wassaw Island in 1892. He spent nearly all of the rest of his life there. He built two shacks on the island, and became a sort of guardian of the Parsons' property and interests on the island. Indeed, in 1917, someone set a fire at the Parsons' place at the north end of the island, and Cap'n Lenoir and some Y. M. C. A. campers helped to fight the fire, saving some of the furniture. Rarely did he visit the mainland, preferring to spend his days quietly on the island. Most accounts of the man indicate that he was an avid reader, and visitors would bring him magazines, books, and newspapers. An avowed animal lover, he had many pets of cats, dogs, and pigs. He once had a puppy he called "Wassaw" and a kitten named "Nellie O."

He also had two pigs which were quite tame, but did not get along well with "Wassaw." He once told how he had to lock "Wassaw" in one of his shacks at night so the pigs wouldn't kill him. [186]

Cap'n Lenoir's idyllic island existence was flawed by the mosquito population, which he detested. In fact, some young men had dubbed his camp "Skeeterhill" because they camped there at a time when the mosquitoes were especially fierce. He called his home "Skeeterhill" from then on. Lenoir enjoyed company, and according to an article in the *Savannah Morning News*, in August of 1926, some ladies in a boating party visited him once at Camp Skeeterhill, and implied that he must not mind the mosquitoes as he had surely become accustomed to them after all this time. This absurdity was countered with this pithy reply, "No, ma'am. I am just like Parsons' bull, and the mosquitoes run him into the surf." [187]

In June of 1931, a weekend boating party which included a physician, came to Skeeterhill. The visitors discovered that Cap'n Lenoir was seriously ill, and contacted the Savannah Fire Department, which in turn, got in touch with William Barbee at Isle of Hope. Mr. Barbee had the old man taken to a local hospital where he died June 25, 1931, at the age of seventy-eight years, thus ending an era of being known as "the recluse of Wassaw Island." [188]

Alex Barbee, the son of William Barbee, told me that he remembered his father referring to Cap'n Lenoir as a squatter who had come to Wassaw and built himself a crude shelter of palmetto fronds. The old man wore ragged clothing, and, according to Alex, it was probable that the stories circulating about Lenoir were exaggerated and idealized. Alex did say that Cap'n Lenoir had requested that he be buried near his hut on the beach at Wassaw. He had also requested that he be buried in a sitting position, facing the sea. Whether these desires were carried out or not is not known. Lenoir's burial place is unknown, but he has retained a niche in the lore of Wassaw.[189]

During the Parsons' long tenure on the island, there was an abundance of deer and other wildlife. Wild cattle roamed the island in the 1800's. Feral pigs also flourished there. In addition to these, there were also numerous small animals, and both terrestrial and marine birds that nested there.

A fort was built on the island in 1898, and troops were garrisoned there during the Spanish-American War. The fort had two mounted 4.7 mm guns, and a large central room for the storage of ammunition and shells for the guns. All that remains of the old fort today are a few ruins which are gradually being reclaimed by the slow actions of the tides.

[185] "Capt. Lanar of Wassaw Island," *Savannah Morning News*, August 22, 1926.
[186] *Ibid.*
[187] *Ibid.*
[188] "Death Ends Solitary Life of Recluse of Wassaw Island; Old 'Cap'n Lenoir' Passes," *Savannah Evening Press*, June 25, 1931.
[189] Telephone interview with Alex Barbee, May 20, 2001.

A Wildlife Refuge

In the 1960's, members of the Parsons family became apprehensive about what might eventually happen to Wassaw Island. Local pressures to develop Wassaw Island and to establish more convenient public access facilities increased an immediate need to take steps to preserve the island in its wild state. After lengthy negotiations with the Parsons Trust of Boston, the Nature Conservancy was able to locate an anonymous donor who purchased the island for a small fraction of its value. It was then conveyed to the United States Fish and Wildlife Service by the Nature Conservancy in 1969.[190] Alex W. Barbee, who had acted as the overseer and agent for the Parsons' estate, was appointed by the Wildlife Service to supervise the refuge. A ban on hunting went into immediate effect. The Parsons family retained one hundred eighty acres, which included their home place and other buildings on the island, for their own use.

This move created quite a stir among local politicians and developers who had been interested in the island for recreational use and for development. The State of Georgia considered a lawsuit against the federal government because the transfer of the property to the federal government was not revealed to the local government until after it became effective. Today, Wassaw, Little Wassaw, and Pine Island comprise the Wassaw National Wildlife Refuge.

[190] Dlugozima, Barbara, "Future's Bright for Wassaw," *Savannah Evening Press*, April 25, 1970.

Anthony Odingsells and His Family

Pine Island, which is a part of the refuge, is the only place where overnight camping is permitted. Since there is no fresh water or sanitation facilities, such camping is very primitive. The earliest mention of Pine Island was in the will of Peter Readdick who died in 1778. Pine Island, according to Readdick's will, was left to his son Jacob Readdick.[191] In later years this island was once owned by a free black man, Anthony Odingsells, who also owned and lived on Little Wassaw.

According to what is known about Anthony Odingsells, he was the son of a white father, quite likely Charles Odingsells Jr., and a black mother, possibly an Odingsells' slave. Anthony's white father, who died when Anthony was very young, made provisions for the education of his son, appointing a guardian, C. O. Screven of Sunbury, to handle the young man's affairs. He also left the boy Little Wassaw Island and eleven slaves.

This inheritance was to be handed over to young Anthony upon reaching his maturity. At some point, Anthony met, and subsequently married, a young mulatto woman, Madeline. Their only child, a daughter whom they named Lucy Ann, was born in 1828. The Odingsells family moved to Little Wassaw in the early 1830's where he made his livelihood by fishing, harvesting oysters, and farming.

Early records, dating from 1834, indicate that Anthony Odingsells hired Ismael Morel to build a large house on Little Wassaw for the sum of one hundred and thirty dollars. In October of 1835, Mr. Odingsells paid fifty dollars to Morel as a down payment for the construction of the house and other buildings. The document indicates that while Anthony Odingsells signed his own name, Ismael Morel signed his with an X. Mr. R. D. Petit DeVillers was Odingsells' guardian, and he also signed the document, giving his approval to the transaction concerning the house and buildings.[192]

An 1836 tax return lists A. Odingsells and his wife, Madeline Odingsells, as the owners of a tract of land consisting of one hundred fifty acres, of which fifty acres were first quality land while the rest was third quality pine land. It also listed one tract of land on Pine Island of fifty acres of third quality land. Odingsells stated on the return that he had eleven slaves.

Although much has sometimes been made of the concept of a free black man who owned considerable property and slaves, this was not an unusual situation. Savannah had always had a relatively large free black population, dating even back to the Colonial period. In the city itself were free blacks such as Jane Deveaux, Simon Mirault, and others who not only owned property, but also in some cases were also slave owners. This same situation existed in other parts of the state and, indeed, in other states as well. Augusta had a small group of wealthy black businessmen who were slave owners, and who sometimes mingled socially with their white counterparts.

During the War Between the States, Odingsells found a profitable market for his oysters and fish by selling to the Confederate troops stationed on Wassaw Island about six miles from the Odingsells' home. This market lasted until the Confederate troops on the island were forced to withdraw when Federal gunboats bombarded the fortifications there. Federal troops moved ashore and occupied the fort.

When the Confederate Army decided that the fortifications at Fort McAllister needed to be strengthened to guard against Federal ships sailing up the Ogeechee River, Odingsells sent his slaves there to help build part of the fort. Eventually, Fort McAllister fell to Sherman's troops. The Odingsells' slaves never returned to Little Wassaw. The Odingsells continued to live on Little Wassaw, but their financial circumstances were greatly reduced by the losses sustained during the war.

Lucy Ann Odingsells had met a young mulatto, by the name of I. M. Barnard, who was both cultured and well educated, much like herself. They married in 1847, and lived on Little Wassaw with the Odingsells until after the War Between the States. When Anthony and Madeline died in the late 1870's, Lucy Ann and her husband became the rightful owners of Little Wassaw. They sold Little Wassaw to the Parsons family and left the island forever.

[191] Will Abstracts. Genealogical Publications.
[192] Walter C. Hartridge Collection, Georgia Historical Society.

OSSABAW ISLAND

Chatham County's southernmost barrier island lies approximately twenty miles southeast of Savannah. It consists of nearly 26,000 acres of what is today an undeveloped sea island. The history of the island, however, goes back more than two thousand years when it was used and inhabited by aboriginal people. Their middens are evident in several locations on the island. This island was set apart in the early days of the colony for the Indian tribes that hunted there. A Spanish mission was established there in the mid-sixteenth century, but it was probably not a permanent one. The Spanish withdrew from the Georgia coast in the 1680's, leaving the island to those tribes who had always inhabited Ossabaw.

Thomas and Mary Musgrove Bosomworth owned the island until about 1760 when it a was sold to Gray Elliott. Elliott bought the entire island. He was the colony's surveyor and owned thousands of acres, including Ossabaw and Sapelo. Gray Elliott served on the Governor's Council, was Speaker of the House of Assembly, and was Grand Master of the Masonic Lodge. Elliott was a Loyalist, and left Georgia about 1772. After the Revolution, he applied for repayment for his Georgia property which he had lost during the Revolution.[193]

Henry Bourquin acquired Ossabaw from Elliott, and in turn, sold it to John Morel, his son-in-law, in 1763. Under the ownership of John Morel, the island was farmed and timber was harvested there. The term "live oaking" was used to refer to the practice of cutting virgin timber for shipbuilding purposes. In 1770, Morel advertised live oak and cedar ship timbers could be brought to the landings on Ossabaw and he would both buy and sell such live oak timber. That same year John Ward built the eighty-four foot *Elizabeth* on Ossabaw for Morel.[194] John Morel's wife, Mary Ann, died on the island in

1765. When Morel himself died in 1776, his three sons, Peter Henry, John, and Bryan Morel, inherited the land which was divided among them into plantations, according to the terms of John Morel's will.

As with many of the offshore and marsh islands, the resulting plantations passed through a succession of various owners. One of the plantation owners on Ossabaw was Benjamin Goldwire who died on Ossabaw in April of 1766. He left a wife, Ann, and a son, Benjamin.

The *Water Witch* was captured on Ossabaw Sound, July 1864.
Photo courtesy Georgia Historical Society.

During the period between 1760 and 1860, much of the island was devoted to the cultivation of cotton. There were approximately twelve hundred slaves living on the island during this time. Of the four original plantations' slave inventories that have survived, one which was compiled about 1812 lists 160 slaves from the Morel era. A second one, the Kollock Plantation Books, 1852-1860, lists fifty-six to sixty-eight slaves living on the south end. George Jones Kollock did not reside on the island full time.[195]

Another absentee owner during this period was Alexander McDonald.

Lt. Thomas Pelot, C.S.A.
Photo provided by Joseph H.
Pelot, USN, Ret.

John Deveaux's grave at
Laurel Grove South.

The period between 1861 and 1865 saw both Confederate and Union troops on the island at various times. No significant military action took place on Ossabaw itself, but it was in the waters of Ossabaw Sound in June of 1864, near Bradley Creek, that Lieutenant Thomas P. Pelot, C.S.A., succeeded in capturing the Yankee gunboat, the U.S.S. *Water Witch,* by means of subterfuge. One of the Confederate boats was piloted by a black man, Moses Dallas, who tricked the Yankees into thinking that runaway slaves were in the unidentified boat that pulled alongside the *Water Witch*. The Confederate boarding party was led by Lieutenant Pelot who was killed instantly when a Yankee bullet struck him in the chest as Pelot was attempting to shield another black Confederate, John Deveaux, from the barrage of gunfire. The capture of the *Water Witch* was successful after a brief and bloody confrontation, but the gunboat would be of little use to the Confederate forces, as it soon became expedient to burn the vessel a little more than ten days later in order to keep it out of enemy hands.

The bravery and valor of Pelot's actions in protecting John Deveaux were not forgotten. John Deveaux survived the war and eventually became head of the United States Customs Office in Savannah. Deveaux regularly tended Pelot's grave in Laurel Grove Cemetery. When Deveaux died in Savannah, June 9, 1909, he was buried

buried near Pelot's grave, in what is today Laurel Grove South.[196]

The *Water Witch* was not the only confrontation to take place in the waters in Wassaw Sound and the Wilmington River. Early on in the war it became necessary to deal with blockaded Southern ports. Savannah was not overlooked by Union troops who were in the process of blockading Savannah to prevent the shipping of cotton to Europe and the subsequent importation of arms and ammunition from England by the Confederate government. Confederate Naval Secretary Stephen Mallory appointed two men, James Bulloch and Caleb Huse, as civilian agents who were to purchase a steamer in Europe. Their choice was the *Fingal*, which was purchased and loaded with weapons and ammunition. The *Fingal* was to sail under the British flag, and its eventual journey from London was on November 2, 1861, bound for the West Indies with a British crew. Although the *Fingal's* official destination was the West Indies, in reality, Bulloch intended to bring the ship into Savannah. On November 6, the steamer reached Bermuda where a Confederate warship was waiting to escort the *Fingal* to Savannah.

The *Fingal* avoided the old whaling ships which had been loaded with stone and scuttled in the shipping channels by Federal troops, and arrived at the port of Savannah with what was said to be the largest single shipment of weapons to reach the Confederacy.

After unloading its cargo, the steamer then moored in the Wilmington River to await an opportunity to slip past the blockade and set sail for Europe once more. When this proved unfeasible, the *Fingal* was refitted as a Confederate warship and renamed the C.S.S. *Atlanta*. On its first naval engagement with the U.S.S. *Weehawken*, the C.S.S. *Atlanta*, which was outgunned, was forced to surrender after a very brief encounter.

Following the War Between the States, the old plantation system was no longer economically feasible, and the islands were left uncultivated and untended. Ossabaw Island slowly reverted to a wild state, the old fields becoming overgrown with various trees, shrubs, and other vegetation.

Two incidents occurred in 1867 which were of local interest. The first was the January attack on the *General Shepley*, a steamer

Two gravestones from the burial ground at Sweet Field of Eden in Pin Point, GA. The hand-lettered stone is that of Margery Devoe, age 80, who died in 1920. The second stone is that of Rev. Peter Joseph Famble, born in 1873, whose family came from Skidaway Island.

that had docked on Ossabaw to take on a cargo of cotton and supplies. The Freedmen on the island at that time believed that the steamer was there to kidnap them and transport them to Cuba. Consequently, they attacked the steamer and burned it.

The second occurred in May of 1867, when a crew member on the U.S. Coast Survey steamer *Endeavor*, which was on its way through Ossabaw Sound, discovered the bodies of two men floating in the water. The crew retrieved the bodies which were then identified as Henry Finnesey of Massachusetts and Thomas McGwiggins of Ireland. They were believed to have drowned when their sail boat capsized. The crew of the *Endeavor* buried the two men at the south end of Ossabaw Island and erected identification markers on each grave.

During Reconstruction, under the control of the Freedmen's Bureau and its agent, Tunis G. Campbell, newly-freed slaves were given land on the island. The few people living on the island at this time were former slaves who eked out a living from small garden plots of land, oystering and fishing, and hunting in the forests. It was an isolated existence. By the time of the 1880 census, there were approximately one hundred and sixty residents, living in about forty houses on Ossabaw.[197]

In the late 1800's, severe hurricanes devastated many of the sea islands, including Ossabaw Island. This disrupted the lives of the former slaves who made the island their home. The great storm of 1889 that flooded several of the sea islands forced the blacks there to move to the mainland. They came into the area known as Pin Point, and there they established the Sweet Field of Eden Church, a successor of the Hinder-Me-Not Baptist Church which they had organized on Ossabaw in the 1870's.[198] They continued to fish and oyster in the nearby river that separated Pin Point from Skidaway Island. The land their descendants occupy today has come to the attention of developers who covet the prime waterfront property that borders the little community of Pin Point, whose most famous son is Clarence Thomas, the first African-American from Georgia to sit on the United States Supreme Court.

The early 1900's saw wealthy investors and private individuals buying tracts of land on Ossabaw to use as hunting retreats. John Wanamaker, a Philadelphia merchant, bought several parcels of land on the island in 1902. He allegedly bought a prefabricated 1876 frame house that was originally built for the Philadelphia Centennial and had it shipped to Ossabaw. Recently, the validity of this claim has been questioned as more information on Ossabaw's past is uncovered. Three tabby slave cabins from the 1840's still exist, though in crumbling condition. Henry D. Weed of Savannah purchased the island in 1906.

In 1913, there was a proposal to colonize Ossabaw. The 25,000 acre island was then owned by U. H. McLaws and Henry D. Weed. It was to be sold for $300,000 to the Ossabaw Island Company, and the plans were to convert part of the island to a pecan orchard. The company also planned to bring in people from other parts of the country to settle there. A charter would give the Ossabaw Island company the right to sell real and personal property and establish a town. According to the plan, they would operate mercantile businesses and fisheries, establish a plantation and truck farms, build a canning plant and a printing business. There were also plans to clear and improve and drain the land, and to operate a dairy. Other plans included the manufacture of lumber ties, shingles, barrels and tubs, waterworks, and a lighting plant. There were rumors that a number of wealthy Englishmen and Canadians wanted to build winter homes on the island.[199] Evidently unforeseen obstacles to this plan prevented it from ever reaching fruition. Weed sold Ossabaw to a shipping firm in 1918, and it was used as a hunting preserve.

By 1920, there were five families, approximately twenty-three people, living on Ossabaw Island. One of these families was that of the farm superintendent, James J. Hineley, his wife, six children and two boarders. A second family consisted of Alexander W. Young, along with his wife and children. Two butchers, James A. Harrison and R. L. Heak and his son, made up two other households. The fifth household was that of a watchman, Charles D. Briggs, his wife and two children.[200] It is interesting to note that one of the boarders who lived with James Hineley was a female school teacher, which seemed to indicate that there was some effort to provide an education for the children on the island at that time.

[193] Reiter, Beth Lattimore, *Historical Narrative* from the National Register Nomination for Ossabaw Island, November 1993.
[194] *Ibid.*
[195] *Ibid.*
[196] Smith, D.
[197] Krueger, Gail, "Ossabaw Island," *Savannah News Press*, October 19, 1950, p. G1.
[198] Reiter, *op. cit.*
[199] "Ossabaw Island Co. Applies For Charter," *Savannah Morning News*, November 20, 1918, p. 10.
[200] Information obtained from the 1920 census records.

The Ossabaw Foundation

In 1924, the island was sold once again, this time to Henry Norton Torrey, a physician, and his wife for the sum of $150,000. The Torreys planned to use Ossabaw Island as a winter retreat. With this in mind, they built a Spanish-style mansion there that boasted nineteen bedrooms. After the death of Dr. Torrey in 1945, and that of his wife in 1959, Ossabaw Island passed into the hands of their daughter, Eleanor Torrey West and her husband, Clifford West of Bloomfield Hills, Michigan, and to the children of Eleanor's brother, the late William F. Torrey.

Clifford West was an artist, and it was this pursuit that gave birth to the idea of making the island accessible to artists, scientists, writers, composers, and others who were inclined to be people of vision. Thus was born the Ossabaw Foundation, which was established as a private non-profit group.

The Ossabaw Foundation was comprised of four important parts, the first of which was dedicated to the idea of permitting composers, linguists, writers, painters, sculptors, scientist, and others to work in a peaceful environment. Those who participated in this segment of the Foundation's program came to the island, stayed in the Torrey mansion, and pursued their individual talents. Their studios were once servants' rooms, garages, and a row of old tabby slave cottages. This was not exclusively an artist colony, but a group of individual thinkers which included ministers, automobile designers, and educators, as well as those dedicated to the arts. No more than ten or twelve members were allowed at one time. The applications for participants were reviewed by a board of advisors.

The governing body of the Foundation was made up of a board of trustees, the membership of which was composed of noted individuals in every field of science and the arts .Aaron Copland, the famed composer, and Harry Bertoia, the noted sculptor, are only two of the well-known and highly-respected personages who have served on the board of trustees.

The second phase was the Genesis Project, which provided an environmental awareness center. Those who participated in this project came to the island and built their own buildings, caught fish for food, milked their own cow, and planted gardens, all the while working on individual university projects. Water for drinking purposes was pumped from a well near an old rice field. This project was located at Middle Place, the only location on the island where nineteenth century construction still exists. Middle Place dates from the period when Ossabaw was cultivated as a plantation. The program came to an end in 1982 for lack of funds.

The Professional Research Project allowed scientists, ecologists, archaeologists, and other like-minded individuals to study the pristine environment unique to Ossabaw, within the context of their various disciplines. A few tabby slave huts, ruins of an old Spanish mission, Indian burial grounds, and ancient plantations draw their attention and study. The famous avenue of live oaks planted hundreds of years ago enhances the attraction for this spot and provides a timeless ambience to the setting.

The Public Use and Educational Project allowed school children, college students, and other groups to visit Ossabaw for a day, or to camp there for several days. Its primary purpose was educational, and was designed to introduce the participants to life on an untouched barrier island.

An interesting sidelight to the Ossabaw story concerns the feral donkeys on the island. It seems that Mrs. West heard of an estate sale on one of the islands off the South Carolina coast. The previous owner of that island had some miniature Sicilian donkeys which his heirs wished to sell. Mrs. West bought the donkeys as a gift for her young son, thinking that they would be interesting pets. She was unprepared for the results of this purchase. The donkeys had a mind of their own. Being very prolific, it was not too long before the feral donkey population exploded, and the number of donkeys roaming Ossabaw reached about eighty. After exploring several solutions for controlling the donkey herd, she finally contacted Penn State which rounded up all of the male donkeys and performed vasectomies on them. This step effectively curtailed the donkey population on Ossabaw.[201]

Recently, the Nature Conservancy developed a plan to rid the island of feral populations of both donkeys and pigs because of the damage they inflict on the ecology of the island. Many of the donkeys are being adopted to individuals who are mostly members of the Conservancy. Those which are considered too old or which tested positive for equine anemia will be allowed to live out their natural lives on their island home.[202] There is a recent movement afoot to rid the island completely of the Sicilian donkeys in a mass extermination. Their fate at this point is highly uncertain.

Rising taxes made it necessary for Eleanor Torrey West to sell the island. Threatened by developers who wanted to open the island to residential development, and fearful for the fate of Ossabaw, she sold the island to the state in 1978 for eight million dollars. The appraised value of the island at that time was sixteen million, but the owners donated half of that sum to the state as a charitable contribution. Ossabaw Island was the first piece of property acquired by the Georgia Heritage Trust. A 1978 executive order by then Governor George Busbee decreed that the island was to be set aside only for cultural and scientific study. It was to be used for research and preservation, and was to be maintained in its natural state. Mrs. West retained a life interest in the house and the twenty-four acres surrounding the house. Government regulations now make it illegal to land on the island in areas other than the beaches. Casual boaters who do land on the island may not cross the high water mark, thus effectively protecting Ossabaw's fragile and pristine wild state.

[201] Phillips, Patti, "Unique Miniature Donkeys flourish on Ossabaw Island," *Savannah Morning News*, August 16, 1996, p. 1B.
[202] Interview with Elizabeth DuBose, The Nature Conservancy.

THE MOREL FAMILY

The Morel family in the Georgia colony began with the arrival of Peter Morel who was born in 1700 in Zurich, Switzerland. He came to America to South Carolina with his wife and two servants. The Peter Morel family moved from South Carolina to Georgia when General James Edward Oglethorpe arrived to establish the new colony. Morel, one of the original settlers of Georgia, received land grants, and in 1751, became a member of the Georgia Assembly. He died in 1754, leaving a son, John, and a daughter, Mary Ann.

John Morel I, who was born in Georgia in 1733, married Mary Ann Bourquin, the daughter of Dr. Henry Bourquin, in 1755. The couple had five children, the last of which, Susannah, was born on Ossabaw Island in 1765. Her mother, Mary Ann Bourquin, died on Ossabaw Island as a result of this birth.

After his wife's death, John Morel I married Mary Bryan, the daughter of Jonathan and Mary Williams Bryan. From this second marriage, six children were born. John Morel was engaged in business with the East India Company. He became a member of the Provincial Congress in 1774, and a member of the Council of Safety in 1775. He died January 3, 1776, leaving Ossabaw Island to his three sons. Under the terms of Morel's will, each son also received one hundred Negroes and three hundred head of cattle. Morel also made handsome provisions in his will for his daughters. The Ossabaw Island plantation was divided among his three sons.

His son, John Morel II, inherited the south end of the island. In 1783, he married Sally Powell, the daughter of Joseph Powell of London. After Sally's death, John Morel II married Henrietta Netherclift O'Brien in 1785. From this marriage, three children were born. Morel was elected president of the Executive Council of the General Assembly for Chatham County in 1785, and served in that capacity, along with George Handley, John Houstoun, James Gunn, and William Gibbons. John Morel II died and was buried at sea in 1802.

Bryan Morel, the son of John I and Mary Bryan Morel, received the north end of Ossabaw under the terms of his father's will. He married Harriet McQueen and had four children.

Peter Henry Morel inherited the middle section of the island, which became known as Middle Place. Peter Morel, who had been sent to England about the time of the Revolution, was educated in Edinburgh where he became a surgeon. He married Tryphena Dunbar, the daughter of Thomas Dunbar of Liverpool, England, in 1778, and had six children, all of whom were born on Ossabaw Island.

Tryphena Dunbar Morel died in childbirth at Ossabaw during a storm that cut off all communication with the mainland. The baby, a daughter who was also named Tryphena, survived. Devastated by his wife's death, Peter Henry Morel moved from Ossabaw Island and never lived there again. He later was married a second time to Ann

Valleau, the daughter of Fauconnier Valleau of New York. From this marriage, twelve children were born. Peter Henry Morel contracted a fever on his Ogeechee River plantation and died May 9, 1812, at Montgomery. His wife, Anne Valleau Morel, died May 19, 1852.

Through the many descendants of Peter Morel, this family became allied, by marriage, with many of the prominent Savannah families, including the families of Deveaux, Walthour, Bryan, Forman, Hartridge, Millen, Wayne, Guerard, Barnwell, and Adler.[203]

[203] This information on the Morel family was provided by Emma W. Adler, a Morel descendant.

Tabby slave cabins dating to the 1840's still stand on old plantation grounds on Ossabaw Island. Photo courtesy of The Ossabaw Island Foundation.

A Sicilian donkey on Ossabaw Island ponders his fate. The long tenure of the feral donkey population on the island is soon coming to an end as the Nature Conservancy makes plans to eliminate it on Ossabaw. Photo courtesy of The Ossabaw Island Foundation.

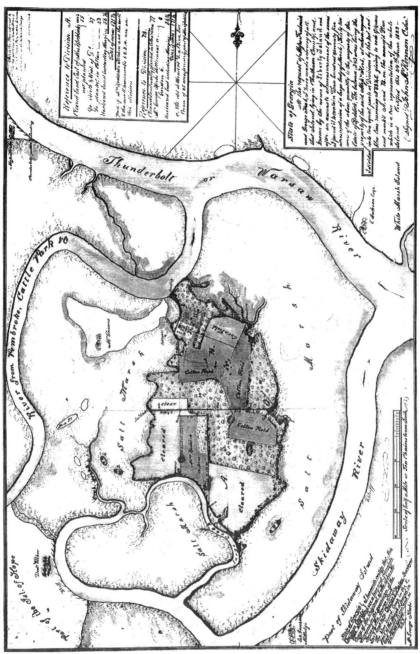

Early map of Dutch Island, 1823. Courtesy of Frank W. "Sonny" Seiler.

DUTCH ISLAND / LIBERTY ISLAND

The story of Dutch Island begins, as do the stories of the other islands, in the 1700's when the colonists arrived and began seeking land on which to live and make a living. The earliest Europeans to come to this small island were probably a group of German settlers, although this is not absolutely certain. In 1756, a grant from King George II of England divided the island into three sections. George and Frederick Herb were the recipients of one section. The other two were granted to the Gnann family and to the Reddick family. Corn and cotton were the main crops grown on the island. Originally called Providence Island in Colonial days, its name has changed several times over the years. Sometime later, after the Revolution, the name of the island was changed to Liberty Island, a name it kept until sometime in the late 1800's or early 1900's, when it began to be referred to as Dutch Island in deference to the German families who first settled there.[204]

The Reddick, or Radick as it is spelled in the early records, family had the longest continuous residency on the island. Their home was on the south end of the island near the cemetery. According to "Sonny" Seiler, the brick and tabby foundations for some of buildings on the Reddick plantation were still visible in the early 1960's. The plantation was described as consisting of slave quarters, barns, other outhouses, and a large, comfortable home.[205]

An 1823 map of the island, created by John McKinnon, Chatham County Surveyor, delineates Mrs. Reddick's property as consisting of a thirty-five acres, which was situated on a large creek, identified on present-day maps as Grimball Creek. The remainder of the island was under cultivation, producing primarily corn and cotton. This portion was owned by George and Frederick Herb, and encompassed more than three hundred forty acres. The old map shows a number of intriguing features, in addition to the layout of the cultivated and cleared fields. Mrs. Reddick's house is shown, as is that of the Gnann family on a hammock to the northwest. In the salt marsh on the western side of the island, a "Saltwell" is marked. Several landings are shown, and a "China tree" is plotted as the site of an old settlement. Other marked features include mulberry, oak and pine trees, dams, a pond, and an old circular bank.

Colonial records show that John Young was granted the north end of the island in 1763. His son, Isaac, acquired the property from his father the following year. A few years later, Isaac Young conveyed the property to Frederick Herb, Sr. and his wife, Ursula.

By 1769, the Herb family owned the entire north end of the island. Henry Danzler, or Denzler, who had received a fifty acre grant on the southwest portion of the island, relinquished his property and it was acquired by the Herb family as well as the other properties they had accumulated.

In 1823, the two sons of Frederick and Ursula Herb, George and Frederick, Jr. and their wives, had Liberty Island surveyed and divided into two equal parts. The portion owned by the Reddick family was excluded from this transaction. Eventually the northern portion of the Herb property was sold to the LaRoche family. By 1867, the Herb heirs had acquired the Reddick property as well. The south end of the island was finally all but abandoned, and the LaRoche family held the title to most of the island, with the exception of the property held by the Kreeger, Cleland and Kruger families. The Gnann family owned Gnann Hammock as well as other property on the island.[206]

In seeking information on Dutch Island, Steven Williams, who has compiled a great deal of information on the old Haven Home School which once stood where Bartlett Middle School stands today, suggested that I contact Mrs. Rita Mae Riley who was born on Dutch Island in 1933, and whose family had once "owned" Dutch Island and were the only people living there on the island in the 1930's.

[204] Seiler, Frank W. *History of Dutch Island*. A paper, October 25, 1994.
[205] *Ibid.*
[206] *Ibid.*

Rita Mae Duncan Riley

The interview with Mrs. Riley revealed much about life on the island during that period of time. Her story, as related to me, is given verbatim here:

> Well, I was born on Dutch Island, May 25, 1933. My family were the only people living on the island then. My daddy was Henry Arthur Duncan. He was born in 1903, and he died in 1951. My mother was Sallie Johnson Duncan. She was born February 5, 1905, on Skidaway Island.
>
> My daddy used to work at the yacht basin that was down here in Thunderbolt. My parents and us children would shell peas and beans to sell at Thunderbolt. We went to school at Haven Home. My daddy's uncles, James and Henry Tatnall, used to live at Isle of Hope at Grimball Point near the water. They all crabbed. And my uncle used to sell crabs on the bluff at Thunderbolt. One of our cousins stayed with us on Dutch Island, and he would row us over to Isle of Hope in the mornings so we could go to school. There used to be a public landing at the Isle of Hope in front of Judge Roote's house. If there was a storm, or the weather was bad, we would stay over at Uncle Henry Tatnall's at Grimball Point. It was understood that we would stay there in bad weather.

Haven Home Industrial School, where Mrs. Riley and her brothers and sisters went to school, was located on the present day site of Bartlett Middle School on Montgomery Crossroads, was established in 1886 as a privately funded boarding school for African-American girls. Girls from all over Chatham County boarded there. Boys were

Rita Mae Duncan Riley, September 2000.

allowed to attend the school as day students. The students came from Skidaway Island, Dutch Island, Pin Point, Sandfly, Ogeecheeville, Tatemville, and other areas of the county. A few came from other states. The subjects taught there included reading, mathematics, science, agriculture, carpentry, masonry, home economics, and music. The Chatham County Board of Education acquired the school in 1932.

> We used to grow all our food. We had lemon, grapefruit, and orange trees on the island. I remember we had one orange tree that was split, and one side had sour oranges and the other side had sweet oranges. I think my daddy did that by putting a piece of the sweet orange tree inside the split. We also had figs and pecan trees. There were lots of berries in the woods. We grew sugar cane and would grind it up to make syrup. I remember you had to stir it with a wooden spoon so it wouldn't burn.
>
> There was always plenty of meat. We raised hogs and chickens, and also had a milk cow, goats, and a horse. We killed hogs when the weather got cold and would hang them up. We made sausage and smoked the hams. We also had turtles and turtle eggs, and all kinds of birds. There were also deer, wild turkeys, and raccoons in the woods. The way you cook coon is to skin it, parboil it, and then put it in a roasting pan

with sweet potatoes, celery, green peppers, and onions and bake it. It was real good.

In the summer, we dried okra and shrimp by putting them on a piece of tin in the sun. You had to turn them every day, and bring them in at night or when it was going to rain, because if they got wet, they would spoil. We also dried butterbeans and onions. We had lots of vegetables, especially sweet corn. Of course, we had all the fish, crabs, and shrimp we wanted.

We used to burn cedar berries in the stove to make the house smell good. My mama used to make the best apple pie. She would roll the dough out on the table, cut up apples on it and sprinkle them with sugar and some spices, and then roll it all up and slice it. She made a cream sauce of curds and poured over it and then baked it.

Our drinking water was artesian water, and it was so cold and good. One part of the island towards the Thunderbolt side, there was brackish water. When we lived over there we had to get ice from Thunderbolt, and we would bury it in sawdust. We had an icebox. We had a good life over there.

I remember once there was a big storm. Our house had wooden shutters, and some of them blew off. Daddy made us all get down on our knees and pray. He said if we didn't know what to say, just say the 'Our Father' prayer over and over. He gave each of us two rows in the garden to take care of at planting time. He didn't care when we did work in the garden just as long as it was done when he came home from Thunderbolt. We would plant and help shell peas and beans, cut okra, and smoke our meat.

> When he came home from work, Daddy used to bring us little bags of candy. He would row over and eat lunch and then row back. Sometimes, he would bring a big 'Washington' pie. There was a big old oak tree in the front yard that looked just like a big parasol. Daddy built benches under it, and we used to eat lunch out under that tree in nice weather. Daddy always cooked on Sundays. Mama cooked all the other times.
>
> There were nine of us children. My brothers were William, Henry, and Arthur. Richard Mungin was a half-brother. My sisters were Ann, Bernice, Cinda, Margaret, and Rosa Lee Stoney. When any of us got sick, Dr. Frazier would come over. He was over here when mama had her babies. My uncle and his wife lived on the island with us. Our first cousins would come over and my grandmamas would come over Thunderbolt and stay a week or so. My mother is still living. She is ninety-five years old, and she has Alzheimer's.
>
> My Uncle Jack Tattnall lived to be a 120 years old. He used to drink water from a 'tesian' well in the river. He was born on Dutch Island, but in later years he started living permanently on Bradley's Island. It wasn't very far from us. He died about nineteen years ago.

When I asked Mrs. Riley why her family left Dutch Island, she had this to say:

> Well, my daddy died in 1951. My mother got sick with cancer, and we were supposed to divide the island among everybody equally. One of my sisters drank a lot of alcohol and always needed money to buy more. She borrowed money from Mrs. Mingledorff against her share. Finally, we had to sell to Mrs. Mingledorff, and we got cheated. We never got paid for Gray's Island

which we also owned, and she didn't pay us for Dutch Island. Now we can't go see where we were born, unless we have a card to go in the gate. My oldest brother Henry is buried over there. When he died, my daddy had to row over and get Dr. Frazier and the coroner to come over and give him a permit to bury Henry. Mrs. Mingledorff is dead now. [207]

I asked Mrs. Riley about the small church on Skidaway Road known as the Wilmington Island Baptist Church. She said that when the older Negroes moved away from the island communities where they had lived so long, the property was given to the community. The part of the property where Myers Middle School is, was all part of the cemetery. She said there used to be a little school and a house near where the church is now. The cemetery where Myers School is now was a very large one, possibly extending all the way back to 48th Street. When the state bought the property for the school, notices were placed in the paper advising people to come and claim the graves there.

Because many of the younger people had moved up North, many of them didn't know about the graves. Some, however, did come back and claim the graves, and they were moved to the site of the present cemetery there. Other graves were just bulldozed and built upon. She said that when the street was built out on Montgomery Crossroads, at Hopecrest Cemetery, some of the graves had to be moved. However, one lady who had relatives buried there said that she was not going to move her people, so the street had to go around one of the gravesites.

As to where her family went to church, she said that they used to come over to Skidaway Baptist Church at what was then known as Baker Crossing, but is now known as Sandfly. That was her mother's church, and it originally came from Skidaway Island.

Property records in the Chatham County Courthouse show that in 1878, Maxine J. Devergers sold property on Liberty Island to Diedrich Grimm. William G. Reddick deeded some of the island property to Jane W. Blois and Elizabeth Herb, who in turn deeded it to Herman D. Lankenau and Mary E. Lankenau. In 1926, Clyde F.

Lankenau sold the property to the Liberty Island Corporation for ten dollars and other considerations. This property consisted of a little more than two hundred acres on the southern end of the island. A family by the name of Krieger or Kreeger formerly owned the remaining north portion. The property transfers specified that a one-quarter acre was used as a cemetery, and this part was reserved by deed from William G. Reddick for this purpose.

The Fred Wessels family bought the island in 1928. Some timber was harvested by Mr. Wessels in the early 1950's, but for the most part the island slept undisturbed. A few Negro families who made their living by oystering occupied Gnann Hammock. Eventually the ownership was contested by Mary Louise Mingledorff, and a lengthy and complicated lawsuit ensued. Mrs. Mingledorff, who asserted that she not only owned Gnann Hammock and Sylvan Island, but took possession of Dutch Island as well, fenced in portions of Dutch Island, and hired a caretaker to protect what she perceived to be her property.

According to "Sonny" Seiler, this caretaker was a very large, rough looking man who lived in a shack on Gnann Hammock. His name was Johnny Ennis. For his services he received fifty dollars a month and provisions brought over once a month by boat. He also had a pack of dogs to aid him in his duties of protecting Mrs. Mingledorff's property.

In the meantime, Mrs. Mingledorff used her resources and other employees to explore Dutch Island. Her explorations included the cemeteries and whatever remained of the old buildings on the island.[208] She adamantly refused to sell Gnann Hammock to Fred Wessels, and at the same time she refused to leave Dutch Island, bolstered in her illegal possession of the island by her formidable caretaker, Johnny Ennis. The case was eventually resolved after several years of litigation. A causeway was constructed that connected Dutch Island to the mainland, and the island property, now owned by Fred Wessels, was subdivided and developed as a gated community of homeowners.

[207] Interview with Rita Mae Riley.

Matthew Batson and the Wonderful Aero Yacht

One interesting facet in the history of this small island took place about 1912. An Illinois aviationist by the name of Captain Matthew Batson chose the island as a location to build his fabled "Aero Yacht."

Matthew Arlington Batson was born in Anna, Illinois. He enlisted in the Army where he attained the rank of First Lieutenant of the Fourth United States Cavalry Unit at Calambra, Luzon, in the Philippine Islands. Batson was awarded the Medal of Honor in March of 1902, for his bravery in swimming the San Juan River under enemy fire and driving the enemy from its entrenchments.[209]

Captain Batson envisioned the departure from Savannah of the first trans-Atlantic aircraft. He organized the Batson Air Navigation Company, and sought investors to finance his dream of an aero yacht capable of transatlantic flights. He sought an isolated area where he could pursue this dream undisturbed. In 1912, Batson purchased land on Dutch Island from Isaac D. and Mary LaRoche. This tract of

Capt. Matthew Batson. From the collection of Frank W. "Sonny" Seiler.

Matthew Batson's staff and crew on Dutch Island in 1913.
Front row, left to right: Karl Monson, A.E. Wells, R.A. Mayer, W.H. Youhill, Matthew Batson, John Ross, Arthur J. Funk, A.D. Middleton (Secretary)
Back row: Gus Elmgren, Yngve Elmgren, R.F. Weston, R.P. Warner.
Photo courtesy of Frank W. "Sonny" Seiler.

land consisted of more than 171 acres, and made up the entire northern half of the island. It was here, on this acreage between the Herb River and Skidaway Island, that he built an aerodrome for the construction of his aero yacht, which he planned to name *Savannah*.

This facility was constructed large enough to contain the aero yacht. It included a marine railway that led to the Herb River

A second tract of land, fifty acres, purchased from Isaac and Mary LaRoche in the same transaction, was located on Whitemarsh Island and was known as the "Brickyard." This tract of land was to be used to house, in hangars, the planes he built at the aerodrome on Dutch Island. This part of Whitemarsh Island is located west of the Savannah Yacht Club and is bounded by the Wilmington River and Long Field Creek, directly across from the mouth of the Herb River.[210]

According to research by Frank W. Seiler, prominent Savannah attorney, Batson hired a native of Sweden, Israel Elmgren, a master boat builder, to build his aero yacht. Elmgren's sons, Gus and Yngve, were part of the workforce, as were other local people from Thunderbolt. Joe DeGracia was the wing-maker. The wireless operator aboard the Aero yacht was Arthur J. Funk. He was the youngest member of

The Batson Aero Yacht Factory on Dutch Island in 1913.
Photo courtesy of Frank W. "Sonny" Seiler.

the team. Other local people involved in the construction were Roy Greg and Raymond Meers, a future Chatham County Commissioner.[211] A number of other Savannah residents were involved as well.

The first Batson hydro-aeroplane was built on Dutch Island about 1912. The craft was completed and ready for its first trip on the Herb River in November of 1913. A limited number of invitations was issued to selected people in Savannah to inspect his flying ship. These guests, most of whom were stockholders in the Batson Company, left on the company's yacht from the Savannah Yacht Club and were transported to Dutch Island. This occasion was for the purpose of inspection only. Batson planned a trial flight later when tides and weather were favorable.[212]

The machine was huge, with twelve wing-planes. It included an enclosed cabin, with a lifeboat underneath. It was painted a steel gray. The twelve wings were so constructed as to be airtight and waterproof. Their mechanism connected with controls inside the cabin.

The strange craft was seventy-four feet long, with a thirty-three foot lifeboat. There was an eleven-foot propeller fastened at either end of the water plane. The wingspread varied nearly thirty feet to thirty-eight feet. Measurements of the tail were given as twenty by thirty feet. Its total weight, when loaded with crew and supplies for a long flight was estimated at nine thousand pounds. The water plane was said to be capable of attaining a speed of forty-five to sixty miles an hour. It was designed to lift off from the water after reaching a speed of forty-five miles an hour, and was equipped with three Emerson aeroplane engines which would raise it from the surface of the water.

Front view of the aero yacht *Savannah* on the Herb River at Dutch Island, 1913. Photo courtesy of Frank W. "Sonny" Seiler.

On November 15, 1913, Batson's flying boat was launched on the Herb River.

Captain Batson demonstrated the craft's perfect equilibrium on the water by having four men stand on one of the pontoons, thereby showing its perfect balance and buoyancy. Batson had kept the initial test launching a secret. Even the workmen in the aerodrome were not aware that it would be launched on the Saturday morning. In spite of the craft's massive weight of nearly three tons, it drew less than twelve inches of water. The radiators, which were custom-made by the Crescent Blowpipe Works of Savannah for the craft, had been installed outside and around the pilothouse, and performed perfectly. This venture was not the official launching, however. Captain Batson was reticent about divulging the names of the flying boat's crew and personnel, nor did he reveal his plans for the official launching. [213]

Mechanical problems plagued the venture. The Aero Yacht was launched into the Herb River by means of a marine railway from the factory to the river, but one of the propellers seriously damaged the aircraft. The Aero Yacht never actually flew. Financial problems added to Batson's woes. A reorganization of the Batson Corporation attracted new investors. A major local stockholder in the company was George F. Armstrong.

Undaunted by the failure of the *Savannah* to be successfully launched, Batson built a smaller version of the "air boat" and named it the *Dragonfly*. Some observers claimed the aircraft did fly for about thirty minutes at an altitude of fifteen feet. One who witnessed this actual trial flight of the *Dragonfly* was Joe DeGracia of Thunderbolt who had been a member of the construction crew from the beginning. [214]

A lawsuit and a sheriff's auction ended Batson's ambitious undertaking on Dutch Island. All of the property of the Batson Air Navigation Company on Dutch Island was sold on the steps of the Chatham County Courthouse on July 6, 1915. Included in the sale was both a large airship and its equipment and one small airship and its equipment. Three Emerson six-cylinder aeronautical motors were also to be sold. The fate of these airplanes and equipment is not known. At least some parts were thought to be in the aerodrome in 1917.

Matthew Batson went to West Virginia, where he served as a recruiter in the Army. He died of pneumonia in Wheeling, West Virginia, in January of 1917, and was buried in Arlington National Cemetery with full military honors. A daughter, Suzanne Batson Shorts, lives in Manchester, Connecticut.

A three-foot replica of the Aero yacht was on display at the now defunct Savannah Science Museum. When the museum closed, the donor, the daughter of Matthew Batson, asked that the model be returned to her. She then donated the model to the New England Aero Museum in Connecticut, according to information obtained from William E. Scarborough of Atlantic Beach, Florida.

In 1969, Fred Wessels, Jr., who was then president of the Southern Union Company and Liberty Island Corporation announced plans for a three million dollar residential development of what was by this time called Dutch Island. The plans included a marina, a golf course, and waterfront residential sites. The marina was to be located on the Skidaway River, and would be the only boating facility between Isle of Hope and the Modena Plantation docks on Skidaway Island. A causeway would connect Dutch Island with the northern section of Isle of Hope. Today, Dutch Island is a gated residential community.

[209] Seiler, Frank W., "Batson And His Magnificent Flying Machine," A paper. June 20, 1996.
[210] *Ibid.*
[211] *Ibid.*
[212] "Batson Flying Boat Finished," *Savannah Morning News*, November 12, 1913.
[213] "Batson Flying Boat Launched," *Savannah Morning News*, November 7, 1913.
[214] Seiler, *op. cit.*

THE MARSHES

The marshes of Chatham County have always provided protection to the mainland from storms, and are also important ecologically as the nurseries for the marine life that is commercially and recreationally vital to the seafood industry. It is only in modern times that the value of these marshlands has been fully explored and understood.

Efforts to fill in marshlands for residential development, dredging for the purpose of draining marshland and the spectre of mining the marshes for phosphates and other mineral materials, have been promoted over the years. Luckily, due to the intervention of those who were aware of the ecological value of the marshlands, most of these efforts were thwarted.

In May of 1968, the Kerr-McGee Corporation, a company based in Oklahoma City, presented a proposal, to lease offshore marshland in Chatham County to mine phosphates, to the State Mineral Leasing Commission for consideration. Their proposal included Little Tybee Island, Wassaw Island, Cabbage Island, and part of Wilmington Island — a total of about 17,000 acres of what was referred to in the proposal as "useless" marshlands. According to this proposal, the material that lay on top of the layer of phosphate would be used to fill up the marsh. Although spokesmen for Kerr-McGee admitted that the mining would destroy the fish nurseries, they said that the state would receive two million dollars annually from the three million tons of phosphates they hoped to recover from the mining operation. Kerr-McGee Corporation sought to obtain a twenty-year lease for $750,000, plus royalties per ton of phosphate, shell, sand, gravel, peat, humus and clay. The plan also provided a clause which would eventually create twenty square miles of high ground suitable for residential development.[215]

The company acknowledged that although much of the salt marsh would be destroyed, they would "rebuild" the salt marsh after mining, but the total area of salt marsh would be reduced. An interesting facet of the plan made provision for Kerr-McGee Corporation to receive more than $54 million worth of landfill material free of charge which would then be used to fill in land owned or leased by the corporation.[216]

One concern brought to the attention of the Mineral Leasing Commission addressed the problem of the ownership of the marshlands. It was believed that the state owned eighty percent of the marsh, but a widespread title search would be necessary to determine exactly who the owners were, and who was entitled to approve the mining or the filling in of the marshland.

In the mid-1900's, many found that the marshlands were a tax burden, and thus, many of the deeds addressed waterfront property in a rather vague manner. Interestingly enough, many of the marshlands in question were part of old Crown grants which defined the property line as being determined by the low water line. A Crown grant is the strongest title to property that exists and is very difficult to break.

As a young staff writer with the *Savannah Morning News-Evening Press*, Bill Carpenter began writing a series of investigative news articles which pointed out the consequences regarding this plan.[217] He discovered that the principal threats advanced by this proposal were the possible destruction of the fresh water supply of Savannah due to the dredging, which could damage the fresh water aquifer, the pollution of the ocean waters which would destroy both the commercial and sport fishing, and the filling-in of marshes which would destroy the seafood industry forever. In addition to these undesirable results, the construction of jetties to protect the mining operation would cause the rapid erosion of Savannah Beach, Tybee Island, and Wassaw Island.

This proposal produced a huge outcry throughout the state. Public hearings were held, and environmentalists joined forces with other prominent spokesmen to defeat this proposal. Commissioners John Rousakis and Tom McCarthy; State Representative Arthur J. Funk; Secretary of State Ben Fortson; John Hoyt, a young marine geologist; and others strongly protested the plan, as did Eugenia Price and Joyce Blackburn of St. Simons Island. Emotions were running high as local citizens, as well as other opponents to the mining operation, pointed out that it took ten thousand years for a salt marsh to form, and that it was highly improbable that it was possible to rebuild one.

This very controversial marshlands issue gave rise to a number of memorable quotes which succinctly stated the speakers' intense feelings over Kerr-McGee's plan to mine the marshes. John Rousakis was quoted in the *Savannah Morning News* as emphatically stating, "We cannot, we will not, take this gamble to possibly destroy our natural resources."[218] Another opponent called Kerr-McGee's proposal of replacing marshlands when the mining operation was completed as "utterly asinine."[219] Still another compared the proposal with the infamous Yazoo Land Fraud of 1784. Perhaps one of the more memorable statements made by an opponent to the mining proposal came in a heated debate in which an engineer for Kerr-McGee made the observation that "God gave us this gift of phosphate." This comment was quickly parried by a Savannah attorney, Ed Hester, with this pithy rejoinder, "That's right, and He put it way down in the ground close to Hades."[220] A petition, signed by two hundred four residents of Wilmington Island, was presented to the Chatham County Commissioners, urging them to vote against the mining proposal.

One of the more intriguing protests came from Frank Downing, who had once been a State Senator from Savannah. Mr. Downing gave spectators and protesters alike a new concern to consider in opposing the mining proposal. His statement told of a Strategic Air Command plane that was given the order to jettison two live atomic bombs in 1958 after colliding with a fighter jet during a training mission in the area where dredging would take place. The pilot was unable to land safely with the bombs on board, and, therefore, the jettison order was issued. Mr. Downing related that, after the bombs were dropped in Wassaw Sound, the Navy sent teams into the marshes to locate the bombs, but the numerous searches over a three-month period were unsuccessful in locating the bombs.[221] Mr. Downing's concern centered on the dredging operation activating the bombs. Although the Air Force confirmed the statement regarding the jettisoning of the bombs, they insisted that the bombs were not armed.

Interestingly enough, the *Savnnah Morning News* ran a story regarding the bombs on November 7, 2000, in which the Air Force reiterated its position that the bombs were not a nuclear threat to the coastal area. Official documents indicate that the bombs were not fully loaded, and did not contain radioactive material. They did confirm that the bombs once held four hundred pounds of TNT to detonate them. Several state politicians had requested that the Air Force re-examine this incident in regard to the location of the bombs and the possible threat to the area.

Dredging results in heavy silting of the water, reducing the oxygen content and affecting the aquatic life and organisms used as food by shell and fin fish. There was a strong possibility that the dredging would break into the fresh water limestone layer, allowing the intrusion of salt water into the aquifer. It was also noted that the phosphate market was glutted and therefore not in great demand, so why mine it? The answer to this questions appeared to lie in the creation of new land for residential use, which would be many times worth more than the two million dollars annually which the state would receive from the mining operations. The consensus was that such an operation would result in damage to many with benefit to only a few.

In light of the fierce opposition to the leasing of marshlands to a mining company, it was finally announced in December of 1968 that because the Georgia Mineral Leasing Commission failed to accept or reject the bid by Kerr-McGee Corporation by the deadline set forth in the proposal, it could not legally consider the proposal.[222] This effectively closed the seven month-long discussion of the proposal. However, it did give impetus to various pieces of legislation aimed at protecting the marshlands from exploitation, mutilation, and destruction.

Dr. Eugene Odum, head of the Institute of Ecology at the University of Georgia, when speaking about the preservation of Ossabaw Island, made comments regarding the importance of the estuarine habitat which is applicable to all of the marsh islands. He stated that the estuaries produce more energy than any other ecosystem. The marshes produce much of the oxygen we breathe. He said that it is imperative that we preserve the marshlands. Destroying the marshes can affect breathing in Atlanta, in Ohio, and even in Viet Nam. As far as recreational lands are concerned, his comment was that "wild is more necessary than recreation."[223]

[215] Cohn, Bob, "Marshlands Stand Gains Supporters," *Savannah Morning News*, November 18, 1970.

[216] Cohn, Bob, "Phosphate Report Called Whitewash," Savannah Morning News, December 11, 1969.

[217] Carpenter, Bill, "Economic Analysis Will Form Heart of Report on Kerr-McGee Proposal," *Savannah Evening Press,* September 29, 1968

[218] Cohn, Bob, "Rousakis, McCarthy Shun Move," *Savannah Morning News*, October 2, 1968.

[219] *Ibid.*

[220] *Ibid.*

[221] Cohn, Bob, "Kerr-McGee Puts Marshlands Issue in Spotlight," *Savannah Morning News*, January 19, 1970.

[222] Cohn, Bob, "Georgia Can't Accept Mineral Leasing Bid," *Savannah Morning News*, December 6, 1968.

[223] Cohn, Bob, "Kerr-McGee Focused Attention on Marshlands," *Savannah Morning News*, January 20, 1970.

HURRICANES

People who choose to live in the Southern coastal areas along the Eastern seaboard of the United States do so with the realization that the climate and the proximity of the sea provide a setting which is often threatened by tropical storms, especially hurricanes at certain times of the year. The storms known as hurricanes are born as tropical depressions in the waters off the coast of West Africa that make their way across the Atlantic, gaining energy from the warm water of the Gulf Stream. If all other conditions are suitable, a hurricane is born. The path the hurricane then travels depends on a large number of variables determined by temperature, wind patterns, air pressure, and even the configuration of the shoreline. Savannah is protected from many of these storms by the marshes and islands that act as a buffer between the city and the ocean. However, all of these factors can change in such a way as to produce a storm that can come in and wreak its destruction on the coastal areas.

The first documented hurricane to cause great damage to this area occurred in September of 1804. There was no warning that a storm of such magnitude was making its way toward the Savannah coastline. In the early hours of September 8, 1804, the winds began increasing, and by the middle of the day had reached full force. The storm would last about thirteen hours.[224]

According to newspaper accounts, an extremely high tide or storm surge pushed its way up the Savannah River, completely inundating Cockspur Island. Houses on that island were smashed by the wind and waves. People who were living on that island at the time found themselves clinging to wreckage in the raging torrent. Some of the survivors from Fort Greene, which was totally destroyed by the storm, managed to hold on to pieces of lumber and eventually washed up on Wilmington Island six miles away.[225] Others were not so fortunate. Eight soldiers garrisoned at Fort Greene lost their lives in the storm. The names of the men who drowned were listed as Corporal Reuben Armstrong, William Crafts, Daniel Lacy, Thomas Moore, Josiah Whitaker, John Glynn, Samuel McWilliams, and James S. Nicoll.[226]

A marker on Cockspur Island bears a description of the 1804 hurricane that destroyed Ft. Greene, the first fort on the island.

This hurricane caused vast destruction of property and life all along the South Atlantic coastline. The *Charleston City Gazette* estimated property damage in Savannah alone at between $350,000 to $500,000.[227] More than thirty vessels tied up at the wharves in the Savannah River were lost. Hutchinson Island had been completely covered, as had many of the rice plantations, and many lives were lost.

On that part of Wilmington Island which is known today as Talahi Island, the sloop *Governor Tattnall* was washed ashore near Bryan's Nonchalance plantation. No lives were lost in that mishap, and several days later the *Governor Tattnall* was refloated and sailed into the port of Savannah.[228] Some of the residents at Nonchalance were not so fortunate. It was this hurricane that caused part of the house at Nonchalance to collapse, killing Mrs. Hannah Proctor Screven and her infant son, John. Mrs. Screven was the daughter of Richard Proctor and Mary Ann Vinson. Her husband was Major John Screven, the son of Lieutenant John Screven and Elizabeth Bryan. The Screven's first child, James Proctor, who had been born in Virginia, would later attain prominence in Savannah as a physician.

Other planters on Wilmington Island were also hard hit by the destructive storm, and many of the plantations on those islands suffered considerably in loss of human lives, property, and livestock.

The next hurricane to be reported in the newspapers occurred on September 10, 1854. This storm, like its violent predecessor in 1804, was one of great violence. At that time, Savannah was in the midst of one of its periodic yellow fever epidemics, and the storm only produced additional problems for the city. A tidal wave produced by the storm completely devastated the sea islands. Hundreds of lives were lost in this storm also. [229]

August of 1871 heralded yet another hurricane, that while noted by the newspapers was not as severe as either earlier ones, or as those which would follow. On Cockspur Island one death was noted, that of Thomas Eagan who drowned when the boat carrying him capsized. Thomas, along with his father Patrick, and his brother, Michael, were attempting to light the beacon at the tip of the island. Patrick and Michael managed to cling to their overturned craft and were eventually washed ashore on a nearby island. The body of Thomas Eagan was never recovered.

The 1881 hurricane occurred on August 27. That particular storm did a great deal of damage on Wilmington Island. Newspaper accounts reported that Mr. Barstow's barn was blown down, and one of his mules was killed. Five Negro houses on the Pinder plantation and one house on Nonchalance plantation were all victims of the storm. Major N. O. Tilton's house on Wilmington Island was blown off its foundation and totally destroyed. At Dr. Oemler's place on Shad Point, the schooner *Daisy* was broken to pieces at the wharf, and the tugboat *Canoochee* was blown ashore about a mile and a half from the Oemler house. The *Canoochee* had traveled over four miles of marshes. It was believed that the *Canoochee* could be salvaged as it was lying about one hundred and fifty feet from a creek and could be dragged off the marsh rather easily.[230]

All of the colored hands on Shad's Island were drowned. Henry Douglas, one of the blacks living there, along with his wife and four children were in their house when the storm struck. He tried to save his family, but some timbers tossed in the raging waters smashed and broke his leg. He managed to struggle ashore, but could not save his family. The family of David Bowens, a wife and six children, were also victims. They all drowned when their cabin, located on Dr. Waring's plantation, was washed into the river.

The newspaper reported a tremendous amount of damage on Wilmington Island, and noted that the woods and fields on the island were littered with wreckage of houses, fences, furniture, boats, and dead cattle. It was also observed that several headboards, which likely came from soldiers' graves on Cockspur Island, were scattered in the woods on Wilmington Island.[231]

On Skidaway Island, houses at the north end belonging to A. N. Miller and to T. W. McNish were carried away by the storm. These two families were forced to spend the night in the fields. On the south end of the island, Captain M. D. Brown's house was washed away, and Mrs. Brown nearly drowned in the swiftly rising waters. The fate of the Negro families living on Skidaway Island was unknown, but it was surmised that they were likely washed away and drowned in the deluge that covered the entire island.[232]

August 31, 1893, saw another hurricane make landfall in Savannah. This storm was to last ten hours without letup. Tybee Island suffered greatly from this storm, being nearly completely submerged, as was Hutchinson Island. On Cockspur Island, the light beacon was filled by the storm surge, forcing Jeremiah Keane and Charles Sisson, the lighthouse keepers, to seek refuge along with others inside a stairwell at Fort Pulaski. The full fury of the storm passed over the sea and marsh islands to the east, and hundreds of Negroes were reported drowned. Bodies continued to wash ashore for days after the storm's passing. This storm lasted about ten hours and inundated the river islands.

In 1895, the local weather bureau received signal flags to be displayed as hurricane warnings. The hurricane flags were two red flags with black centers. These flags were to be used by several vessels which would, upon receipt of a hurricane warning, sail out along the coast and among the sea islands, flying the hurricane warning flags. This would alert residents along the coast and on the islands to make what preparations they could for the approaching hurricane.[233]

On September 29, 1896, yet another hurricane vented its fury on the Georgia coast. This storm was unusual because it lasted less than an hour, according to the reports. The loss of life in the area from this storm was given as fifteen, with five people being killed in the city of Savannah. An article in the *Savannah Morning News* dated October 3, 1898, gives a brief mention of Skidaway Island as being completely submerged by this storm. The article states that two white families lived on the portion of Skidaway directly opposite Isle of Hope. Most of the other residents on Skidaway Island at that time were Negroes. There was no report on whether there were fatalities there, or whether these people had been able to escape the storm. It was known that the causeway to Isle of Hope was under water at one stage of the storm, and Mr. Barbee's yacht *Neptune* was blown up on the bluff, but the cottages themselves appeared to have sustained only minor damage.[234]

---

[224] *Columbian Museum & Savannah Advertiser*, September 12, 1804, p. 3.

[225] *Ibid.*

[226] *Charleston City Gazette*, September 19, 1804.

[227] *Ibid.*

[228] *Columbian Museum & Savannah Advertiser*, September 15, 1804, p. 3.

[229] Lee, F.D. and J. L. Agnew, *Historical Record of the City of Savannah*, Printed and published by J. H. Estill, Morning News Steam-Power Press, 1869, p. 79.

[230] "Terrific Tempest, The Fiercest Gale Ever Known," *The Morning News*, August 29, 1881.

[231] "Horrors of the Cyclone," *The Morning News*, August 30, 1881.
[232] *Ibid.*
[233] *The Morning News,* July 28, 1895, p.8, c. 4.
[234] *Ibid.*

SHIPWRECKS

The men who go down to the sea in ships, those who are born with the taste of the sea on their lips, are by and large an adventuresome, independent breed. Savannah's geographic situation made sea trade mandatory. We think nothing today of boarding a plane and flying around the world, but in the beginning pages of our history there was always the sea, the early interstate, so to speak. General Oglethorpe, and those early explorers and colonists who came to the shores of this country long before the *Ann* made her first voyage, looked upon the sea as the highway to a new way of life.

Life aboard those old sailing vessels was not easy. In addition to the problems of adequate drinking water for a long voyage, preservation of the food supplies, the inevitable diseases and illnesses, and even piracy or mutiny on the high seas, the threat posed by raging storms was an ever-present danger. The annals of history contain numerous accounts of ships foundering and capsizing in hurricanes or other storms at sea. Too often the verdict rendered on a ship that failed to reach port was "lost at sea." The fact that so many ships did indeed make port safely with little or no loss of life or cargo is a tribute to the men who captained and manned these old ships, and to their seafaring skills.

Chatham County's coastline, with the Savannah River emptying into the sea at Tybee and the Wilmington River opening into Wassaw Sound, created ample opportunity for maritime disasters. The various wars fought in the vicinity also made their contributions to the growing number of wrecks that litter many of our waterways.

Unidentified shipwreck on Wilmington Island.

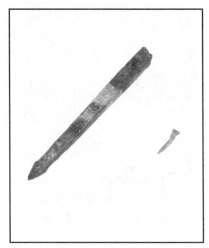

Muntz metal spike from Wilmington Island wreck.

The genesis of this book occurred when I was invited to visit the remains of an old wreck on private property on Wilmington Island. Little did I know when I happily took photographs and made inquiries, that I was awakening interest in an unidentified wreck whose location had been noted and recorded on the Georgia State Site File. The wreck had been discovered and reported by Charles Martin of Wilmington Island, whose title to his property is traced to a Crown grant that establishes the property lines to the low water mark. The old wreck appeared to have been burned at some point. It was investigated by Dr. Lawrence E. Babits and Rick Anuskiewicz about 1980, and they filled out a site form and recorded the wreck with the state. One of the interesting aspects of this wreck, which Dr. Babits tentatively identified as nineteenth century, were the unusual fasteners used to hold the planking to the futtocks. While barbed points were used in the old fasteners so that they did not easily work out of the wood sheathing, but gripped the wood, these fasteners were approximately ten inches long with a rounded top and a strange diamond-shaped point, which seemed to offer little gripping power.

Dr. Babits suggested that these strange fasteners were composed of Muntz metal, an alloy of high zinc brass content with approximately

sixty percent copper and forty percent zinc. In a telephone conversation, he did admit that he had found some artifacts from the period of 1740 to 1750, which would perhaps indicate an earlier vessel. He did not believe that the ship was burned for salvage. He stated that when a ship was purposely run ashore for salvage and burning, it is usually driven on shore bow first on a low tide, and is then burned to the waterline. The Martin wreck went in broadside, which suggested it may have been blown ashore. Some mid-eighteenth century artifacts were discovered in the archaeological survey conducted by Dr. Babits and Armstrong College in 1982. These were primarily china and pottery fragments. All that remains of the old wreck today are a number of partially burned timbers, visible only at very low tide.
According to Dr. David J. Killick of the Department of Anthropology at the University of Arizona, Muntz metal was patented in 1832, but it is quite possible and likely that there were examples of this alloy used in ship construction prior to the patent date. He described Muntz as being fairly corrosion-resistant in a marine environment, and thus well-suited for shipbuilding. He told me that it is a commonly used alloy for ships' fittings.

A number of early settlers on the islands engaged in some shipbuilding. John Penrose, John Morel, and others did build some ships in this area. Is the Martin wreck one of these, or is it what remains of some other ship that was tossed ashore in a storm?

Its caretakers have been the Martin family for over twenty years, but it is slowly succumbing to the ravages of time and of natural erosion. Its existence has tantalized a number of seriously interested individuals, but it seems determined to remain an enigma. It is registered with the state as a protected site.

Other ships were known to have wrecked in the waters of eastern Chatham County. A few of these are listed here for those who are fascinated with maritime disasters. Some of these were victims of storms, some were lost as a result of military engagements, and others were sunk because of exploding boilers or other causes such as human error or miscalculation.

SHIPWRECKS

Audacia, Portuguese Bark — 27 August 1893
Wrecked on Tybee Island

Aurora — Lost, cause unknown
30 December 1888, Wassaw Sound

Frank Harrington, Schooner — 28 January 1890
Wrecked on Tybee Island

General Shepley, 144-ton Sidewheel steamer
27 January 1867 — Fire — Ossabaw Island

Harold, Norwegian Bark — 27 August 1893
Wrecked on Tybee Beach.

Lampedo — Stranded on Wassaw Beach — 1866

Leila Smith, Schooner — 27 August 1893
Wrecked on Tybee Island.

C.S.S. *Water Witch*, 378-ton side wheel steam gunboat
19 December 1864 — Fire — Near White Bluff

PROHIBITION

One additional piece of island lore and history needs to be told. That is the role the islands played in that very controversial period of United States history known as the Prohibition Era. The concept of prohibiting the production and sale of alcoholic beverages goes back to the mid-1800's, when the state of Maine passed legislation prohibiting alcohol. As the nineteenth century began, the opposition to alcohol became more widespread. The Women's Christian Temperance movement was at the forefront in encouraging the enactment of prohibition measures to close the many saloons that dotted the faces of most of the cities in America. The National Prohibition Party, organized in 1869, won a seat in the House of Representatives in 1890. Great pressure was exerted by churches and other anti-alcohol organizations on the various legislative bodies and lawmakers. The Anti-Saloon League was formed in 1899. Most of us are familiar with the images of very stern-faced, determined, axe-wielding women, with leaders such as Carry Nation of Kansas, marching resolutely into a saloon and wreaking havoc with the merchandise there. Some of the cartoons during this period are not flattering at all, and these forerunners of women's liberation tolerated jeers and physical restraints with great aplomb.

While these early efforts awakened the people's growing awareness of how widespread was the abuse of alcohol, it was during World War I that a Temporary Wartime Prohibition Act was passed by Congress. The object was to divert the stores of grain in this country to food rather than to the distillation of spirits. Most Americans cooperated with this act in the interest of the wave of patriotism that swept the country. By 1920, total prohibition was in effect in thirty-three states.

Ruins of an old moonshine still on Skidaway Island show the gashes made by government agents in their efforts to destroy the stills which produced illegal whiskey during Prohibition.

The Eighteenth Amendment to the Constitution was passed in 1910. This amendment took away licenses to do business from breweries, distillers, and saloonkeepers. A bill known as the Volstead Act was passed and went into effect in 1920.[235] This bill prohibited the manufacture and sale of alcoholic beverages. Druggists were still permitted to sell alcohol for medicinal uses, as long as the patron had a prescription from a doctor. Such prescriptions were quite often forged.

Prohibition came to Savannah in 1908. The Anti-Saloon League obtained a large Curtis bi-plane which took off from Daffin Park and flew over the city, scattering the ashes of "John Barleycorn," along with the league's anti-saloon literature. At almost the same time, the United States Marshal in Savannah led a group of federal agents into the Ogeechee swamp where they destroyed three large stills. Forty-nine barrels of sour mash and one thousand gallons of brew were poured out on the ground.[236]

Georgia, which had been "dry" since 1911, rose to the challenge, so to speak. The independent farmers, who had found a lucrative market for the corn crops they grew, adapted very easily to constraints imposed by the law. Across the state, there were those enterprising souls who were quick to seize the opportunity to profit by the prohibition law. Many had bought out the entire stock of saloons before they closed down. According to the records published in the *Savannah Morning News* in 1924, thousands of gallons of contraband whiskey poured into the state through Savannah. Some of this whiskey was good; some was not. In fact, some of the whiskey was actually poisonous due to the materials and conditions under which it was distilled. A popular saying in vogue throughout Georgia at this period was, "All people are divided into two classes; those who have a little still, and those who still have a little."[237] This was the advent of the "Golden Era of Bootleggers."

Real estate prices for waterfront property around Savannah increased, due to the fact that the irregular coastline and marshes with their winding, lonely waterways were ideal for smuggling bootleg whiskey into the state. Moonless night brought the sound of speedboats, moving surreptitiously through the water off Wilmington, Tybee, Whitemarsh, and Skidaway, and throughout the marsh coves and inlets. These swiftly moving crafts were used to unload contraband liquor from vessels outside the three-mile limit, and then transport the illegal cargo into the marshy hide-aways where

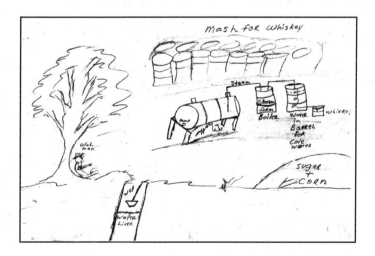

Drawing done by the last moonshiner on Skidaway Island, showing his construction plans for his still. Drawing courtesy Skidaway Island State Park.

waiting trucks would then transport the cargo to eager buyers. The Savannah newspaper called Skidaway Island "a veritable nest of moonshine stills."[238] This activity on that island, at least, so intimidated the Negroes who lived there that they were forced to move away to the mainland.

This era gave rise to the self-styled "Bootleg Princes" who operated fleets of fast cutters between the West Indies and Tybee Island. Some were even bold and daring enough to sail their illegal cargoes up the Savannah River and unload at the city wharves. Skidaway Island became a transport point for rumrunners bringing in cargo from the West Indies.[239]

The restrictions against alcohol created many headaches for the law officers who were sworn to uphold the law. Roadhouses, similar to the "speakeasies" of the larger, more cosmopolitan Northern cities, flourished in Chatham County. Men and women who were caught drinking in these roadhouses usually had their names recorded and then were paroled by the county officers who first extracted a promise from each of them to appear in court when the cases were called. The owners of the roadhouses were formally charged with keeping liquor for sale in their places of business, thereby being guilty of violating the prohibition laws.

The *Savannah Morning News* carried a lengthy story on October 30, 1922, on the so-called "King of the Bootleggers." Anthony Cassese, known as a millionaire bootlegger, was arrested in Savannah by federal officers on the charge of transporting whiskey from the Bahamas and bringing it in through Tybee Island. Cassese was extradited to New York where there was a prior pending warrant for his arrest in Brooklyn.[240]

In 1923, the fines collected in Chatham County for liquor violations totaled more than $13,000. The city government records for 1924 report eighty-three persons, in one day alone, convicted for some phase of bootlegging, were sent in two chartered cars from Savannah to the federal penitentiary in Atlanta. Those same records for the year, ending in June 1926, reported that the local district court had 851 liquor cases pending, 284 cases in the works, and 419 cases resolved.[241]

"Moonshiners" were also prime targets for the marshals. Often local officials looked the other way in many cases and did not seek warrants, unless some other individual swore out a warrant, thus forcing the local officials to serve it. In fact, Sheriff Meldrim made the statement that he would not issue any warrants, but he would uphold the law and serve any warrants that were brought to him.[242]

The moonshine stills on Skidaway, Whitemarsh, and Wilmington Islands continued to operate throughout the prohibition era. In fact, some of these predated prohibition, and they operated well into the twentieth century. Making "shine" was a quite lucrative pursuit, not requiring a lot of expensive machinery, and always finding a ready market.

Marion Boyd chuckled when questioned about the stills on Wilmington Island. His grandfather owned two stills, he told me. One was for personal use, while the other was for sale. Although other people ran the operation, it was grandfather Rhines who paid for them and owned them. Boyd remembered camping and fishing on the various islands and hammocks from Tybee to Ossabaw as a boy. It was not unusual to come upon a still on an isolated hammock. It was just a part of island living then.

Walter Schaaf had the following commentary on prohibition and moonshiners:

> During Prohibition there was a lot of bootlegging of whiskey going on out here and on Screven Island which is now called Talahi. Just before you get to the bridge going over to Oatland Island, there used to be an old building which we called the Casino. It was a Prohibition era speakeasy. We (young Walter and other neighboring children) used to go out in the woods and watch the bootleggers working their stills. Mr. Goette had a pig farm nearby, and once when one of the stills was shut down by law officers, all of the mash had to be disposed of. This problem was solved by feeding it to the pigs. "We had three hundred drunk pigs out here. There were squealing and cavorting out here. I went there with some other kids to watch them.

The Prohibition Act was finally repealed in 1933, and those who had profited from that illegal trade turned their attention to other pursuits. The federal agents, who had waged such a losing battle against many of the illegal rumrunners, now directed their attention to those evading taxes through the sales of untaxed alcohol. The age of the moonshiner was far from over, but the illegal smuggling of spirits from the West Indies and elsewhere was no longer a lucrative pursuit for local entrepreneurs. The making and selling of the local product known by various names such as "white lightning," "shine," "scrap," and other colorful designations, would continue up through the 1960's, much to the chagrin of the Treasury Department. Then, as now, the taxing of certain items seems to adhere to the scientific law of action and reaction.

[235] Behr, Edward, *Prohibition, Thirteen Years That Changed America*," Arcade Publishing, New York, 1996, p. 78.
[236] "They Scattered His Ashes From A Coffin Aloft," *Morning News*, January 12, 1938.
[237] *Ibid.*
[238] *Ibid.*
[239] *Ibid.*
[240] "Marshal Surprised At Army Reporters That Met Cassese," *Savannah Press*, October 30, 1933.
[241] *Ibid.*
[242] *Morning News*, January 12, 1938.

AUTHOR'S COMMENTS

Chatham County's islands still bask in the summer heat, but for many of them, that sleepy existence has vanished. Shopping centers, increased traffic, vacationers, and developers seem to conspire to destroy the ambience of a former time. Visitors are no longer happy to spend part of a summer in an old wooden summer home on the beach or river. Instead, condominiums rise high above the surrounding marshes. The old bateau that once provided dependable transportation, has been replaced by outboard motors and jet skis. The old fish camps have fallen into ruin. Even some of the waterways have vanished, victims of man's increasing desire to wield power over nature.

Luckily, a few of the islands, such as Ossabaw and Wassaw, seem to have escaped that frenzy we call progress. The marshes won a reprieve in the matter of the phosphate mining proposal, but clean and plentiful drinking water faces serious challenges as I write.

We can only abuse our natural resources so long, until they are irreparably destroyed. Man cannot create marshlands, nor can he reclaim a depleted aquifer. We tread on very dangerous ground when we play God with our resources.

The people who first came to these islands were seeking to carve out a place for themselves amid the vast live oak forests. They came to terms with a rural environment which enabled them to provide for their families from the resources at their backdoor. These people were determined to create a home for themselves. They were intensely family-oriented, and they live through their descendants, many of whom still remain in the area.

Though it is totally unrealistic, nor is it desirable, to return to the lifestyle of the first colonists who came to these shores, it is not too difficult to see that we have lost a valuable chunk of our birthright in our desire to exploit our own planet. In doing so, we destroy ourselves. We cannot recreate what has been lost, but we can recognize the loss, and strive to curb it. Each time a lonely gravestone or abandoned cemetery is plowed under, or bulldozed for construction, a part of our heritage is irreparably lost. Our ancestors, who gave us life, are obliterated by the desire for quick profits. In the long run, it is ourselves we are systematically destroying.

The young man in this early 1900's photo holds a black otter and a duck, both of which he trapped on Wilmington Island. Otter pelts were in demand by furriers in Savannah during this period. A properly prepared black otter skin would bring $10 to $16 in local markets. Photo courtesy of the Lynes family.

In this undated photo, an oysterman, with oars in hand, stands near the Oelmler Oyster plant on the Shad River. Photo courtesy of the Lynes family.

APPENDICES

Appendix A

ISLAND MARRIAGES

The following list of marriages involving island families came from a number of sources, including *Marriages of Chatham County, Georgia, Vol. 1*, compiled by the Genealogical Committee of the Georgia Historical Society, as well as from various published genealogies, family Bible records, newspaper accounts, and other family documents.

Adams, Samuel and Miss Mary Louisa Barnard (d/o William Barnard) 25 February 1820.
Amorous, Miss Kate and John Goette.
Amorous, Matthias and Miss Sarah Ann McCall, 17 January 1843.
Amorous, Matthias and Catherine Venghen, 15 May 1854.
Amorous, Matthias and Mary Sowney, 13 April 1855.
Arkwright, Mary and Henry Clay Houstoun, 4 September 1872.
Arkwright, Thomas and Lydia Lachlison, 25 January 1846.
Arkwright, Thomas and Martha Stanley of Philadelphia, 18 July 1860.
Arthur, John and Mrs. Susan S. Quarterman Barnard, 28 September 1838.
Barnard, Amelia Wash and Major John L. Morgan, 24 March 1864.
Barnard, Andrew Fuller and Fannie E. Turner, 19 October 1877.
Barnard, Ann Matthews, of Wilmington Island, and William W. Wash, 1 June 1829.
Barnard, Caroline Catherine and William P. Rowland of Macon, 27 May 1843.
Barnard, Florence Augusta (d/o Dr. James & Margaret W. Barnard) and W. L. Fulton.
Barnard, Frances (d/o William Barnard of Wilmington Is.) and John Cooper, 28 June 1803.

Barnard, Henry J. of Duval County, Florida Territory and Henrietta Bilbo, 4 January 1843

Barnard, Henrietta and Stephen S. Williams, 20 March 1817.

Barnard, James and Miss Catherine G. Guerard, 23 January 1811.

Barnard, James (widower of Catherine G. Guerard) and Miss Margaret C. Williams, 26 April 1819.

Barnard, John "Jack" and Ann Catherine Shad, 20 April 1814.

Barnard John and Lucy C. Turner

Barnard, John Bradley and Miss Martha J. Law, 4 May 1829.

Barnard, John Bradley and Miss Ann P. Law (Liberty County) 22 July 1837.

Barnard, John Daniel and Harriet Moore of Huntsville, Alabama.

Barnard, John Washington, and Miss Ann C. Shadd, 21 April 1814.

Barnard, Julia Persis (d/o Dr. James Barnard) and L. S. Quarterman, 30 September 1862.

Barnard, Miss Louisa T. and John Rowland, 23 October 1814.

Barnard, Lucy Washington (d/o Maj. John Barnard) and (1) Rev. Henry Charles Jones

Barnard, Lucy Washington (d/o Maj. John Barnard) and (2) Charles Odingsells Screven

Barnard, Margaret Louisa and George Washington Hardee, 13 August 1844.

Barnard, Miss Martha Ann and Keeland Tyner, 20 October 1803.

Barnard, Miss Mary Ann and James Dickson, 18 February 1835.

Barnard, Miss Mary Ann, spinster (d/o John w. Barnard, dec.) and Elias Butts Barstow, 17 December 1839.

Barnard, Miss Mary S. and Samuel Adams, 25 February 1820.

Barnard, Nathaniel Law and (1) Frances Elizabeth Dougherty, 5 October 1853.

Barnard, Nathaniel Law and (2) Augusta "Gussie" Walthour (d/o George Washington Walthour of Walthourville, Georgia), August 1888.

Barnard, Miss Sarah H. and John Everingham, 11 May 1819.

Barnard, Solomon S. and Miss Ann Mary Walthour (d/o Hon. George Walthour) 7 May 1846.

Barnard, Mrs. Susan S. Quarterman and John Arthur, 28 September 1838.

Barnard, Dr. Timothy G. and Miss Mary Ann Naylor Mongin, 23 April 1835.

Barnard, Timothy and Amelia Guerard.

Barnard, Timothy and Catherine E. Shadd, 30 June 1814.

Barnard, Virginia Clancy and Louis Demere, 19 July 1842.
Barnard, Virginia Margaret and William R. Pritchard, 3 May 1849.
Barnard, Vernon Rosa and James l. Hines, 12 December 1860.
Barnard, William E. W. and Miss Mary Ann Dawsay, 29 January 1828.
Barstow, Elias Butts and Miss Mary Ann Barnard, spinster (d/o John W. Barnard, dec.) 17 December 1839.
Bessett, William and Ann Shad (d/o Solomon Shad, Sr.).
Bexley, Simon and Catherine Readick, both of Liberty Island, 11 October 1810.
Bilbo, Henrietta and Henry J. Bryan, of Duval County, Florida Territory, 4 January 1843.
Bourquin, Mary Ann (d/o Dr. Henry Bourquin) and John Morel I (s/o Peter Morel), 1755.
Bower, Mary (d/o William & Martha Hext Bower) and John Williamson.
Bower, William and Martha Hext (d/o Hugh Hext of South Carolina)
Bradley, Col. John and Jane Bradley, 10 December 1743, South Carolina.
Bryan, Conrad S. of Twiggs County and Catherine Herb, 29 July 1828.
Bryan, Hannah Georgia of Wilmington Island, and James Proctor Screven, 9 March 1827.
Bryan, Henry J., of Duval County, Florida Territory, and Henrietta Bilbo, 4 January 1843.
Bryan, Jonathan (s/o Joseph & Janet Bryan) and Mary Williamson, 13 October 1737.
Bryan, Joseph and Delia Forman (d/o Gen. Thomas Forman of Cecil Co., Maryland)
Bryan, Josiah (s/o Jonathan Bryan) and Elizabeth Pendarvis, 14 August 1770.
Bryan, Mary (d/o Jonathan Bryan) and (1) John Morel, 24 January 1767
Bryan, Mary and (2) Richard Wylly, 3 June 1784.
Bryan, Thomas Marsh (s/o Joseph & Delia F. Bryan) and (1) Florida Troup. *Note: Thomas M. Bryan changed his name to Forman, 1846.
Butts, Eliza and John Robert Shad (s/o Solomon & Mary G. Shad)
Calhoun, Katherine Miller and Joseph Claghorn Saffold, 11 February 1942.
Carruthers, Dr. William A. and Louisa Catherine Gibson (s/o Robert S.& Sarah T. Gibson) 30 June 1823.
Cooper, John and Frances Barnard (d/o William Barnard of Wilmington Is.), 28 June 1803.

Cowling, Mr. Slaughter and Miss Betsey Herb/Hext, 26 December 1793.
Dawsay, Miss Mary Ann and William E. W. Barnard, 29 January 1828.
Delegal, Ann Rebecca and Tobias Thompson. 6 September 1842.
Delegal, Catherine and Capt. John Lightenstone.
Delegal, Edward and Miss Jane Delegal, 19 January 1809.
Delegal, Miss Sarah Jane and Thomas Canaday, 23 June 1832.
Demere, Louis and Virginia Clancy Barnard, 19 July 1842.
Demere, Raymond and Miss Mary Miller (eld. d/o late Samuel Miller, Esq.), 19 December 1784.
Demere, Raymond P. and Miss Susan J. Maxwell, 14 January 1819.
Densler, Mary A. E. (d/o David R. Densler, dec.) and Christopher C. Thompson, 23 July 1838.
Dews, John J. and Miss Harriet Gugel, 1 May 1828.
Dews, Robert J. and Miss Eliza M. Gray, 12 December 1816.
Dews, William and Mary————.
Dickson, James and Miss Mary Ann Barnard, 18 February 1835.
Dixsee, James and (1) Susannah Rogers.
Dixsee, James and Mrs. Isabella Rogers, May 1774.
Dougherty, Frances Elizabeth and Nathaniel Law Barnard, 5 October 1853.
Downey, Ellen and George Sweet Gray, 2 May 1842.
Everingham, John and Miss Sarah H. Barnard, 11 May 1819.
Fleetwood, Green and Miss Mary Morgan (of Effingham Co.), 5 December 1832.
Forman, Delia and Joseph Bryan (s/o Josiah & Elizabeth P. Bryan) 9 April 1805, in Maryland.
Forman, Thomas Marsh Bryan and (2) Helen Brooke, 1847. Note: (See Bryan, Thos. M.).
Fulton, W. L. and Florence Augusta Barnard (d/o Dr. James & Margaret C. Williams Barnard).
Fahm, Frederick and Sophia————.
Friend, Jacob and Georgianna Verdell, 20 February 1843.
Garbet, Mary Ann and Col. Solomon Shad., Jr.
Gibson, Louisa (d/o Robert S. & Sarah T. Gibson) and Dr. William A. Carruthers, 30 June 1823.
Gibson, Robert Stewart and Sarah Turner of Turner's Rock.
Gilbert, Mary Ann, of Wilmington Island, (d/o William, dec. & Ann Gilbert) and John Hughes, 31 March 1808.
Gilbert, William and Ann Ready.
Gnann, David and Miss Maria Sophia Reddick, 28 June 1820.

Gnann, Joseph and Caroline E. Bexley, both of Liberty Island, 16 March 1829.
Goette, Joseph and Miss Bridget Barrett, 3 April 1856.
Goldwire, Benjamin, Planter on Burnt Pot Island and Elizabeth——.
Goldwire, Elizabeth (wid./o Benjamin Goldwire, Jr.) and Captain Charles White, 22 September 1785.
Gray, Miss Eliza M. and Robert J. Dews, 12 December 1816.
Gray, George Sweet and Ellen Downey, spinster, 2 May 1842.
Gray, Mary Ann (d/o Tobias V. & Margaret Hartstene Gray) and Pierce Butler Prendergast, 6 February 1834.
Gray, Tobias Vanzant and Miss Ann Margaret Hartstene, 18 May 1809.
Gray, Tobias, Vanzant and Miss Margaret Coe, 23 March 1826.
Guerard, Amelia and Timothy Barnard, (s/o Major John Barnard.)
Guerard, Miss Catherine G. and James Barnard, 23 January 1811.
Gugel, Miss Harriet and John J. Dews, 1 May 1828.
Harstene, Ann Margaret and Tobias Vanzant Gray, 18 May 1809.
Hardee, G. W. and Margaret L. Barnard, 13 August 1844.
Henderson, Mary Elizabeth and Solomon Sigismund Shad (s/o Solomon & Mary G. Shad.
Herb, Catherine and Conrad S. Bryan of Twiggs County, Georgia, 29 July 1828.
Herb, Frederick and Ursula Peters.
Herb, George and Miss Sarah Shaffer (d/o Balthasar Shaffer), 9 February 1802.
Herb, John and Miss Sarah W. Potter, 8 April 1811.
Herb, Louisa Carpenter (d/o George Herb, late of Liberty Island, dec.) and Thomas Kreeger, 25 January 1841.
Herb, Mary (d/o late Frederick Herb) and John Kreiger, 28 June 1792.
Herb, Mary Ann (d/o George Herb, late of Liberty Island, dec.) and John Hunter, 3 August 1838.
Herb/Hext, Betsey and Slaughter Cowling, 26 December 1793.
Hext, Martha (d/o Hugh Hext of South Carolina) and William Bower.
Heyward, Elizabeth Pritchard (d/o John & Constantia Pritchard Heyward) and Armenius Oemler.
Hines, James R. and Vernon Rosa Barnard, 12 December 1860.
Houstoun, John (s/o Sir Patrick Houstoun) and Hannah Bryan.
Hughes, John and Mary Ann Gilbert (d/o William Gilbert, of Wilmington Island, dec. & Ann Ready Gilbert), 31 March 1808.
Hunter, John and Mary Ann Herb, 3 August 1838.

Johnston, William Martin and Lightenstone (Lichtenstein), Elizabeth, 21 November 1779.

Jones, Rev. Henry Charles and Lucy Washington Barnard, (d/o Major John Barnard).

Jones, James and Sally Eppinger Millen (wid./o John Millen), 2 August 1792.

Kreeger, Thomas and Louisa Carpenter Herb, 25 January 1841.

Krieger, John and Mary Herb, 28 June 1792.

Lachlison, Lydia and Thomas Arkwright, 25 January 1846.

Law, Miss Ann P. (d/o Nathaniel Law of Liberty County, Georgia) and John Bradley Barnard, 22 July 1837.

Law, Miss Martha J. (d/o Nathaniel Law) and John Bradley Barnard, 4 May 1829.

Lightenstone (Lichtenstein), Elizabeth (d/o Capt. John & Catherine Delegal Lightenstone) and William Martin Johnston, 21 November 1779 in Savannah.

Lightenstone, Capt. John and Catherine Delegal (d/o Col. Philip Delegal).

Lucas, Elizabeth and Charles Pinckney, 1744, in South Carolina.

McClesky, George A. and Mary Ann Shad, 5 May 1842.

McDonell, Edgar M., Jr. and Miss Sallie Gignilliat of McIntosh County, Georgia, 29 June 1869.

Mathers, William H. and Margaret Shad (d/o Solomon Shad, Sr.).

Maxwell, Miss Susan J. and Raymond P. Demere, 14 January 1819.

Mongin, Miss Mary Ann Naylor and Dr. Timothy G. Barnard, 30 June 1814.

Mongin, Susan F. and Solomon Sigismund Shad (s/o Solomon & Mary G. Shad).

Moore, Harriet (of Huntsville, Alabama) and John Daniel Barnard, 1854.

Morel, John (s/o Peter Morel) and Mary Ann Bourquin (d/o Dr. Henry Bourquin), 1755.

Morel, John (s/o Peter Morel) and Mary Bryan (d/o Jonathan & Mary Williams Bryan), 24 January 1767.

Morel, John Henry (s/o Peter H. & Tryphena Dunbar Morel) and (1) Mrs. Katherine Millen Waldburg.

Morel, Mary Bryan (wid./o John Morel) and Colonel Richard Wylly, at Brampton Plantation.

Morel, Peter Henry (s/o John & Mary Bourquin Morel) and Tryphena Dunbar, 1778.

Morel, Peter Henry (s/o John & Mary Bourquin Morel) and Anne Valleau, 25 February 1790.
Norton, Isaac and Miss Margaret Shad, 6 April 1819.
Norton, Thomas and Mrs. Tamar Waters (wid.) 16 March 1792.
Oemler, Allan Norton (s/o John N. & Marie C. Oemler) and Mary Teasdale.
Oemler, Armenius (s/o August G. & Mary Shad Oemler) and Elizabeth P. Heyward.
Oemler, August (s/o Armenius & Elizabeth Oemler) and Frieda Rauers.
Oemler, August Gottlieb and Mary Ann Shad (d/o Solomon & Mary Garbet Shad), 23 July 1838.
Oemler, Constantius Heyward (s/o Armenius & Elizabeth Oemler) and Sarah Pindar.
Oemler, Elizabeth Heyward (d/o John N. & Marie C. Oemler) and Villa Dale.
Oemler, Elizabeth L.(d/o Armenius & Elizabeth Oemler) and Fleming Yonge.
Oemler, John Norton (s/o Armenius & Elizabeth Oemler) and Marie Conway.
Patterson, Capt. William and Miss Henrietta Turner, 2 November 1841.
Pendleton, Phillip and Ann Catherine Cecilia Tebeau (d/o Frederick & Catherine Tebeau), 23 November 1841.
Pendleton, Phillip Coleman, and Miss Catharine Sarah Melissa Tebeau (d/o Frederick E. Tebeau), 14 November 1842.
Pinckney, Charles and Elizabeth Lucas, 1744, in South Carolina.
Pindar, Joseph W. and Miss Ann M. Tebeau, 14 December 1815.
Potter, Sarah W. and John Herb, 8 April 1802.
Preston, Henry and Miss Jane Delegal (d/o Col./ Philip Delegal, 1 June 1774 at Skidaway Island.
Pritchard, William R. and Virginia Margaret Barnard, 3 May 1849.
Provost, Peter and Ann Treutlen (d/o Frederick & Margaret Schadd Treutlen).
Provost, William (s/o Peter & Ann T. Provost) and Ann Cater (d/o William Cater), 1819, in Barnwell, South Carolina.
Putnam, Augustus H. (s/o Benj. & Anna Malcolm Putnam) and Mary Alice Tebeau (d/o John R. & Catherine T. Tebeau), 13 April 1815.
Quarterman, L. S. and Julia Persis Barnard (d/o Dr. James Barnard), 30 September 1862.
Rahn, Miss Ann E. Rahn and William Reddick, 9 May 1838.

Readick, Catherine and Simon Bexley, 11 October 1810.
Readick, William and Mrs. Mary Salfner, 1 July 1832.
Ready, Ann and William Gilbert of Wilmington Island.
Reddick, Ann and John Verdell, 21 March 1809.
Reddick, William and Miss Susan Densler, 25 May 1831.
Reddick, William and Miss Ann E. Rahn, 9 May 1838.
Saffold, Joseph Claghorn and Katherine Miller Calhoun, 11 February 1942.
Salfner, Mrs. Mary and William Readick, 1 July 1832.
Screven, Charles Odingsells and Lucy Washington Barnard Jones (d/o Maj. John Barnard).
Screven, James Proctor (s/o Maj. John & Elizabeth P. B. Screven) and Georgia Hannah Bryan, Wilmington Island, 9 March 1827.
Screven, Col. John (s/o James Proctor & Hannah B. Screven) and Mary White Footman, 1849.
Screven, Lt. John and Elizabeth Pendarvis Bryan, 13 January 1776.
Screven, Maj. John (s/o Lt. John & Elizabeth P. B. Screven) and Hannah Proctor.
Schadd, Margaret (d/o Col. Solomon Schadd) and Frederick Treutlen, ca. 1752.
Shad, Ann and William Bessett.
Shad, Ann C. and John "Jack" Washington Barnard (s/o Maj. John Barnard), 20 April 1814.
Shad, Catherine (d/o Solomon S. Shad) and Jack Barnard.
Shad, Catherine E. and Timothy Barnard, Jr., 30 June 1814.
Shad, John Robert (s/o Solomon & Mary G. Shad) and Eliza Butts of North Hampton, Massachusetts, 5 December 1827.
Shad, Mary Ann (Anna), of Whitmarsh Island, and George A. McClesky, 5 May 1842.
Shad, Miss Margaret and Isaac Norton, 6 April 1819.
Shad, Mary Ann and August Gottlieb Oemler, 17 February 1825.
Shad, Margaret and William H. Mathers, Sheriff of Chatham County, Georgia.
Shad, Margaret and Frederick Treutlen.
Shad, Solomon and Catherine————.
Shad, Solomon Sigismund, III (s/o Solomon & Mary G. Shad) and (1) Susan Frances Mongin.
Shad, Solomon Sigismund, III (s/o Solomon & Mary G. Shad) and (2) Mary Elizabeth Henderson.
Shad, Solomon, Jr. and Mary Ann Garbet.

Shadd, Margaret Norton and Francis Waver of Wilmington Island, 20 May 1851.
Shaffer, Sarah (d/o Balthasar Shaffer) and George Herb, 9 February 1802.
Stanley, Martha, of Philadelphia, and Thomas Arkwright, 18 July 1850.
Stark, Ebenezer and Mrs. Alathea Call (wid./o Col. Richard Call), 16 January 1800.
Tebeau, Miss Ann Margaret, and Joseph William Pinder, 14 December 1815.
Tebeau, Miss Catharine Sarah Melissa (d/o Frederick E. Tebeau) and Phillip Coleman Pendleton, 14 November 1842.
Tebeau, Frederick, of Wilmington Island, and Miss Huldah Lewis of New York.
Tebeau, Susannah (gr.dau./o Frederick Treutlen, dec.) and Lewis Turner, 27 November 1804.
Tebeau, John (s/o James Tebeau) and Catherine Treutlen (d/o Frederick & Margaret Schadd Treutlen).
Tebeau, Mary Alice (d/o John R. & Catherine Tebeau, Sr.) and Augustus H. Putnam (s/o Benj. F. & Anna Malcolm Putnam), 14 April 1815.
Torlay, Alfred E. and Miss Mary Elizabeth Thomas, 18 November 1844.
Thompson, Christopher C. and Mary A. E. Densler (d/o David R. Densler), 23 July 1838.
Treutlen, Ann (d/o Frederick & Margaret Schadd Treutlen) and Peter Provost, ca. 1780.
Treutlen, Catherine (d/o Frederick & Margaret Schadd Treutlen) and John R. Tebeau.
Treutlen, Frederick (bro./o John Adam Treutlen) and Margaret Schadd (d/o Col. Solomon Schadd), ca. 1752.
Troup, Florida (d/o Gov. George M. Troup) and Thomas Marsh Bryan, 1834.
Turner, Fannie and Dr. Andrew Fuller Barnard, 19 October 1877.
Turner, Miss Henrietta and Capt. William Patterson, 2 November 1841.
Turner, Lewis and Susannah Tebeau (gr.dau./o Frederick Treutlen, dec.), 27 November 1804.
Turner, Lucy C. and John Barnard.
Turner, Sarah and Robert Stewart Gibson.
Tyner, Keeland and Miss Martha Ann Barnard, 20 October 1825.
Verdell, Georgianna and Jacob Friend, 20 February 1843.
Verdell, John and Miss Ann Reddick, 21 March 1809.
Verdell, Peter and Miss Sophia Reddick, March 1812.
Verdell, Peter and Ann Reddick, 26 April 1815.

Vincent, Thomas and Hannah————.

Walthour, Augusta "Gussie" (d/o George Washington Walthour of Walthourville, Georgia) and Nathaniel Law Barnard, August, 1888.

Walthour, Mary Ann (d/o Hon. George Walthour) and Solomon S. Barnard, 7 May 1846.

Wash, William W. and Ann Matthews Barnard of Wilmington Island, 6 April 1830.

Waver, Francis of Wilmington Island and Margaret Norton Shadd, 20 May 1851.

Williams, Stephen S. and Henrietta Barnard, 20 March 1817.

Williams, Miss Margaret C. (d/o Stephen S. Williams) and James Barnard, 26 April 1819.

Williamson, John and Mary Bower (d/o William & Martha Hext Bower).

Williamson, Mary (d/o John & Mary Bower Williamson) and Jonathan Bryan, 13 October 1737.

Wylly, Col. Richard and Mary Bryan Morel (wid./o John Morel), 3 June 1784.

APPENDIX B

VITAL RECORDS
OF ISLAND FAMILIES

The following vital records came from the Barnard family Bible; the Morel family register; early Savannah newspaper records; early death register; private papers; and cemetery records and tombstones.

Amorous, Capt. Antonio. Died after Civil War.
Amorous, Mary.(wid./o Capt. Antonio Amorous). Born ca. 1823; Died in Atlanta, Georgia, 11 June 1888, age 65.
Amorous, Martin Ford. (s/o Capt. Antonio and Mary Amorous). Born 23 October 1858, in Savannah, Georgia.
Amorous, Matthias Oliver. Born 22 April 1810, in Minorca, Spain; Died 29 August 1864, in Savannah, Georgia.
Amorous, Sarah Ann McCall. (w/o Matthias O. Amorous). Born 9 June 1824; Died 20 July 1853.
Arkwright, Ann Ellen. (d/o Thomas and Lydia Lachlison Arkwright). Born March 1849 in Savannah; Died 6 February 1860 in Savannah; Burns; Buried in Laurel Grove Cemetery.
Arkwright, Lydia Lachlison. Born July 1833 in England; Died 10 May 1855 in Savannah; Buried in Laurel Grove Cemetery.
Arkwright, Martha Stanley. Born 1837 in Pennsylvania; Died 23 November 1877; Buried in Bonaventure Cemetery.
Arkwright, Thomas. Born 14 October 1821 in Preston, Lincolnshire, England; Died 16 July 1881; Anthrax; Buried in Bonaventure Cemetery.
Arkwright, William. (bro./o Thomas Arkwright) Born 1790 in Scotland; Died 20 October 1847 in Savannah; Engineer.
Arkwright, William Preston. (s/o Thomas and Lydia Lachlison Arkwright). Born January 1847 in Savannah; Died 14 July 1849; Mercury Poisoning. Buried at Laurel Grove Cemetery.
Arkwright, Thomas, Jr. s/o Thomas and Martha Stanley Arkwright). Born 10 July 1866 in Georgia; Died 10 October 1891; Opium Poisoning; Buried in Bonaventure Cemetery.

Armstrong, Corp. Reuben. Died September 8, 1804. Drowned at Fort Greene.

Bacon, Scott. Black. Died 27 August 1893. Drowned, with his son, during hurricane at Tybee Island.

Barnard, Dr. Andrew Fuller, (s/o Dr. James & Margaret C. Williams Barnard); Born 6 April 1839; Died 11 January 1908.

Barnard, Amelia Wash. (d/o Timothy G. & Mary Ann Naylor Mongin Barnard); Born 1838 on Wilmington Island; Died 25 May 1919 in Atlanta, Georgia.

Barnard, Ann C. Shad (w/o John W. Barnard; d/o Solomon & Mary G. Shad). Born 1782; Died 4 October 1850. Drowned on the *Isaac Mead*.

Barnard, Ann Catherine. Born 1 April 1820; Died December 1882. Never married.

Barnard, Ann P. Law (w/o John Bradley Barnard; d/o Nathaniel Law). Born 1819; Died 17 December 1891.

Barnard, Ann Mary Walthour. Born 18 January 1827; Died 16 April 1901 in Walthourville, Georgia.

Barnard, Bradley G. Born 2 February 1818.

Barnard, Catherine Elizabeth (w/o Timothy Barnard; d/o Solomon & Mary G. Shad). Born 1786; Died 1 September 1861.

Barnard, Mrs. C. Died 4 October 1859 on the *Isaac Mead*.

Barnard, Catherine G. Born 17 October 1813; Died 18 February 1818.

Barnard, Catherine L. Died 4 October 1850 on the *Isaac Mead*.

Barnard, Charles. Black. Died 4 November 1888. Accidentally shot & killed on Whitemarsh Island.

Barnard, C. J. Died July 1889.

Barnard, Clifford Victoria (d/o Dr. James & Margaret C. Williams Barnard). Born 15 February 1837; Died 30 March 1907. Never married.

Barnard, Edward. Born 1722 in England; Came to America ca. 1743; Died ca. 1775.

Barnard, Elizabeth (d/o Col. John & Jane Bradley Barnard). Born 14 July 1753.

Barnard, Florence Augusta (d/o Dr. James & Margaret C. Williams Barnard).

Barnard, Mrs. F. E. Died 1911.

Barnard, Godin G. Born 24 December 1815; Died 28 April 1816.

Barnard, Henrietta (d/o Maj. John & Lucy C. Turner Barnard). Born 31 October 1789.

Barnard, Isabella Zenobia (d/o Dr. James & Margaret C. Williams Barnard). Born 9 January 1835; Died July 1879. Never married.

Barnard, James (s/o Maj. John & Lucy C. Turner Barnard). Born 20 December 1789; Died February 1859.

Barnard, James Campbell (s/o Dr. James & Margaret C. Williams Barnard). Born 1 May 1830.

Barnard, James S. Born 9 December 1811; Died 25 October 1817.

Barnard, Jane (d/o Col. John & Jane Bradley Barnard). Born 19 August 1755.

Barnard, Jane Bradley (d/o William Bradley of London). Died 9 October 17?? At Wilmington Island.

Barnard, John Bradley (s/o Timothy & Amelia Guerard Barnard). Born 12 October 1807 on Wilmington Island; Died 25 December 1861; Buried at Laurel Grove Cemetery.

Barnard, John (s/o Col. John & Jane Bradley Barnard). Born 12 November 1750.

Barnard, John (s/o John & Jane Bradley Barnard). Born 10 January 1757.

Barnard, John (s/o William Barnard of Wilmington Island). Born 1781 on Wilmington Island; Died 20 October 1808 in Savannah.

Barnard, Col. John. Born 29 January 1720 in England; Died 1784.

Barnard, John Daniel (s/o John Bradley & Ann Law Barnard). Born 17 August 1830; Died 2 April 1860 in Huntsville, Alabama; Buried Laurel Grove Cemetery.

Barnard, John "Jack" Washington. Born 1783; Died between 6 November 1826 & 11 February 1827. Died in duel.

Barnard, John w. (s/o John & Lucy C. Turner Barnard). Born 23 December 1783.

Barnard, Julia Persis. Born 7 October 1831.

Barnard, Lucy Wilmington (d/o John & Lucy C. Turner Barnard). Born 13 August 1777.

Barnard, Margaret C. Born ca. 1701; Died November 1777.

Barnard, Margaret Louisa. Born 23 August 1826.

Barnard, Mary Ann. Born 1815.

Barnard, Mary E. (d/o Maj. John & Lucy C. Turner Barnard). Born 17 January 1780.

Barnard, Mary Henrietta. Born 2 May 1810.

Barnard, Nathaniel Law (s/o John Bradley & Ann Law Barnard). Born 15 April 1832 on Wilmington Island; Died 28 June 1910 in Savannah; Buried in Laurel Grove Cemetery.

Barnard, Robert (s/o Col. John & Jane Bradley Barnard). Born 10 January 1757.

Barnard, Sarah (w/o William Barnard of Wilmington Island). Born 1762; Died 9 January 1808 in Savannah at house of John Cooper, Chairmaker. Age. 40.

Barnard, Solomon Shad (s/o Timothy & Catherine E. Shad Barnard). Born 19 February 1821 on Wilmington Island; died 14 February 1875; Buried in Walthourville Cemetery.

Barnard, Timothy (s/o John & Lucy C. Turner Barnard). Born 2 November 1775; Died 1839. Buried in a vault on Wilmington Island.

Barnard, Timothy (s/o John & Jane Bradley Barnard). Born 3 November 1745.

Barnard, Timothy Rowland (s/o John Bradley & Ann Law Barnard). Born 1834; Died 1853.

Barnard, Vernon Rosa. Born 21 November 1824; Died 29 December 1907.

Barnard, Virginia Clancy (d/o Dr. James & Margaret C. Williams Barnard). Born 7 November 1821.

Barnard, William (s/o James & Margaret C. Williams Barnard). Born 1834; Died 1853.

Barnard, Dr. Williams (s/o James & Margaret C. Williams Barnard). Born 1834; Died 26 July 1864 at Fancy Bluff, Georgia. Never married.

Batson, Matthew Arlington. Born 24 April 1866 in Anna, Illinois; Died 16 January 1917 in Wheeling, West Virginia.

Barstow, Elias Butts, Jr. (or Eben E.). Born 1843; Died 1898.

Barstow, John Washington. Died 4 October 1850 on the *Isaac Mead*.

Bryan, Jonathan (s/o Joseph & Janet C. Bryan). Born 1708 in South Carolina; Died 1788 at Brampton Plantation, Chatham County, Georgia.

Bryan, Joseph. Born 18 August 1773; Died 5 September 1812 at Nonchalance, Wilmington Island.

Buchenau, Margaret (wid./o Nicholas Buchenau). Died 3 June 1800.

Buchenau, Nicholas (h/o Margaret). Died 25 June 1793 on Skidaway Island.

Cant, John. Born ca. 1804 in Scotland; Died 16 July 1860 on Wassaw Island. Age 56 yrs.

Clark, Ann (w/o William Clark). Died 9 February 1786 on Wilmington Island.

Coleman, Sam. Born 1848 on Wilmington Island. Died 25 June 1886; Age 38. Buried Colored Section of Catholic Cemetery, Savannah, Georgia.

Cooper, John. Born 1763 in Massachusetts; Died 5 October 1808 at Mr. Barnard's on Wilmington Island. Chairmaker.

Crafts, William. Died September 8, 1804. Drowned at Fort Greene in hurricane. Musician.

Davidson, Henry C. Born ca. 1840 in South Carolina; Died 7 August 1861 on Tybee Island; Age 21 yrs.

Dawson, Richard. Born ca. 1789 on Dutch Island; Died 16 July 1815 in Savannah; Age 26 yrs.

Demere, Frances Ann. Born ca. 1790; Died 11 September 1849; Age 59 years; Buried on Turner's Rock.

Demere, Mary Elizabeth. Born ca. 1759; Died 31 October 1783; Age 24 yrs. Buried Colonial Cemetery, Savannah, Georgia.

Demere, Mary E. Died, age 75 years. Buried on Turner's Rock.

Demere, Raymond (h/o Mary Demere). Died 22 May 1791; thrown from horse on Maj. Harden's plantation at Great Ogeechee.

Demere, Raymond P. Born 27 March 1791; Died 25 August 1885. Buried Turner's Rock.

Demere, Susan Jefferson Maxwell (w/o R.P. Demere). Born 10 July 1802; Died 29 March 1857. Buried on Turner's Rock.

Demere, Mrs. Virginia C. Died October 1900.

Deveaux, James. Died 27 June 1771.

DeVeaux, John. Born 1848 in Savannah; Died June 9, 1909 in Savannah.

DeVoe, Margery. Born ca. 1840; Died 20 April 1920; Buried in Sweet Field of Eden, Pin Point, GA.

Dixsee, James (h/o Isabella). Died 5 November 1785 on Burnt Pot Island.

Downy, John B. Born 1827 in Georgia; Died 4 September 1860 at Springfield Plantation on Skidaway Island.

Duncan, Henry Arthur. Black. Born 1903; Died 1951 on Dutch Island.

Duncan, Rita Mae. Black. (d/o Henry Arthur & Sallie Johnson Duncan). Born 1933 on Dutch Island.

Duncan, Sallie Johnson. Black. Born 5 February 1905 on Skidaway Island.

Dye, Sarah. Born 1842 in South Carolina; Died 3 February 1860 on Wassaw Island.

Fahm, Frederick. Died April 1796.

Feely, Michael. Born 1833 in Ireland; Died 10 August 1861 on Tybee Island; Age 28 yrs.

Finnesy, Henry. Born Massachussetts; Died May 1867 near Ossabaw Island. Drowned; Buried on south end of Ossabaw Island.

Fleetwood, Green. Died 3 November 1856 on Whitmarsh Island; Buried Laurel Grove Cemetery.

Fogarty, Eliza. Black. Died 1915 at Long Point, Whitmarsh Island. Buried on Whitmarsh Island.

Forumi, Lucy R. Born 1838; Died 30 July 1855 at Isle of Hope. Buried at Laurel Grove Cemetery.

Forumi, Mary. Born 1805 on Wilmington Island; Died 23 November 1855 in Savannah; Buried at Laurel Grove Cemetery.

Garbet, Mr. George (bro. in law/o Solomon Shad). Born ca. 1759; Died 23 January 1799 on Wilmington Island, at Mr. Shad's.

Gartelmann, Mildred K. L. Born 26 June 1899 in Savannah; Died 29 July 2001 in Savannah. Age 102 years. Buried in Bonaventure Cemetery.

Gibson, Daniel (s/o Robert & Sarah S. Gibson).

Gibson, Robert. Died 1790; Emigrated from Ireland 1755; Buried on Whitemarsh Island.

Gibson, Robert Stewart (s/o Robert & Sarah S. Gibson).

Gilbert, William. Died ca. 1796 on Wilmington Island.

Goette, Walter B. (s/o Joseph Goette). Born 1879; Died 7 October 1898.

Gray, Tobias Vansant (s/o George S. & Ellen Gray). Born January 1851; Died 3 April 1853; Buried at Laurel Grove Cemetery, Savannah, Georgia.

Greenman, Francis H. Born 1824; Died 26 August 1858 at Tybee Roads.

Haist. George (f/o Elizabeth Haist and George Haist). Died 16 October 1799.

Hardee, Mrs. Margaret L. Died November 1885.

Hartstene, Benjamin (s/o Catherine Harstene; bro./o Jacob Harstene). Died 27 January.

Herb, Ann Catherine (relict/o John Herb). Born 1764; Died 12 October 1823. Buried Colonial Cemetery, Savannah, Georgia.

Herb, Frederick (h/o Ursula Herb). Born 4 March 1728 in Germany; Died 26 October 1790 in Savannah; Age 62 yrs. Buried Colonial Cemetery, Savannah, Georgia.

Herb, Frederick. Born 1763 in Savannah; Died 28 February 1837; Buried Colonial Cemetery, Savannah, Georgia.

Herb, George A. Born ca. 1794; Died 25 October 1812; Buried Colonial Cemetery.

Herb, Sarah. Born 19 April 1785; Died 8 November 1802; Buried on Dutch Island.

Herb, Ursula Peters (w/o Frederick Herb). Born 28 October 1741 in Germany; Died 9 November 1814; Age 73 yrs. Buried Colonial Cemetery, Savannah, Georgia.

Heyward, Elizabeth Pritchard (d/o John & Constantia Pritchard Heyward). Born 31 July 1832.

Heyward, John (s/o Miles & Charlotte Villepontoux Heyward). Born 1807 in Pocotaligo, South Carolina.

Heyward, Thomas Wilson. Born 20 February 1834; Died 26 October 1868; Buried on Wilmington Island.

Higgins, Martha. Born ca. 1756 in Edenton, North Carolina; died 15 July 1808, Savannah, Georgia; Age 52 yrs.; The principal owner of Tybee Island.

Hines, Mrs. V. R. Died 29 December 1907. (see Barnard, Vernon Rosa).

Hopkins, Catharine T. Born 15 June 1833 on Wilmington Island; Died 27 June 1860; Buried in Laurel Grove Cemetery.

Hughes, Mary Ann (w/o John Hughes, Wilmington Island Planter). Born 1791 on Wilmington Island. Died 15 May 1813. Childbirth.

Hughes, Terrence (s/o John & Mary Ann Hughes of Wilmington Is., gdsn./o Edward Hughes) Born ca. Apr. 1813. Died 14 July 1813.

Hunter, Cassius. Black. Born abt. 1820 on Whitemarsh Island; was 78 yrs. old in 1898.

Hunter, Miss H. A. Born abt. 1709 in Georgia; Died 4 November 1820 on Whitemarsh Island; Age 11 yrs.

Jarvis, John. Died 10 December 1795 on Skidaway Island.

Johnson, Amanda. Black. Born ca. 1810, slave on the Barstow plantation. Died ca. 22 September 1888 on Wilmington Island & buried on Barstow estate. Some of her descendants were still living on the estate at her death. (SMN).

Johnston, Elizabeth Lichtenstein (Lightenstone). (w/o William Martin Johnston; d/o Capt. John & Catherine Delegal Lightenstone). Born. 28 May 1764 at Little Ogeechee; Died 1848 in Halifax, Nova Scotia.

Lacy, Pvt. Daniel. Died September 8, 1804. Drowned in hurricane, Fort Greene, Cockspur Island.

Lang, Lottie. Born 26 March 1885; Died 25 March 1945; Buried in Bonaventure Cemetery, Savannah, Georgia.

Lightbourn, John H. Born 1822 in Savannah; Died 5 October 1860 at Wassaw Island.

Lightbourn, Margaret E. Born 2 February 1858 in Savannah; Died 13 December 1859 on Wassaw Island.

Lucas, Elizabeth. (d/o George Lucas). Born 1722 in Antigua, West Indies; Died 1793 in Phildelphia, PA.

Lysaught, Dennis. Born 14 January 1854.

Madan, Robert. Born in England; Died October 1801 on Skidaway Island; lightning.

Martin, Patrick. Born 1835 in Ireland; Died 14 August 1861 at Skidaway Island; Struck by lightning.

McGwiggins, Thomas. Born in Ireland; Died May 1867 near Ossabaw Island. Drowned. Buried at the south end of Ossabaw Island.

McIntosh, George (s/o Lachlan McIntosh, the Elder). Born 1766; Died 5 May 1805 at Skidaway Island; Buried Colonial Cemetery, Savannah, Georgia.

McWilliams, Samuel. Died September 8, 1804. Drowned in hurricane at Fort Greene, Cockspur Island.

Mayer, John Hover. Born January 1860; Died 25 April 1860 at Skidaway Island.

Milledge, John. Born 1757 in Savannah; Died 1818.

Moore, Pvt. Thomas. Died September 8, 1804. Drowned in hurricane at Fort Greene, Cockspur Island.

Morel, Anne V. (d/o Peter H. & Anne V. Morel). Born 7 October 1801; d. 4 July—.

Morel, Anne Valleau. Died 19 May 1852.

Morel, Charles Harris (s/o Peter H. & Anne V. Morel). Born 31 October 1798; Died 18 October 1820; Buried Colonial Cemetery.

Morel, Edward (s/o Peter H. & Anne V. Morel). Born 13 September 1807.

Morel, George Dunbar (s/o Peter Henry & Tryphena Dunbar Morel). Born 24 May 1784 at Ossabaw Island; Died 4 November 1784.

Morel, Hannah Bryan (d/o John Morel I). Born 20 August 1776; Died 5 April 1790 from fall from her horse; Buried Colonial Cemetery.

Morel, Henry II (s/o Peter Henry & Tryphena Dunbar Morel). Born 22 July 1779 at Ossabaw Island; Died 12 August 1779.

Morel, James Seagrove (s/o Peter H. & Anne V. Morel). Born 4 July 1811; Died in Savannah.

Morel, John I (s/o Peter Morel). Born 17 February 1733 in Georgia; Died 3 January 1776.

Morel, John II (s/o John Morel I). Born 1 January 1759 in Savannah.

Morel, John Henry (s/o Peter Henry & Tryphena Dunbar Morel). Born 15 August 1780 at Ossabaw Island.

Morel, Harriet (d/o Peter H. & Anne V. Morel). Born 19 December 1804; Died 1 April 1868.

Morel, Henry III (s/o Peter H. & Anne V. Morel). Born 12 September 1794; Died 12 August 1807.

Morel, Louisa II (d/o Peter H. & Anne V. Morel). Born 16 August 1792; Died 15 July 1795.

Morel, Louisa I (d/o Peter Henry & Tryphena Dunbar Morel). Born 14 February 1783 at Ossabaw Island; Died 19 August 1784.

Morel, Louisiana (d/o Peter H. & Anne V. Morel). Born 27 June 1803; Died 8 August 1812.

Morel, Margaret (d/o Peter H. & Anne V. Morel). Born 1 August 1812; Died 1818; Buried Colonial Cemetery.

Morel, Mary (d/o Peter H. & Anne V. Morel). Born 6 May 1809.

Morel, Mary Ann Bourquin (w/o John Morel). Died 15 August 1765 at Ossabaw Island.

Morel, Peter. Born bef. 1700 in Zurich, Switzerland; Died 5 October 1754 in Georgia.

Morel, Peter Henry. Born 20 February 1754 in Savannah; Died 9 May 1812 at Montgomery, Georgia.

Morel, Susan Eliza (d/o Peter H. & Anne V. Morel). Born 1 December 1790; Died 28 December 1791.

Morel, Susannah (d/o John and Mary Bourquin Morel) Born 10 or 14 August 1765.

Morel, Thomas Dunbar (s/o Peter Henry & Tryphena Dunbar Morel). Born 13 September 1785 at Ossabaw Island; Died 5 October 1785.

Morel, Tryphena Dunbar (d/o Peter Henry & Tryphena Dunbar Morel). Born 21 January 1787 at Ossabaw Island.

Morel, Tryphena Dunbar (w/o Peter Henry Morel). Died 21 January 1787 at Ossabaw Island.

Morel, William (s/o Peter H. & Anne V. Morel). Born 12 May 1796; Died 6 August 1868 in Savannah.

Muse, Archibald. Remains moved from Green Island to Laurel Grove Cemetery 14 March 1854.

Nicoll, James S. (s/o Capt. Nicoll). Died 8 September 1804. Fort Greene on Cockspur Island.

Norton, Sarah Wilmington "Willie". Born 26 April 1827; Died in either Baltimore or New York where she was attending boarding school; Buried in Shad vault on Wilmington Island.

Norton, Tamar Waters (m/o John Waters). Born 1748; Died 5 January 1808.

Odingsells, Anthony. Mulatto. Born ca. 1784; Died 15 January 1878. Age 94 yrs.

Odingsells, Charles (h/o Sarah). Born ca. 1754; Died 4 June 1809 on Skidaway Island. Buried in Colonial Cemetery. Revolutionary War Patriot.

Odingsells, Charles Spencer (s/o Maj. Charles Odingsells). Born 1811; Died 17 October 1817; Buried in Colonial Cemetery.

Odingsells, Mary A. Free Black. Born 1780; Died 6 March 1860; Age 80 yrs.

Odingsells, Mary Susannah (d/o Maj. Charles Odingsells). Born 1808; Died 6 November 1817; Buried in Colonial Cemetery.

Oemler, Armenius. Born 12 September 1826; Died 8 August 1897; Buried on Wilmington Island.

Oemler, August Gottlieb (h/o Mary Ann Shad). Born ca. 1773; Died December 1852 on Wilmington Island.

Oemler, Augustus (h/o Frieda Rauers Oemler). Born 3 February 1857; Died 21 November 1927. Buried in Bonaventure Cemetery.

Oemler, Constantius. Born 8 March 1859; Died 6 April 1896; Buried on Wilmington Island.

Oemler, Frieda Rauers (w/o Augustus Oemler). Born 17 January 1879; Died 15 December 1916; Buried in Bonaventure Cemetery.

Oemler, Mary Ann Shad (w/o August G. Oemler). Born 1790.

Pelot, Thomas P. Born in South Carolina; Died June 4, 1864.

Pendarvis, Elizabeth (d/o Joseph Pendarvis). Born 23 May 1755; Died 5 April 1804.

Pinder, Ann Margaret Tebeau. Born 1790; Died 1800.

Priester, Lawton M. Born March 1860; Died 11 February 1861 at Springfield Plantation.

Pritchard, Constantia (d/o William Richard & Mary Ann Carney Pritchard). Born ca. 1881. Buried in Bonaventure Cemetery.

Provost, William (s/o Peter & Ann Treutlen Provost). Born 17 January 1783 in South Carolina.

Provost, Ann Margaret Treutlen (w/o Peter Provost; d/o Frederick & Margaret Shad Treutlen). Born 1754; Died 20 October 1827.

Provost, Peter. Died ca. 1830.

Quarterman, Mrs. L. S. Died 1906.

Readick, Peter. (h/o Catterenah; bro./o Michael Readick); Died bet. 21 August 1778 and ???

Richardsone, Cosmo P. Born ca. 1805; Died 8 February 1852; Buried on Whitemarsh Island; Moved to Laurel Grove Cemetery in 1856.

Robe, Francis. (gr.f./o John Milledge, Mary Elizabeth Demere, w/o Raymond Demere); Died bet. 16 April 1778 and 7 November 1782. Skidaway Island Planter.

Roberts, Addie. Born 1919.

Roberts, Samuel Capers. Born 1910; Died 17 January 2000 in Savannah.

Robertson, Susannah L. Born 7 December 1841 on Ossabaw Island; Died 30 August 1857 in Savannah.

Rowan, Lt. Robert. Born 1775 in North Carolina; Died 3 March 1800 at Fort Pulaski. Lieutenant in 1st Regt. Of Artillery & Engineers in U.S. Troops.

Saffold, Katherine Miller Calhoun. Born 21 April 1915.

Saffold, John Barnard. Born 27 February 1951.

Saffold, Joseph Claghorn, Sr. Born 21 April 1913 in Madison, Georgia.

Saffold, Thomas Peter. Born 23 September 1888 in Davisboro, Georgia. Died 9 May 1958 in Savannah, Georgia.

Savage, John. Died March 1879; Boat captain. Drowned in Wilmington River off Freeborn's Cut.

Schadd, Margaret (d/o Col. Solomon Schadd). Born 1726 in Switzerland. Died 1807 on St. Simon's Island, Georgia.

Screven, Hannah Proctor (w/o Maj. John Screven). Born 1778 in South Carolina; Died September 1804 on Wilmington Island.

Screven, Maj. John Richard (h/o Hannah Proctor). Born 1777 in South Carolina; Died 23 November 1830 in Savannah. Buried on Wilmington Island. Moved to Laurel Grove Cemetery 23 April 1878.

Screven, John (s/o Maj. John & Hannah P. Screven). Born 1803 on Wilmington Island; Died September 1804 on Wilmington Island.

Screven, James Proctor (s/o Maj. John & Hannah P. Screven). Born 1799; Died 1859.

Screven, James P., Jr. Born ca. 1836. Died 7 November 1854. Drowned at Wilmington Island; Buried in Laurel Grove Cemetery.

Schad, Margaret (d/o Solomon Schad). Born ca. 1728 in Switzerland; Died 1861.

Sellmer, Charles Howard (Inf. s/o Charles Marion Sellmer). Born 21 April 1872 at Fort Pulaski; Died 15 June 1872 at Fort Pulaski.

Shad, Annie. Born 1872 in Georgia; Died 21 July 1888. Age 16 years. Buried Laurel Grove Cemetery.

Shad, Catherine (w/o Solomon Shad Sr.). Died ca. 1790.

Shad, Edward. Born 1875 in Georgia; Died 21 May 1888. Age 13. Buried Laurel Grove Cemetery.

Shad, Elias Butts (s/o John R. & Eliza Butts Shad). Born aft. 1833; Died 1861.

Shad, Han Joachim, Jr. Born 1725 in Switzerland.

Shad, Harriet (d/o John R. & Eliza B. Shad). Died 1842; Never married. Engaged to Wm. Patterson who defeated Jack Barnard in duel.

Shad, John Robert (s/o Solomon & Mary G. Shad; h/o Eliza Butts. Born ca. 1794; Died bef. 1838.

Shad, Lydia (d/o John R. & Eliza B. Shad). Died bef. 1837.

Shad, Mary Ann Garbet (w/o Col. Solomon Shad, Jr.). Born 1750; Died aft. 1825.

Shad, Sarah (d/o Solomon & Mary G. Shad). Born 1788.

Shad, Solomon, Sr. (h/o Catherine Shad). Died 1768.

Shad, Solomon, Jr. Born 1750; Died 23 April 1833.

Shad, Solomon Sigismund III (s/o Solomon & Mary G. Shad). Born 1792; Died 2 July 1857; Buried in one of the Shad vaults on Wilmington Island.

Shaffer, Harriet S. Born 1805 on Wilmington Island; Died 5 September 1874; Age 69. Buried Lot 1077, Laurel Grove Cemetery.

Stevens, Henry. Born 23 October 1856 in Savannah; Died 3 October 1859 at Springfield Plantation on Skidaway Island.

Stewart, Fred. Died 27 August 1893. Drowned during hurricane on Hutchinson Island.

Stibbs, Ann; Born 1776 in New Jersey; Died 17 June 1858 on Wassaw Island; Buried Laurel Grove Cemetery.

Stiles, Margaret V. Born February 1860 in Savannah; Died 29 August 1860 on Green Island.

Tattnall, Jack. Black. Born ca. 1860 on Dutch Island; Died ca. 1981 on Bradley's Island; Age 120 yrs.

Tebeau, Ann Catherine Cecilia (d/o Frederick & Catherine Tebeau). Born 9 April 1818.

Tebeau, Ann Margaret. Born 1790; Died 1800.

Tebeau, Catherine Sarah Melissa (d/o Frederick & Catherine Tebeau). Born 28 May 1822; Died 12 May 1889.

Tebeau, Catherine Treutlen (w/o John Robert Tebeau). Born 3 June 1756; Died 16 1836;

Tebeau, Charles Watson (s/o John R. & Catherine T. Tebeau). Born 30 September 1796; Died 11 December 1823.

Tebeau, Daniel (f/o John Robert Tebeau). Died bef. 1757.

Tebeau, Frederick Edmond (s/o John R. & Catherine T. Tebeau). Born 6 December 1792; Died 6 April 1869.

Tebeau, James E. Born ca. 1825; Died 24 January 1851.

Tebeau, John Robert (h/o Catherine Treutlen; f/o Frederick Edmund & Charles Watson Tebeau). Born 17 November 1747; Died 12 October 1807; Buried in Tebeau vault in Colonial Cemetery.

Tebeau, Mary. Born August 1844; Died 7 October 1844; Age 2 months.

Tilton, Millie E.(youngest d/o N. O. & L. A. Tilton). Born March 1886; Died 20 February 1891.

Tilton, Maj. Nathaniel O. Born 1830; Died 11 February 1902; Age 72. Buried in Bonaventure Cemetery. CSA.

Torlay, Mary Elizabeth (d/o Alfred E. & Mary F.. Torlay). Born October 1849 in Savannah; Died 17 July 1852. Teething.

Torlay, Mary Elizabeth Thomas (w/o Alfred E. Torlay). Born 1823 in South Carolina; Died 19 October 1852. Childbed fever. Buried in Laurel Grove Cemetery in 1853.

Treutlen, Frederick (bro./o John Adam Treutlen). Born in Holland; Died ca. September 1793.

Turner, Elizabeth (d/o Richard Turner). Born ca. 1781 on Whitmarsh Island; Died 16 July 1816.

Turner, Elizabeth. Born 1819 in Georgia; Died 11 October 1861 on Green Island.

Turner, Lewis (h/o Jesten). Died bet. 22 July 1784 and 9 March 1786. Whitemarsh Island Planter.

Turner, Lewis. (bro./o Elizabeth Whiting; unc./o Lewis T. Whiting). Died bet. 11 July 1800 and 28 July 1803.

Turner, Lewis Tattnall. Born 5 November 1846; Died 30 September 1903; Buried in Laurel Grove Cemetery.

Turner, Mary Wylly Newell. Born 25 August 1846; Died 13 December 1916. Buried in Laurel Grove Cemetery.

Turner, Richard (s/o Lewis & Susan Turner). Born January 1814; Died 5 November 1816.

Ulmer, A. C. Died 27 August 1893. Drowned during hurricane on Hutchinson Island.

Vallotten, James. Born 1754 in Virginia; Died 25 May 1805 at Whitemarsh Island; Shoemaker. Buried in Colonial Cemetery.

Verdell, Sophia Reddick (w/o Peter Verdell). Born 2 March 1770; Died 10 June 1813. Buried on Dutch Island.

Verdell, Elizabeth (d/o Peter Verdell). Born 8 April 1806; Died 20 September 1809.

Verdell, Josephalia (d/o Peter Verdell). Born 7 April 1809. Died 25 April 1809.

Verdell, Maria. Born 26 September 1807; Died 8 October 1807.

Verdell, Peter. (s/o Peter Verdell). Born 8 April 1806. Died 11 April 1809.

Vincent, Thomas. Born ca. 1728; Died September 1767; Buried Colonial Cemetery.

Waters, Alicia "Elecy" (w/o John B. Waters). Born ca. 1782; Died 17 March 1808 in Savannah; Buried on Skidaway Island.

Walker, Mary Gertrude. Born April 1856; Died 5 July 1856 on Wassaw Island; Buried at Laurel Grove Cemetery.

Waters, John B. (s/o Tamar). Born ca. 1769 in Scotland; Died 17 September 1835; Buried Colonial Cemetery; Moved to Laurel Grove Cemetery 16 May 1859 to Lot # 1110.

Waters, John B., Jr. (s/o John B. & Alicia Waters). Born 1802; Died 25 December 1804; Buried on Skidaway Island.

West, Alfred James. Born 1852 in New York' Died 10 September 1858 at Cockspur Island.

Whitaker, Joseph. Died September 8, 1804. Drowned in hurricane at Fort Greene, Cockspur Island.

Williams, Jane (w/o David D. Williams). Born 1780 on Wilmington Island. Died 7 February 1816. Childbirth.

Williamson, Mary (d/o John & Mary Bower Williamson).

Wilson, Peter. Died 14 May 1858; Drowned at Wassaw Island.

Yonge, Daniel Fleming. Born 5 August 1855; Died 12 March 1937; Buried on Wilmington Island.

Yonge, Elizabeth Oemler. Born 23 October 1860; Buried on Wilmington Island.

APPENDIX C

LIST OF SOME BLACKS WHO WERE ISLAND-BORN AND LATER MOVED TO SANDFLY, PINPOINT, AND OTHER MAINLAND LOCATIONS

The following information was provided by Mr. Kemp of Sandfly.

Barney, Mrs. Hattie Hargroves (d/o Balaam & Mary Hargroves; w/o 1st William Green, 2nd Prince Barney). Born 8 June 1882 on Skidaway Island; Died 20 January 1964.

Baker, Pearl Famble (d/o Rev.& Mrs. Peter J. Famble, the 9th of 12 chdn.; w/o Joseph Baker). Born 10 November 1911 on Skidaway Island; Died 15 November 1976.

Bivens. Deacon Daniel (s/o John & Alice Bivens; h/o Ellie Newton). Born 20 January 1910 on Skidaway Island; Died 13 August 1980.

Brown, Clara Bivens (d/o John & Alice Bivens; m. George Brown 15 June 1950). Born 12 May 1906 on Skidaway Island; Died 27 January 1974.

Chisholm, Rena Bonds. (d/o Lizzie & Shed Bonds; w/o Johnny Chisholm, 1928; 2 chdn.). Born 1 May 1897 on Skidaway Island; Died 7 November 1972; Member of Sweet Field of Eden Church at Pin Point.

Famble, Cornelia W. "Ms. Whoshoo" (w/o 1st Paul Martin, 2 chdn.; 2nd Joseph Famble, 6 chdn.) Born 24 December 1903 on Skidaway Island; Died 2 July 1987.

Golden, Isaac "Ike" (s/o Hattie Slee & Esau Golden; h/o Mrs. Grace Battey, 28 July 1946). Born on Skidaway Island; Died 30 October 1989; Veteran of W.W.II.

Golden, Isaac Leon (s/o Betsy & Jacob Golden); Born on Skidaway Island; Died 25 September 1967.

Golden, Jacob (s/o Sylvia & Peter Golden; h/o 1st Bette Hargroves, 8 chdn., 2nd Mrs. Florence Perry, 1955). Born Skidaway Island;

Died 2 March 1970.

Martin, Clyde "Cheater", Sr.(s/o Sarah Martin Smith; h/o Dorothy Martin, 5 chdn.) Born 13 November 1926 on Skidaway Island; Died 5 February 1994.

Martin, Nelson (s/o Charles & Katie Martin) Born 1 April 1909 on Skidaway Island; Died 1 June 1984. Had 4 chdn.

Mitchell, Katie Slee. Born 1900 on Skidaway Island; Died 1981.

Moses, Phyllis Simmons, "Ms. Fibbie" (d/o John & Claw Simmons; w/o Eddie Moses, 5 chdn.). Born 1 October 1882 on Skidaway Island; Died 20 August 1986.

Riley, Rita Mae Duncan. (d/o Henry Arthur & Sallie Johnson Duncan). Born 1933 on Dutch Island.

Williams, Cyrus (s/o Andrew & Patience Williams; h/o 1st Helen Wright, 5 chdn.; 2nd Susie George). Born 1 March 1910 on Skidaway Island.

Williams, Louise Golden (d/o Jacob "Papa Jake" & Betty Hargroves Golden; w/o Clarence Williams, 9 May 1933; no chdn.). Born 24 December 1904 on Skidaway Island; Died 9 September 1997.

Wright, Patience Parker (d/o Andrew & Clara Parker; w/o 1st Andrew Williams; 2nd John Wright). Born 19 July 1888 on Skidaway Island; Died 3 August 1975.

Appendix D

GRAVE SITES ON THE ISLANDS

Known Grave Sites

Bryan, Joseph on Talahi Island.
Bryan, Delia on Talahi Island.
Delegal, Philip on Skidaway Island.
Gibson, Robert on Whitemarsh Island.
Gibson, Sarah Stewart on Whitemarsh Island.
Herb, Sarah on Dutch Island.
Heyward, Thomas Wilson on Wilmington Island.
Oemler, Armenius on Wilmington Island.
Oemler, Constantius on Wilmington Island.
Rowan, Robert on Cockspur Island
Sellmer, Charles Howard on Cockspur Island
Verdell, Sophia Reddick on Dutch Island.
Waters, Alicia "Elecy" on Skidaway Island.
Waters, John B., Jr. on Skidaway Island.

Lost Grave Sites

African cemetery on Wilmington Island.
Barstow vault on Wilmington Island.
Duncan cemetery on Dutch Island.
Finnesy, Henry on the south end of Ossabaw Island
Fogarty, Eliza on Whitemarsh Island.
Gnann cemetery on Dutch Island.
Herb cemetery on Dutch Island.
Hunter cemetery on Wilmington Island.
Jenkins, Mollie on Whitemarsh Island.
McGwiggins, Thomas on the south end of Ossabaw Island
Norton, Sarah Wilmington "Willie" on Wilmington Island.

Reddick/Readick/Radick cemetery on Dutch Island.
Shad, Col. Solomon S. on Wilmington Island.
Shad vault on Wilmington Island.
Verdell cemetery on Dutch Island.
Yonge, Daniel Fleming on Wilmington Island.
Yonge, Elizabeth Oemler on Wilmington Island.

Appendix E

ISLANDERS WHO WERE <u>KNOWN</u> VICTIMS OF MAJOR HURRICANES THAT SWEPT THE ISLANDS

Note: In each of these cases there were hundreds of victims who were not named. These names were gleaned from the newspaper accounts of the storm, and represent people who were known to be on the islands at that particular time.

Hurricane of 1804:

Armstrong, Corporal Reuben. Drowned at Fort Greene on Cockspur Island.

Bones, Reuben. Died of wounds received in storm on Cockspur Island.

Crafts, Pvt. William. Drowned at Fort Greene on Cockspur Island.

Glynn, John. Drowned at Fort Greene on Cockspur Island.

Lacy, Pvt. Daniel. Drowned at Fort Greene on Cockspur Island.

McWilliams, Samuel. Drowned at Fort Greene on Cockspur Island.

Moore, Pvt. Thomas. Drowned at Fort Greene on Cockspur Island.

Moxham, John. Overseer. Drowned with his wife on Hutchinson Island.

Nicoll, James C. Drowned at Fort Greene on Cockspur Island.

Screven, Hannah Proctor. Killed when house collapsed on Screven Island[+]

Screven, John. Infant. Killed when house collapsed on Screven Island[+]

Whitaker, Joseph. Drowned at Fort Greene on Cockspur Island.

Hurricane of 1871:

Thomas Eagan. Drowned on Cockspur Island when boat capsized.

Hurricane of 1881:

Bowens, David. Black. Drowned with wife & six children on Shad's Island.*
Brown, Dido. Black. Drowned on Hutchinson Island.
Douglas, Mrs. Henry. Black. Drown with her four children on Shad's Island.*
Forrester, Mrs. Boston. Black. Drowned with her three children on Shad's Island.*
Falk, Joshua. White. Died on Tybee Island.
Helback, Aldoph. Black. Died from falling trees on Hutchinson Island.
Morton, Valentine. Fisherman. Drowned on Long Island.
Page, Albert. Black. Injured — Broken back & leg on Tybee Island.
Pinckney, Lizzie. Black. Drowned on Hutchinson Island.
Spring, Hannah. Black. Injured — Burned leg on Tybee Island.
Watson, Rena. Black. Drowned on Hutchinson Island.
Wolf, Mrs. Georgianna. White. Died of fractured skull on Tybee Island.
Wolf, Halle. White. Child. Died on Tybee Island.

Hurricane of 1893:

Baker, Scott. Black. Drowned with his son on Tybee Island.
Butler, Mrs. Ed. Black. Drowned on Hutchinson Island.
Driver, H. P. Missing, presumed drowned at Tybee Island.
Fender, Harry. Missing, presumed drowned. Left from Thunderbolt on a maroon.**
Fincken, Theodore. Missing, presumed drowned at Tybee Island.
Gradot, C. A. Missing, presumed drowned. Left from Thunderbolt on a maroon.**

Green, Mrs. Thomas. Black. Drowned on Hutchinson Island.

Holmes, Tony. Black child. Crushed by falling roof on Hutchinson Island

Robider, Walter. Missing, presumed drowned. Left from Thunderbolt on a maroon.**

Schwarz, George. Missing, presumed drowned. Left from Thunderbolt on a maroon.**

Squire, Taylor. Black 6-yr. Old child. Drowned on Hutchinson Island

Stewart, Fred. White. Drowned on Hutchinson Island.

Ulmer, A. C. White. Drowned on Hutchinson Island.

Williams, John. Black. Drowned on Hutchinson Island.

+ Talahi Island
* Probably Elba Island
** A maroon was a camping trip.

Appendix F

A LIST OF UNION SOLDIERS KILLED OR WOUNDED IN THE SKIRMISH ON WHITEMARSH ISLAND

Andrews, Lyman A. - Co. C. -Wounded in right hip.
Atherton, Asa - Co. A. - Killed by a shot through the head.
Ayres, Edwin - Co. I - Killed by a shot in the left thigh.
Bailey, Charles A. - Co. B - Killed by a shot in the throat.
Barton, James F. - Co. H - Killed by shot to right cheek and head.
Bunting, John R. - Co. I - Wounded in left ankle.
Caldwell, Henry W. - Co. A - Wounded in right breast and back.
Carlin, Nicholas - Co. D - Wounded in right thigh.
Cole, Warren - Co. D - Wounded in both hips.
Collins, Barney - Co. A - Wounded in right hand.
Colt, William B. - Co. I - Wounded in right shoulder and back.
Conden, Levi - Co. A - Killed by shot to left temple.
Cooper, James - Co. D - Wounded in right thigh.
Cramer, Ezekiel - Co. C - Wounded in right hand.
Delong, Carlos - Co. A - Wounded in left arm and hip.
Hadger, Lt. - Co. C - Wounded in body, mortally.
Harkinson, P.H. - Co. D - Wounded in left wrist.
Jennings, Aylmer - Co. A - Wounded in left thigh.
Jennings, Second Lt. George - Co. K - Wounded in left leg.
Kapple, D. - Co. B - Killed by shot to back and heart.
Larner, Silas - Co. C - Wounded through the body.
Moore, Franklin - Co. C - Wounded in left foot.
Myers, Eli - Co. K - Killed by shot to lungs and back.
Osborne, Andrew J. - Co. D - Wounded in inferior maxillary.
Peatya,―――― Co. K - Killed by shot to left side.
Piper, Lewis - Co. C - Wounded in left thigh.
Plinstock, Thomas - Co. I - Wounded in left hand.
Pratt, Minor, Capt. Adjutant - Co. A - Killed.
Ryans, Walter S. - Co. I - Wounded in hypogastric region.
Schloppi, Constantine - Co. C - Wounded in left leg.

Shillinger, Fred - Co. A - Wounded in left thigh.
Smith, Walter D. - Co. D - Engineer Corps. Wounded in left arm and back.
Spurbuck, George - Co. B - Killed by shot to right lung.
Vandenstack, A. - Co. B - Killed by shot to right lung and right arm.
Walker, Amos C. - Co. C - Wounded in left thigh.

Appendix G

SOME ISLAND PLANTATION OWNERS IN 1865 WHOSE LAND WAS TAKEN BY THE FREEDMEN'S BUREAU

Wilmington Island

J. M. Pinder - 95 Acres.
John Screven - 155 Acres. Restored.
William or James Hunter - 195 Acres.
William Shad - 92 Acres.
William W. Wash - 140 Acres.

Whitemarsh Island

John Fleetwood - 110 Acres.
George Gray - 270 Acres.
R. F. Gibson - 170 Acres.
Turner/Screven - 485 Acres. (Turner's Rock).

Skidaway Island

Waring - 750 Acres. Restored. Dr. William R. Waring owned more than 2800 acres on the island.
White - 10 Acres.
Ziegler - 295 Acres. Restored.
Jones - 90 Acres (Long Island).
W. R. Symons - 250 Acres. Restored

Appendix H

A LIST OF SOME FREED NEGROES WHO WERE GIVEN ACREAGE ON THE ISLANDS IN 1865 BY THE FREEDMEN'S BUREAU

Wilmington Island Plantations

Andrews, Jesse - 30 Acres - Screven Plantation.
Brown, Abner - 30 Acres - Hunter Plantation.
Carr, Augustus - 20 Acres - Hunter Plantation.
Cumming, Sanney - 15 Acres - Hunter Plantation
Dukes, Joseph - 40 Acres - Wash Plantation.
Garrett, Charles - Hunter Plantation - (He did not live on the plantation.)
Harris, Clayborn - 15 Acres - Hunter Plantation.
Prophet, James - 40 Acres - Shad Plantation.
Lord, Melrose - 15 Acres - Screven Plantation.
Mackey, William - 40 Acres - Shad Plantation.
McQueen, April - 40 Acres - Screven Plantation.
Simmons, Bella - 10 Acres - Shad Plantation.
Stewart, Hartwell - 30 Acres - Screven Plantation.
Straight, William - 20 Acres - Shad Plantation.
Tattnall, King - 40 Acres - Pinder Plantation.
Tattnall, King - 10 Acres - Pinder Plantation.
Williams, Dan - 20 Acres - Pinder Plantation.
Williams, James - 40 Acres - Wash Plantation.
Williams, John - 40 Acres - Wash Plantation.
Winkler, Tom - 40 Acres - Screven Plantation.
Young, George - 10 Acres - Pinder Plantation.

Whitemarsh Island

Barnard, Cato - 40 Acres - Fleetwood Plantation.
Bird, James - 40 Acres - Gray Plantation.
Bolding, Andrew - 30 Acres - Gray Plantation.
Borshine, Charles - 40 Acres - Gray Plantation.
Bryant, Polydore - 20 Acres - Gray Plantation.
Bryant, Seylon - 30 Acres - Gray Plantation.
Campbell, Henry - 20 Acres - Turner Plantation.
   (This acreage was never planted.)
Dixon, John - 10 Acres - Turner Plantation.
Doyle, Richard - 40 Acres - Fleetwood Plantation.
Edwards, David - 10 Acres - Gray Plantation.
Ferguson, Henry - 20 Acres - Turner Plantation.
Frazier, Will - 20 Acres - Turner Plantation.
Gibbons, Alfred - 40 Acres - Turner Plantation.
Giles, Jack - 20 Acres - Gibson Plantation.
Giles, William - 40 Acres - Gibson Plantation.
Hutchison, Sam - 20 Acres - Gibson Plantation.
Jackson, Green - 40 Acres - Turner Plantation.
Jackson, Nancy - 15 Acres - Gibson Plantation.
Jenks, Robert - 30 Acres - Fleetwood Plantation.
Lloyd, Bonaparte - 25 Acres - Gibson Plantation.
Ross, John - 20 Acres - Turner Plantation.
   (This acreage was never planted.)
Stiles, Joseph - 40 Acres - Gibson Plantation.
Stiles, Frank - 40 Acres - Turner Plantation.
   (This acreage was never planted.)
Waltower, Ben - 30 Acres - Gibson Plantation.
Williams, Peter - 40 Acres - Turner Plantation.

Skidaway Island

Brown, Augustus - 30 Acres - Waring Plantation.
Brown, Prince - 40 Acres - Waring Plantation.
Chisholm, Jacob - 10 Acres - Ziegler Plantation.
Clifton, Joe - 15 Acres - Waring Plantation.

Colic (Kollock ?), Ernest - 30 Acres - Waring Plantation.
Drayton, Bristow - 40 Acres - Jones Plantation.
Eddy, James - 40 Acres - Lymons Plantation.
Elon, Ben - 20 Acres Waring Plantation.
Gibbs, J. L. - 15 Acres - Waring Plantation.
Gordon, Jack - 20 Acres - Ziegler Plantation.
Green, Joseph - 30 Acres - Waring Plantation.
Hammond, Joe - 20 Acres - Waring Plantation.
Hardaway, Lewis - 40 Acres - Waring Plantation.
Harris, Stephen - 10 Acres - White Plantation.
Houston, G. Z. - 10 Acres - Waring Plantation.
Houston, W. - 40 Acres - Lymons Plantation.
Howell, Lymus - 40 Acres - Waring Plantation.
Hurburt, Paul - 15 Acres - Waring Plantation.
Jackson, Prince - 20 Acrcs - Jones Plantation.
Jones, Austin - 40 Acres - Waring Plantation.
Jones, Sarah - 20 Acres - Waring Plantation.
Maxwell, John - 40 Acres - Lymons Plantation.
McQure, Thomas - 40 Acres - Lymons Plantation.
Mopson, Jack - 40 Acres - Waring Plantation.
Mopson, John - 40 Acres - Waring Plantation.
Roberts, Robert - 40 Acres - Waring Plantation.
Screven, Dick - 40 Acres - Waring Plantation.
Screven, Henry - 40 Acres - Waring Plantation.
Shellman, Cuffy - 10 Acres - Ziegler Plantation.
Steele, Charles - 30 Acres - Jones Plantation.
Walcott, Jacob - 40 Acres - Waring Plantation.
Wallace, Hercules - 15 Acres - Waring Plantation.
Washington, William - 40 Acres - Lymons Plantation.
Williams, York - 40 Acres - Waring Plantation.
Winn, Isaiah - 25 Acres - Ziegler Plantation.
Wright, Martha - 30 Acres - Waring Plantation.
Young, Phillip - 40 Acres - Waring Plantation

Appendix I

NEGRO SLAVES BURIED IN LAUREL GROVE SOUTH WHO BELONGED TO ISLAND FAMILIES

The following slaves, buried in Laurel Grove Cemetery South, were owned by island families. These were gleaned from *Volume 1* of *Laurel Grove Cemetery, 12 October 1852 - 30 November 1861,* which was compiled by the Genealogical Committee of Georgia Historical Society, Savannah, Georgia. I did not list stillbirths or infants of less than one year, unless they were named, although they were also buried there. It is likely that there are others in that publication who should have been included, but only those of whom I was certain are listed here.

Undoubtedly, there were many more slaves on the islands, but they most certainly would have been buried near their island homes. Why some were brought into the city for burial is unknown. They may have been living in the city at the time of their death. I have separated them by their owners.

Shad Slaves

Bob — Born 1770; Died 3 December 1860; Age 90 years ; Measles — E. B. Shad

Clarissa — Born January 1861; Died 29 August 1861; Age 7 months; Cholera Infantum — Estate of E. B. Shad

Ella — Born 1841; Died 12 September 1859; Age 18 years ; Consumption — Elias Shad

Ellen — Born 1856; Died 19 November 1859; Age 3 years; Typhoid — E. B. Shad

Elsie — Born 1856; Died 16 October 1861; Age 4 years; Congestive Chills — E. B. Shad

Ferdinand — Born 1826; Died 28 April 1861; Age 28 years; Congestion in Lungs — Estate of John Shad

Lavinia — Born 1858; Died 4 December 1859; Age 1 year; Typhoid — E. B. Shad

Scipio — Born 13 December 1859; Died 23 December 1859; Age 10 days ; Spasms — Robert Shad

Tenah — Born 1849; Died 26 May 1856; Age 7 — E. Shad

Oemler Slaves

John — Born 1855; Died 28 September 1857; Age 2 years; Convulsions — Dr. A. Oemler

Prince — Born 1847; Died 12 October 1857; Age 10 years; Consumption — Dr. A. Oemler

Rose — Born 1781; Died 7 June 1861; Age 80 years; Old Age — Dr. Oemler

Barnard Slaves

Ben — Born 1845; Died 27 October 1860; Age 15 years; Typhoid; Brought in from the country — E. J. Barnard

Joe — Born 1852; Died 9 May 1856; Age 4 years; Inflammation of Lungs — James Barnard

Judy — Born 1824; Died 23 April 1861; Age 37 years; Childbed —Mrs. Barnard

Henry — Born 1796; Died 24 February 1861; Age 65 years; Paralysis — Mrs. T. Barnard

Lizzy — Born 1853; Died 8 May 1856; Age 3 years; Sequelae of Measles — James Barnard

Maria — Born 1811; Died 14 November 1861; Age 50 years; Hemoptisis — Mrs. M. A. Barnard

Morel Slaves

Betsey — Born 1830; Died 1 December 1854; Age 24 years; Peritonitis — W. Morel

Jim — Born 1823; Died 22 April 1861; Age 38 years; Consumption — W. Morel

Louisa — Born August 1857; Died 10 October 1858; Age 1 year, 2 months; Thrash — E. H. Morel

Matilda Simpson — Born 1800; Died 13 November 1859; Age 59 years; Congestion of Brain — E. H. Morel

Minty — Born 1791; Died 17 June 1855; Age 64 years; Inflammation of Bowels — H. Morel

Sandy — Born 1748; Died 31 August 1854; Age 106 years; Old Age — William Morel

Solomon — Born 1806; Died 16 April 1854; Age 48 years; Pleurisy — W. Morel

Bryan Slaves

Cato — Born 1846; Died 20 September 1861; Age 15; drowned — C. S. Bryan

John — Born 1795; Died 17 July 1860; Age 65 years; Dropsy — Joseph Bryan

Katy — Born 1836; Died 30 January 1856; Age 20 years; Dropsy — Mrs. H. Bryan

Louisa — Born 1780; Died 5 February 1856; Age 76 years; Pneumonia — J. Bryan

Ned — Born 1807; Died 16 February 1857; Age 50 years; Killed by car at C. R. R. — Joseph Bryan

George A. McClesky

Juliet — Born 1797; Died 3 September 1857; Age 60 years; Congestion of Bowels

Primus — Born 1847; Died 17 April 1857; Age 10 years; Convulsions

Sue — Born 1836; Died 6 February 1856; Age 20 years; Childbed

Others

Annette — Born 1804; Died 14 April 1856; Age 52 years; Consumption — James Hunter

George — Born 1824; Died 13 March 1859; Age 35 years; Consumption — Estate of Frederick Herb

Eliza — Born 1826; Died 5 October 1854; Age 28 years; Bilious — Misses McNishes

Flora — Born 1771; Died 3 June 1853; Age 82 years; Dropsy — Mrs. M. T. Pinder

Jack — Born 1832; Died 25 January 1854; Age 22; Cholera — George S. Gray

John — Born 1851; Died 5 October 1854; Age 3 years; Worms — T. J. McNish

John Gardner — Born 1811; Died 27 August 1856; Age 45 years; Consumption — James Hunter

Juliette — Born 1826; Died 19 September 1859; Age 22 years; Ruptured Spleen — Mrs. F. Waver

Peter — Born 1801; Died 14 April 1861; Age 60; Dropsy — M. N. Waver

Rhoda — Born 1770; Died 2 March 1855; Age 85 years; Old Age — George S. Gray

Sarah — Born 1853; Died 6 May 1855; Age 2 years; Croup; Mrs. Gray.

Appendix J

SOME ADDITIONAL BIOGRAPHICAL SKETCHES

Budreau

Joseph Lindly Budreau was born June 16, 1884, in Maine. He came to Savannah in 1907 as a young man and established a successful farm produce business which was nationally known. He operated a rather extensive truck farm on Whitmarsh Island and was considered a progressive individual by local businessmen and acquaintances. In 1933, he was elected to the board of directors of The Citizens and Southern National Bank. He was also a director of the Macon, Dublin, and Savannah Railroad. He was active in a number of civic and state projects, and was well-known hunter of big game animals. Mr. Budreau was a member of several organizations, including The Hibernian Society, the Savannah Golf Club, and the Savannah Rotary Club. In 1918, Mr. Budreau organized the Savannah Truckers' Exchange. He was married to Mattie Woods and had four children: Joseph Lindly Budreau Jr., John M. Budreau, Lt. Remer Lane Budreau, and a daughter, Mary Louise, who married Walter Lee Mingledorff Jr. Mr. Budreau died September 10, 1946. (SMN)

Goette

Clarence R. Goette was born January 12, 1880, in Savannah. His family established a funeral parlor in Savannah which was later taken over by his brother, Albert Goette. Clarence Goette married Annie Keys and had two daughters, Mary Bernard Goette and Catherine Goette. In 1916, Mr. Goette was appointed superintendent of playgrounds for the city of Savannah. It was in this capacity that he developed a summer camp for boys and girls on Whitmarsh Island. After retiring from the city in 1946, Mr. Goette raised flowers at his Bluffton, South Carolina, farm. Clarence R. Goette died in Savannah, April 6, 1949, at the age of 69.

Parsons

George Parsons was born November 1, 1826, in Kennebunk, Maine. He came to Savannah in 1848, but returned to the North in 1860. After the Civil War, Parsons bought Wassaw Island, and was associated with the Savannah street car system. He sold his Savannah interests in 1902 and returned to New York where he died in 1907. George Parsons' brother, Charles Parsons, was born in Alfred, Maine, February 6, 1829. He was a railroad magnate and a Savannah businessman. His son, Charles Parsons, Jr., born in 1878 in Savannah, was the principal owner of the Savannah-Thunderbolt-Isle of Hope Railway.

Tilton

Major Nathaniel O. Tilton was born March 1, 1830, in Charleston, South Carolina. He was the son of a Wadmalaw Island, South Carolina, cotton planter. In 1857, he moved to Savannah as the manager of the Habersham Rice Mill. Serving in the Confederate Army in the Forest City Rangers, he attained the rank of major and was instrumental in leading a detachment of soldiers to bring the abandoned Confederate guns on Tybee Island into Savannah. As part of his military duties, Major Tilton saw to the placement of obstructions in the Savannah River to deter Union ships from reaching Savannah by water. After the war, he continued to live in Savannah and, by the late 1890's, owned a large portion of Wilmington Island where he maintained a summer home. He was an honorary member of the Georgia Hussars. He died February 11, 1902, and is buried at Bonaventure Cemetery.

Walthour

Henry Clayton Walthour was born in Opelika, Alabama, on February 22, 1874. He was the son of Mr. and Mrs. A. M. Walthour. Mr. Walthour received his education at Auburn College in Alabama and moved to Savannah in 1893 to work as cashier with the Florida Central and Peninsular Railroad. In 1897, he entered the cotton business with a local cotton exporter, and in 1907 he bought an interest in the Espy Cotton Company. According to his obituary, Mr. Walthour was one of five owners of the Tybee Land Development Company, and at one time owned half of the waterfront on Wilmington Island, as well as a large amount of property on Whitemarsh Island, much of which he eventually sold. In 1932, he opened a real estate office, Walthour & Lynes Realty Company. He was quite active in civic and local affairs, being a member of Alee Temple of the Shrine, the Oglethorpe Club, the Rotary Club, Savannah Golf Club, and the Elks Club. Henry Walthour served as a Chatham County Commissioner for a short time before resigning to become United States Marshal, an office he held until his death.

Mr. Walthour was married to Helen Buckman, with whom he had four children, a son and three daughters. His son, John P. Walthour, became a minister and was living in Tampa, Florida, when his father died. Of the daughters, two of them lived in Savannah, Mrs. Sarah Walthour Rainey and Mrs. Nephew K. Clark. The third daughter, Mrs. Ozelle Moss, lived in Southern Pines, North Carolina. Henry Clayton Walthour died at home on Wilmington Island, September 21, 1940.

BIBLIOGRAPHY

BOOKS

Behr, Edward. *Prohibition: Thirteen Years that Changed America*, Arcade Publishing, New York, 1996.

Blair, Ruth. *The 1806 Tax Digest of Georgia*. The Georgia Department of Archives and History. 1926.

Bowden, Haygood S. *Two Hundred Years of Education 1733-1933 Savannah, Chatham County, Georgia*. The Dietz Printing Company, Publishers. Richmond, Va. 1932.

Burt, Virginia Barnard and William Franklin Barnard. *History of One Branch of the Barnard Family*. Barnard Printing Company, Gordo, Alabama. 1961.

Cooper, Sherwin H. *The Rural Settlement of the Lower Savannah River Basin in Georgia. Ph.D. Dissertation*. University of Michigan. 1959.

1850 Census of Georgia Slave Owners. Comp. By Jack F. Cox. Clearfield Company, Inc. Baltimore, Maryland. 1999.

Davis, Curtis Carroll. *Chronicler of the Cavaliers: A Life of the Virginia Novelist Dr. William A. Caruthers*. The Dietz Press, Inc. Richmond, Virginia. 1953.

Drums and Shadows: Survival Studies Among the Georgia Coastal Negroes. W.P.A.Georgia Writers Project. University of Georgia Press. Athens. 1947.

Early Deaths in Savannah, Georgia, 1763-1803: Obituaries and Legal Notices. Comp. By the Genealogical Committee of Georgia Historical Society, Savannah, Georgia. 1993.

Encyclopedia Americana, Volume 15. "Indigo." Grolier Company, Danbury, CT. 2000 Edition

Flynn, Charles L. *White Land, Black Labor: Caste and Class in Late 19th Century Georgia.* Louisiana State University Press. Baton Rouge. 1983.

Gallay, Alan. *The Formation of a Planter Elite: Jonathan Bryan and the Southern Colonial Frontier.* University of Georgia Press. Athens. 1989.

Gamble, Thomas. *Duels and Duellists, 1733-1877.* Reprint. The Oglethorpe Press 1997, pp. 216, 226.

Godley, Margaret. *Historic Tybee Island, Savannah Beach, Georgia.* Savannah Beach Chamber of Commerce. 1958.

Harden, William. *A History of Savannah and South Georgia. Volume II.* Cherokee Publishing Company. Atlanta, Georgia. 1981.

Johnson, Whittington B. *Black Savannah 1788-1864.* University of Arkansas Press. Fayetteville, Arkansas. 1996.

Johnston, Edith Duncan. *The Houstouns of Georgia.* University of Georgia Press, Athens. 1961.

Johnston, Elizabeth Lichtenstein. *Recollections of a Georgia Loyalist,* written in 1836. The De La More Press, 52 High Holborn, London.

Jones, George Fenwick. *The Georgia Dutch, From the Rhine and Danube to the Savannah, 1733-1783.* University of Georgia Press. Athens.

Kelly, V. E. *A Short History of Skidaway Island.* 1980.

Lattimore, Ralston B. *Fort Pulaski.* National Park Service Historical Handbook Series No. 18. Washington, D. D. 1954.

Lawrence, Alexander A. *Storm Over Savannah, The Story of Count d'Estaing and the Siege of the Town in 1799.* The University of Georgia Press. Athens. 1951.

Lee, F. D. and J. L. Agnew. *Historical Record of the City of Savannah.* Printed and published by J. H. Estill, Morning News Steam-Power Press, Savannah 1869.

Leckie, George G. *Georgia: A Guide to Its Towns and Countryside.* Tupper & Love. Atlanta, Georgia. 1954.

Linn, C. A. *History of the German Friendly Society, 1837-1937.* Savannah. 1937. pp. 47-51.

O'Connell, Rev. J. J. O. S. B. *Catholicity In the Carolinas and Georgia.* 1879.

Radasch, Arthur Hitchcock. *Barstow-Bestor Genealogy: Descendants of John Barstow and George Barstow.* Boston Public Library. 1964.

Savannah River Plantations. Mary Granger, Editor. Savannah Writers' Project. Georgia Historical Society. Savannah. 1947.

Shad, Terri Bray. *The Genealogy of The Shad Family of Georgia.* Gateway Press, Inc. Baltimore. 1990.

Stokes, Thomas L. *The Savannah.* Rinehart & Company, Inc. New York. 1951.

Smith, Derek. *Civil War Savannah.* Frederic C. Beil. Savannah, Ga. 1997.

Smith, Julia Floyd. *Slavery and Rice Culture in Low Country Georgia 1750-1860.* University of Tennessee Press. Knoxville. 1985. pp. 1460-1465.

Suchlicki, Jaime. *Cuba, From Columbus To Castro and Beyond.* 4th Edition., Brassey's, Washington & London, 1997.

Wood, Virginia Steele. *Live Oaking: Southern Timber for Tall Ships.* Northeastern University Press. Boston. 1981.

World Book Encyclopedia. Volume 10. *Indigo.* World Book, Inc. Chicago. 1998 Edition.

Papers and Documents

Babits, Lawrence . *Phase II Archaeological Investigation Long Point, Whitemarsh Island, Chatham County, Georgia.* Center for Low Country Studies, Armstrong State College. October 10, 1983.

Baker, Mrs. George Mallard. Handwritten copy of a telephone interview, January 1, 1971 regarding Barstow family. Genealogy files of the Georgia Historical Society.

Barnard Family Bible. Georgia Historical Society.

Barstow, Elias B., Jr. Abstract of Estate Proceeding. Chatham County Ordinary's Office, File Number B 812.

Barstow, Mary Ann. Letter dated Sept. 30, 1891 to her cousin, Dr. A. Fuller Barnard. From the Genealogy Files of the Georgia Historical Society.

Bulloch, J. G. Letter to Dr. Andrew Fuller Barnard, St. Mary's, Ga. nd.

Chatham County Superior Court. Injunction: *Goette vs. Desvergers*. July 27, 1898.

Dexter Realty Co. Advertisement. n.d. "Beautiful Riverfront Home."

Estill, J. H. *Tales of Tybee (From Savannah Morning News, Feb. 12, 1905)*. Savannah, Georgia. 1906.

Gamble, Thomas. "First Benedictines Came To Savannah Isle 62 Years Ago." *Georgia Miscellany. Vol. 4.*

Gamble, Thomas. *Georgia Miscellany. Vol. 4*, p. 85. Legal Papers With Reference To Monastery Tract.

Gamble, Thomas. *Savannah's Interest In Filibustering Expeditions To Free Cuba*, March 1935.

Lattimore, Ralston B. *Destruction of Fort Greene* September 26, 1951.

Letter to Thomas Gamble from Joseph D. Mitchell regarding Benedictines on Skidaway. February 2, 1938.

Indenture - Liberty Island. Chatham County Courthouse. Plat Book 9 p.

Johnson, Robert E. *Archaeological Testing of the Exchange Tract Parcel, Skidaway Island, Chatham County, Georgia. The Branigar Organization. May 1990.*

Legal Paper. Deed of Conveyance from William Wade to Rt. Rev. John Barry, Bishop, for monastery tract on Skidaway. Vol. 4 of *Georgia Miscellany* by Thomas Gamble.

Morel, Ellen. *The Morel Family Register Collected by Ellen Morel.* 1890

Notes on the Barnard Family. Genealogy File of the Georgia Historical Society.

Pamphlet. *Daniel G. Purse.* November

Plat Book 9 P. Chatham County Courthouse.

Rebellion Record 1862. Doc. 140 "Skirmish At Wilmington Island, Ga." Lt. Wilson's Report., pp. 500-501.

Rebellion Record 1862. Doc. 140. "Colonel Fenton's Report." p. 501.

Seiler, Frank W. *Batson and His Magnificent Flying Machine.*

Seiler, Frank W. *History of Dutch Island.* Written and presented at a meeting of the Dutch Island Club, October 25, 1994.

Schriver, George H. *The Historical Pilgrimage of The Evangelical Lutheran Church of the Ascension, Savannah, Georgia.*

Simpson, John. *Thomas Arkwright.* A paper. November 12, 1986.

Smith, Fae Oemler. *A Sea Island Plantation. China Grove, Wilmington Island, Georgia.* Georgia Historical Society. Savannah, Georgia. Undated, but probably 1959.

Sutherland, Marjorie. *Wilmington Island.* A Paper. No date.

The Lutheran Church of the Redeemer, Wilmington Island. No author. No date.

Workman, M. S. Letter dated 1893. From the files of the Chatham-Effingham-Liberty County Library.

PERIODICALS:

The Georgia Historical Quarterly.

Delegals of Skidaway: Is Philip Alone on the 13th Hole Palmetto? By Shari Lee Laist. TWATL, Vol. XVIII, No. 28, pp. 28-32.

Gillette, Jane Brown. "Enchanted Isle," Historic Preservation, November-December 1995.

Fossil News, Journal of Avocational Paleontology, Volume 6, Number 7, July, 2000. pp. 14-15' "Plentifully Charges With Fossils: The 1822 Discovery of the Eremotherium at Skidaway," by Todd Womack.

Osier, David R. "Ossabaw Miracle," Georgia Journal. January-February 1997, pp. 12-24.

The Southern Cross. "Skidaway Island Footnote: A Tragic Halloween Misadventure," by Rita H. DeLorme. November 2, 2000.

Collections:

Abstract of Wills, Chatham County, Georgia. Genealogical Publications.

Barnard Family Notes. Walter C. Hartridge Collection. Georgia Historical Society

Gamble, Thomas. *Georgia Miscellany*, Volume 4, pp. 34, 79, 80, 86.

Gamble, Thomas. *Savannah's Interest in Filibustering Expeditions To Free Cuba.* March, 1935.

M. H. & D. B. Floyd Collection Georgia Historical Society. Collection 1308.

Shad family information. Letters regarding Elba Island. Walter C. Hartridge Collection. Georgia Historical Society.

Newspapers:

Atlanta Journal:
"Marshlands Have Feet of Clay, Shrimp Industry Uneasy," by Estelle Ford. April 27, 1969.

Charleston City Gazette, September 19, 1804.

The Columbian Museum and Savannah Advertiser: September 15, 1804. p.3, c.3.

Daily Morning News:
Advertisement of William P. Rowland regarding shipment of oranges from Wilmington Island. January 15, 1851, p.3, c.4
"Arrival Yesterday in Savannah of Capt. Robt. T. Brown, late commander of ill-fated bark *Isaac Mead*," November 5, 1850, p.2, c.2.
"Fire on Wilmington Island," December 4, 1852, p.2, c.1.
Obituary Notice. Henry Shad. 22, September 1858, p.2, c.3.
Shad Residence Sold. June 23, 1858 p.2 c.1.
The Sinking of the *Isaac Mead*, October 7, 1850, 2, c.3.
December 31, 1857; p.2 c.2.

Georgia Gazette:
Barnard, Jane. Obituary. October 9, 1794.
Observer Smyth. July 28, 1895., p. 8. C.4.
For Sale: Green Island. 1764.
June 9, 1980

The Morning News:
"Ancient Order of Hibernians Picnic at Wilmington Island." July 24, 1895. p.8 c.6
"Horrors of the Cyclone." August 30, 1881. n.p.
"Capt. Judkins Given Presentation." July 26, 1895. P. 8 c.4.
"Charles Jemdal, et. al. vs. Wilmington Island Pleasure and Improvement Company." July 31. 1895. p. 5 c.4.
"E. J. Dawson Dead of Exposure," March 1, 1891. p.8 c.2.
"Jemdal Verdict," August 1, 1895. p. 8 c. 4.
"Jemdal Final Decree," August 4. 1895. p. 8 c. 2.
"Memories of Savannah' Greatest Hurricane Fifty Years Ago Recalled." by Thomas Gamble, August 22. 1943.
"Turner Killed By Lightning," July 2,1895. p.2 c.2 October 3, 1898.

New Orleans Times Democrat:
Gonzales, Ambrosio Jose. "The Cuban Crusade," April 6, 1884.

Savannah Evening Press:

"Anvil's Previous Ties Cloud Mining Report," by Bill Carpenter. November 18, 1969. p.1D.

"Artifacts Discovered," by Barbara Dlugozima. September 14, 1972. Local Page.

"Associates in Bellanca Buy Gen. Oglethorpe." March 13, 1956.

"Clarence R. Goette Died This Morning." April 6, 1969.

"Conservation Group Maps Plan For Preservation of Little Tybee," by Brad Swope, June 24, 1990, p. 6A.

"County: Go Slow on Mining," by Kathy Haeberle. September 13, 1968.

"Economic Analysis Will Form Heart of Report on Kerr-McGee Proposal." by Bill Carpenter. September 29, 1968. p. 1B.

"Fine Oranges Grown On Tybee Island." November 25, 1913. p. 13.

"Gen. Oglethorpe To Be Center for Retirement." May 24, 1956.

"Gen. Oglethorpe Hotel Purchased By. S. L. Albert." March 22, 1933. p. 36.

"Group To Develop Dutch Island Area." June 27, 1969. p.1A.

"Harpoon in Skull of Whale Dug Up At Savannah Beach." n. d.

"Hundreds of Oranges Load Tree On North End Tybee, " November 21, 1932.

"Kerr-McGee Head Vows To Continue," by Bill Carpenter. October 2, 1968.

"James A. Duncan Drowns while On Fishing Trip." November 30. 1953.

"Marshal Surprised At Army Reporters That Met Cassese," October 30, 1922. p.11968. P.1

"Mining Lease Gives Free Fill," by Bill Carpenter. September 14, 1968.

"Old Tybee Centered on Pavilion." by Archie Whitfield. May 23, 1967. p. 1 B.

"Oglethorpe Hotel Co. Bankrupt." January 1, 1961.

"One Man's Family," by Cliff Sewell. June 6, 1971.

"Opposition Kills Marshlands Bill," by Bill Carpenter. February 12, 1970.

"Ossabaw Island." October 29, 1951, p. G1.

"Paddy, the Sea-going Mule, is Dead." January 10, 1934.

"Phosphate Market Glutted," by Bill Carpenter. September 28, 1969. p. 1.

"Reorganization of Oglethorpe Hotel." February 2, 1937.

"Senator's Problem: Leaving the Island." by Bill Carpenter. October 9, 1970. p.23.

"Sleep of Gibson Family Disturbed." May 13, 1959.

"Slimes Forever A Plague To Phosphate Miners." by Bill Carpenter.

"State Official Blasts Phosphate Hearings, Deposits Set At Billions," by Bill Carpenter. November 11, 1969. p.1.

"Sleep of Gibson Family Disturbed," by Eugene Wright. May 13, 1939.

"Teamsters Take Over Oglethorpe," December 6, 1961.

"Teamsters Union Buys Savannah Inn." February 3, 1970.

"Vandals Stripped Barnard Vault of Parts of Caskets," August 20, 1920.

"Wessels To Develop Dutch Isle," June 28, 1969.

September 10, 1946

January 27. 1970

Savannah Morning News:

"Barnard Street Named For the Man Who Could Not Be Bought," by Thomas Gamble, March 17, 1918, p.30.

"Batson Airship Inspected To-Morrow,", p. 14; November 11, 1913

"Batson Flying Boat Finished," November 12, 1913, p. 17.

"Batson Flying Boat At Anchor On Herb River," November 18, 1913, p.14.

"Batson Flying Boat Launched," November 17, 1913.

"Dr. Armenius Oemler Dead." August 1898. p.8.

"Dr. Oemler Dying." August 8, 1897. p. 7.

"Finish Survey of Historical Forts," April 24, 1951.

"Finds Skeleton On Whitmarsh," July 30, 1937. p.14.

"Gen. Oglethorpe Opens Tomorrow." November 29, 1935.

"Ghouls Robbed Barstow Grave," December 22. 1904.

"Group Wants Phosphate Mining Facts," September 7, 1968.

"Hasn't Abandoned Tybee Road Project." October 22, 1918.

"Horse Racing on Wilmington," Dec. 29, 1938.

"Hotel Sale By Union Reported." January 18, 1963.

"Hoyt Warns of Erosion," by Bob Cohn. October 2, 1968.p.1

"Island Lighthouse May Be Repaired." June 16, 1960.

"Kerr-McGee Focuses Attention on Marshlands." by Bob Cohn. January 20, 1970, p. 3B.

"Kerr-McGee Case Puts Marshlands Issue in Spotlight," by Bob Cohn. January 19, 1970. p. 4B.

"Marshland Unit Rejects Skidaway-Green Project," by Ann Marshall. March 16, 1972

"Mining Firm Pledges Rebuilding of Marsh: Some Loss Seen." by Bob Cohn. September 30, 1968. p.1

"Mining Proposal Ripped at Meet," by Bob Cohn. September 16, 1968, p. 1.

"Natural Beauty Marks Proposed Site of Park." by Phil Smith. April 4, 1965. p. 1B.

Obituary and Funeral Notice. Elias B. Barstow, Jr. November 3, 1898. p. 6.

Obituary. Amanda Johnson, September 22, 1888. p. 2, c. 6.

"Orange Groves Flourished Here," June 3, 1937.

"Ossabaw Decision Delayed," May 18, 2000. p. 1C.

"Ossabaw Island Co. Applies For Charter." November 20, 1918. p.6.

"Our Quietly Dynamic Salt Marshlands," March 23, 1975.

"Phosphate Report Called Whitewash," by Bob Cohn. December 11, 1969. p. 12 D.

"Remove Scaffolding From Batson Craft," November 7, 1913. n.p.

"Road Houses Are Raided By Sheriff." November 23, 1913. b. 28.

"Rousakis, McCarthy Shun Move," by Bob Cohn, October 2, 1968.

"Scientists Feel That Marshlands Could Be Rebuilt," by Bob Cohn. December 6, 1968, p. 1D.

"Senators Propose Stronger Marshlands Protection Bill," January 20, 1970. p. 3B.

"Skidaway Potential Lab Site," by Barbara Dlugozima. March 5, 1967. p.1B.

"The General Oglethorpe, South's Newest Hotel, Will Open on Monday." October 16, 1927. n.p.

"The Open Tomb," by Lillian C. Bragg. June 5, 1960.

"The Skidaway Island Trouble." February 21. 1868.

"Sleep of Gibson Family Disturbed," by Eugene Wright. May 13, 1939.

"Teamsters Take Over Oglethorpe," December 6, 1961

"Teamsters Union Buys Savannah Inn." February 3, 1970.

"Thieves Scatter Bones To Loot A Burial Vault," May 6, 1939. p. 12, c.2 .

"To Colonize Wilmington," December 24, 1891. p.8, c.3.

"Trappers Ready For Fur Season." November 23, 1913. P. 9

"Trouble On Skidaway Island—The Negroes Firing on Fishing Boats," December 18, 1868.

"Unique Miniature Donkeys Flourish on Ossabaw Island." by Patti Phillips. August 6, 1996. p. 1 B.

"Vandals Stripped Barnard Vault of Parts of Caskets," August 20, 1920.

"Very Few Things on Skidaway Remain Unchanged," by Kay Giese. January 28, 1973. p.17

"Wilmington Island Scene of Activity," May 24, 1922.

February 27, 1883; p.4. c.4
March 31, 1883; p.4; c.2
May 11, 1883;
January 20, 1884; p.2, c.2
May 1, 1897; p.8
October 7, 1898
September 24, 1905; p. 19
November 20, 1913; p. 1F
November 23, 1913; p.9
November 23, 1913, p. 28
October 30, 1922;
January 12, 1938;
October 25, 1957; p.2, c. 1
February 16. 1958; p. 6C
March 5, 1961
April 4, 1965; p. 1B
December 21, 1968
March 16, 1972;
January 28, 1973;
August 6, 1996; p.1B
July 7, 1999; *Intown Closeup*, p.7A

Savannah Press:

"Carl Stahmer Victim Accidental Shooting," December 11, 1922.

"Exercises at Wilmington," August 5, 1889.

Fogaley, Richard, "Deal Could Give Georgia Title to Little Tybee, Cabbage Islands," p.5, January 25, 1990,

"Gay Wilmington,", nd.

"Marshal Surprised At Army Reporters That Met Cassese," p. 1, October 30, 1922.

"Nimrods Haled To Court-Say Were Accompanied On Chase By Diana Duo." November 1921.

"Stahmer Dies," December 15, 1922.

"Three Shot, One Dead As Result." December 11, 1922

GENERAL INDEX

Akron, Ohio, 101
Alachua County, Florida, 110
American Revolution, 27, 28, 49, 52, 55, 106, 108, 112, 114, 115, 127, 156
American Hotels Corporation, 99
Ancient Order of Hibernians, 87, 248
Anti-Saloon League, 200
Archaeological excavations, xvi, xvii, 9
Arkwright Cotton Manufacturing Company, 132, 133
Arkwright's Village, 130-134
Arlington National Cemetery, 182
Armstrong College, xviii, 197
Artesian water, xvi, 40, 41, 147, 175
Atlantic Beach, Florida, 182
Augusta, Georgia, 48, 94, 107, 154
Baker Crossing, 176
Bartlett Middle School, 172
Batson Air Navigation Company, 180, 182
Battery Crescent, 13, 15, 25
Battery Point, xvii, 11, 13, 15
Battle of Bloody Marsh, 111
Beach Hammock, 130, 132, 133
Beaufort, South Carolina, 46, 95
Beaulieu, 7, 19
Bellanca Aircraft Corporation, 101
Belmont Abbey, North Carolina, 122
Benedictine Military School, 24
Benedictine monastery, 109, 120, 121, 122
Bluffton, South Carolina, 248
Bolton Hotel, 129
Bona Bella, 70, 87

Boy Scouts, 149
Bonaventure Cemetery, 222, 224, 226, 229, 249
bootleggers, 62, 202, 203
Bradley Point, 32
British Marines, 106
Bryan County, Georgia, 122
Bryan Woods Road, 27
Budreau site, xvii
Bureau of Refugees, Freedmen, and Abandoned Lands, 117
Calibogue Sound, 95
Camp Venture, 27
Camp Walleila, 14, 16
Cardenas, Cuba, 67
Catholic Cemetery, 220, 221
Center for Low Country Studies, xviii
Central of Georgia Railroad, 129, 142
Charleston, South Carolina, 14, 71, 72, 136, 150
Chatham Artillery, 116
Chatham County Recreation Department, 25
Chippewa Square, 23
Citadel, The, 24
citrus trees, 72, 108
Civil War (see also War Between the States), 11, 13, 24, 29, 30, 32, 35, 55, 57, 73, 79, 85, 97, 116, 154, 159
Cleveland, Ohio, 100
Clinch County, Georgia, 97
Coastal Heritage Society, 25
Code duello, 50
Colonial Cemetery, 22, 110, 115, 222, 223, 224, 226, 229, 230
Columbian Museum and Savannah Advertiser, The, 107
Conductors' Home, 27
Confederate fortifications, 11, 13, 15, 35, 37
Confiscated Estates, xviii, 28
corn, 10, 35, 170, 200
cotton, 1, 5, 6, 10, 35, 107, 108, 160, 170
Cotton Hammock, 26, 27, 28
Crescent Blowpipe Works of Savannah, 181
Cronstadt, Russia, 113
Crown Land Grants, xix, 35, 43, 48, 56, 146, 185, 196

cucumbers, 11
Dad's Place, 26
Daffin Park, 200
Daily Morning News, The, 11
Darien, Georgia, 45
Davisboro, Georgia, 16
Daytona, Florida, 41
Dragonfly, Aero Yacht, 182
Depression, The, 26
DeSoto Hotel, 61
DeSoto Beach Hotel, 102
Dexter Realty Company, 89
Dresden, Germany, 57
Earl of Wilmington, the, 39
East India Company, the, 107, 166
earthworks, military, 11, 13, 15, 35, 37, 116, 117, 132
Ebenezer, Georgia, 52
Ecuador, 105
Eighteenth Amendment, 200
Eighth Michigan Infantry, 12
Emancipation Proclamation, 117
Eppinger house, 2
Eremotherium, 116
Espy Cotton Company, 250
Eureka Club, The, 81
Fee Simple Title, xix
feral donkeys, 164, 168
Fifty-Seventh Georgia Infantry, 12
Forest City Rangers, 249
Fort Deleware, 136
Fort Graham, 138
Fort Greene, 134, 189, 190, 230, 235
Fort Jackson, 50
Fort Oglethorpe, 94
Fort McAllister, 154
Fort Pulaski, 127, 135, 136, 192, 227
Fort Screven, 138, 143
Fourth Georgia Battery, the, 116
Freedman's Bureau, 117, 119, 160

Fresh Air Home, the, 142
fur trapping, 13, 80
General Oglethorpe Hotel, The, 17, 98, 99, 101, 102, 103
Genesis Project, 163
Georgia Mineral Leasing Commission, 187
Georgia Heritage Trust, 165
Georgia Hussars, 249
Georgia Writers' Project of the W. P. A., 96
Georgian, The, 116
German Club, the, 87
Giant Ground Sloth, 116
Gibson's Plantation, 12
Gibson's Point, 11
Girl Scouts, 14, 15, 16, 147, 149
Goette Funeral Home, 74
Gordon, Georgia, 59
grapefruits, 72, 173
Graham House, 129
Green Door Tea Room, 88
Green's Fish Camp, 38
Grimball Point, 172
Habersham Rice Mill, 249
Halifax, Nova Scotia, 114, 223
Hampstead, 52
Havana, Cuba, 67
Haven Home Industrial School, 171, 172
Hinder-Me-Not, 161
Hopecrest Cemetery, 176
hurricanes, 139, 161, 189, 190, 191, 192, 193
Immortal Six Hundred, the, 136
"Indian Fort", 106
Indian mounds, xvii, 15, 98
Indian trails, 27
indigo, 1, 4, 5, 10, 35
Indigo suffructiosa, 4
International Monetary Conference, 101
Island Investments, Inc., 125
Islands
    Arkwright's, 130, 132, 133

Baillou's, xx
Bradley's, 228
Broughton's, 45, 46
Burnt Pot, 211
Butt, 39
Cabbage, 184
Cockspur, 114, 129, 134, 137, 138, 184, 189, 190, 191, 192, 224, 225, 230
Daufuskie, 70
Dutch, 172, 173, 175, 176, 177, 179, 180, 183, 221, 228
Elba, 55, 56
Fenk, 31
Gnann Hammock, 177
Goette, 26
Green, 125, 226, 228, 229
Hutchinson, 190, 192, 228, 229, 236
Lacy's, 35
Liberty, 170, 171, 176, 177, 182, 211
Little Tybee, 61, 63, 130, 132, 146, 184
Little Wassaw, 146, 153, 155
Oatland, 26, 38, 131, 156-167, 203
Ossabaw, 6, 81, 132, 147, 157, 160, 161, 203, 205, 225
Pigeon, 15
Pine Island, 146, 154
Providence, 170
Sapelo, 156
Screven, 45, 47, 235
Shad, 192, 236
Skidaway, 80, 105-112, 115, 116, 118, 119, 121-125, 192, 193, 201, 202, 203, 231, 232, 233, 240
St. Simons, 186
Sylvan, 177
Talahi, xxi, 20, 45, 79, 190, 204
Turner's Rock, 2, 24, 36, 39, 222, 211
Tybee, 39, 106, 128, 129, 130, 202, 236, 237
Wassaw, 15, 141, 146-155, 184, 205, 230
Whitemarsh, xv, xvii, xviii, xxi, 7, 9, 10, 30, 35, 39, 73, 180, 202, 204, 215, 230, 238, 240
Wilmington, xv, xvii, xxi, 2, 6, 7, 9, 35, 39, 74, 184, 186, 192, 197, 202, 204, 227, 231

Isle of Hope, 117, 120, 121, 150, 183, 193
Joe's Cut, 58
Johnny Harris' Restaurant, 26
Kerr-McGee Corporation, 184, 185, 186, 187
Kessel's Pavilion, 79
Kollock Plantation Books, 157
Landings on Skidaway Island, The, 108, 109
Laurel Grove Cemetery, 49, 110
lazaretto, 134
Liberty Boys, 107
Liberty County, Georgia, 217
Liberty Island Corporation, 177, 182
Liberty Hall, 82, 83
live oak trees, 6, 7, 156, 164
Long Point, xviii, 11, 28, 29, 31, 32, 33
Lovell Station, 143
Lutheran Church of the Ascension, 84, 85
Lutheran Church of the Redeemer, 86
Mackey's Point, 94
Macon, Georgia, 14, 67, 68, 103, 148
Mafia, the, 62, 103
malaria, 27, 135
Manchester, Connecticut, 182
Manchester, England, 49
Marine Resource Center, 124
maroon trips, 83, 149, 236, 237
Marshlands Protection Agency, 125
martello tower, 134
mastodon, 116
Meldrim site, xvi
melons, 11, 26, 31, 72, 73
Mickve Israel, 147, 149
Montgomery Crossroads, 172
moonshine, 13, 201, 202, 203, 204
Morningside Drive, 62, 79
mosquitoes, 62
Mulberry trees, 4, 10
Muntz metal, 196, 197
Myers Middle School, 176

National Park Service, 135
National Prohibition Party, the, 199
Nature Conservancy, the, 152, 164, 168
New England Aeronautical Museum, 182
New Orleans, Louisiana, 66
New York, 71
Oakridge Golf Club, 110
Ocean House, 129
Oemler Oyster Company, 58, 59, 60, 206
Oemler's Point, 62
Ogeecheeville, Georgia, 173
Oglethorpe Club, the, 250
Oglethorpe's Rangers, 48, 111
Oklahoma City, 184
Olympics, 103, 130
oranges, 20, 72, 108, 143, 173
Ossabaw Foundation, 162, 164, 168
Ossabaw Island Company, 161
oysters, xviii, 31, 58, 59, 154, 160, 161
Paddy the Mule, 27, 28
Palmetto Golf Course, 112
Philadelphia, Pennsylvania, 161
Pin Point, Georgia, 160, 161, 173, 174
Plantations
   Bloomsbury, 109
   Brampton, 43, 220
   Burleigh tract, 47
   Cedar Grove, 109
   China Grove, 55
   Delegal, 108, 111, 112, 113
   Gibson's, 12, 20, 21, 23
   Hampton Place, 109, 120, 121
   Hibernia, 109
   Hunter, 47, 48
   Jones, 117
   Long Point, 29, 31, 32
   Mayer, 47
   Middle Place, 166
   Modena, 108, 123, 183

    Mulberry Grove, 6
    Nonchalance, 12, 43, 44, 45, 46, 190, 191
    Orangedale, 109
    Pinder, 191
    Skidaway Island, 1, 109
    Springfield, 108, 123
    Wakefield, 109
    White, 118
    Wormsloe, 116
    Ziegler, 117
Planters' Rice Mill, 132
Professional Research Project, 164
Prohibition era, 199-204
Priest's Landing, 116
Public Use and Educational Project, 164
Quarantine Station, 142
Reconstruction, 160
Repealing Act of 1750, 1
rice, 1, 5, 10, 35
Riceboro, Georgia, 41
rivers and creeks
    Adams, 106
    Back, 144
    Bradley, 35
    Bull, xv, 38, 45
    Burnside, 59
    Camuse, 45, 47
    Delegal, 112
    Gibbons, 60
    Grimball, 170
    Half Moon, xv, 39, 94, 96, 97
    Herb, 179, 180, 181
    Jenkins, xx
    Lazaretto, 12
    Little Half Moon, xvi
    Little Tybee, 12, 63, 118
    Ogeechee, 52, 154
    Richardson, xv, 11, 14, 20, 25, 26, 27, 28
    San Juan, 178

Satilla, 68, 70
  Savannah, xv, 50, 55, 70, 80, 126, 127, 134, 136, 144, 195
  Shad, xv, 60, 62, 63, 206
  St. Augustine, xv, 68
  Thunderbolt, 68, 118
  Turner's, xv, 45, 38, 97
  Tybee, 12, 45, 47, 127, 130, 195
  Vernon , 59
   Wilmington, xv, xvi, 12, 49, 83, 96, 102, 108, 195
Romerly Marsh, 109
Rose Dhu, 16
Saffold Field, 16, 17, 18, 19, 20
"salt meadow", 62
Sampson's Point, 62
Sandfly, Georgia, 174, 177
sassafras, 126
Savannah Aero Yacht, 179, 181, 182
Savannah Beach Club, 61
Savannah Corps of Engineers, 24, 125
Savannah Morning News, The, 74, 75, 81, 89
Savannah Motor Lodge, 102
Savannah Science Museum, 182
Savannah Theatre, 132
Savannah Yacht Club, 179, 180, 181
Scott Paper Mill, 41
"Scrap Iron", 26, 204
Schoenebeck, Germany, 91
schools, 2, 20
Screven's Ferry, 50
Sea Island cotton, 1, 6, 107, 108
Shad Point, 191
sheep, 108
Shellman's Bluff, 40
Sheraton Savannah Resort, 103
ships and steamers
  Alpha, steamer, 148
  Ann, 195
  CSS Atlanta, 159
  Audacia, bark, 198

Aurora, steamer, 198
Bewlie, schooner, 7
Camusi, steamer, 59
Canoochee, tugboat, 191
Cleopatra, steamer, 67, 69
Clivedon, steamer, 95
Daisy, schooner, 192
Doretta, steamer, 59, 148
Endeavor, steamer, 160
Elizabeth, 157
Fingal, steamer, 159
Flora, steamer, 87
Forest City, steamer, 139
General Shepley, sidewheel steamer, 159, 198
Governor Tattnall, 46, 190
Harold, bark, 198
Honduras, 12
Ina Louise, yacht, 82, 83
Isaac Mead, steamer, 71, 218
James, 106
Lampedo, 198
Leila Smith, schooner, 198
Magnolia, 69
Mary Draper, steamer, 133
Mermaid, steamer, 74
Neptune, yacht, 193
H.M.S. Scarborough, 128
Southerner, steamer, 71
C.S.S. Water Witch, gunboat, 157, 159, 160, 198
U.S.S. Weehawken, warship, 159
silk, 4
Sisters of St. Joseph, 133
Skeeter Hill, 151
skeletons. 13, 144
Skidaway Baptist Church, 176
Skidaway Institute of Oceanography, 123
Skidaway Island State Park, 116
Skidaway Narrows, 116, 124
slaves, 29, 66, 244

slave burials, 244
Southern Natural Gas Company, 56
Southern Union Company, 182
Spanish-American War, 135, 138, 152
Spanish Guale, 126
St. Mary's, Georgia, 35, 70
State Coastal Marshland Protection Agency, 125
State Mineral Leasing Commission, 184
Sweden, 179
Sweet Field of Eden Church, 160, 161
Switzerland, 121, 165
Tail male, xix
Tatemville, Georgia, 173
Teamsters' Union Pension Fund, 102, 103
Temporary Wartime Prohibition Act, 199
Thirteenth Georgia Infantry, 11, 12
Thunderbolt, 39, 80, 82, 83, 96, 148, 174
Tidecraft, 2
truck farms, 13, 26
Twenty-Fifth Regiment of the Georgia Infantry, 116
Twenty-Seven Oaks, 89
Tybee Island Light, 127, 129
Tybee Land Development Company, 250
Tybrisa Pavilion, 129, 130, 143, 144
Union Camp Corporation, 122, 123
Union Mission Church of Wilmington Island, 85, 86
Union Mission Sunday School, 84
United States Fish and Wildlife Service, 146, 152
University of Georgia, 108, 123
Valdosta, Georgia, 148
vandals, vandalism, 21, 22, 23
Vernonburg, Georgia, 83
Vernon Oyster Company, 59
Vietnam, 188
Vietnam War, 27
Volstead Act, 200
Wall's Corps of Artillery, 115
Waltham Watch Company, 101
Walthour site, xvii

Walthourville, Georgia, 208, 216
Wangen, Germany, 52
Warsaw, Georgia, 83
Wassaw National Wildlife Refuge, 146, 153
Wassaw Sound, 96, 97, 116, 130, 146, 195
War Between the States, the (see also Civil War), 29, 30, 32, 35, 55, 57, 73, 79, 97, 116, 121, 128, 154, 159
Wilkinson County, Georgia, 58, 59
Wilmington Island Baptist Church, 176
Wilmington Island Pleasure and Improvement Company, 81, 84, 86
Wilmington Park Association, 95
Wheeling, West Virginia, 182
Women's Christian Temperance Union, 199
Works Projects Administration (W.P.A.), xvi, xvii, 13, 96, 97
World Fund and Bank, 101
Yamacraw, 114
Yazoo Land Fraud, 186
Y.M.C.A., 149, 150

FULL NAME INDEX

Abbott, A. E., 139
Adams, David E., 109, 115
Adams, Samuel, 207
Adler, Emma M., 167
Albert, Sidney L., 101
Ambos, Mr., 31
Amorous, Antonio, 217
Amorous, Kate, 207
Amorous, Mary, 7, 29, 217
Amorous, Mary Sowney, 32, 207
Amorous, Martin Ford, 217
Amorous, Matthew, 11, 207
Amorous, Matthias, 29, 30, 207, 217
Amorous, Sarah Ann McCall, 207
Andrews, Jesse, 241
Andrews, Lyman A., 238
Anthony, Rev. Bascom, 148
Anuskiewicz, Rick, 196
Arkwright, Ann Ellen, 132, 217
Arkwright, Thomas, 132, 133, 207, 213, 132, 133
Arkwright, Thomas, Jr., 207, 217
Arkwright, Lydia Lachlison, 132, 133, 217
Arkwright, Martha Stanley, 132, 217
Arkwright, Mary, 207
Arkwright, William, 217
Arkwright, William Preston, 217
Armstrong, George F., 182
Armstrong, Reuben, 190, 218, 235
Arthur, John, 207, 208
Artley, William H., 88
Astor, Lady Nancy, 101
Atherton, Asa, 238
Audubon, John James, 7
Ayres, Edwin, 238

Babits, Lawrence E., xviii, 196, 197
Bacon, Scott, 218
Bailey, Charles A., 238
Bailey, David, 68, 71
Baillou, Peter, xix, xxi, xx, 9, 10
Baker, J. O., 88
Baker, Joseph, 231
Baker, Pearl Famble, 231
Baker, Scott, 236
Barbee Alex W., 151
Barbee, William, 151
Barnard, Amelia Wash, 207
Barnard, Andrew Fuller, 207, 218
Barnard, Ann Christianna Shad, 52, 54, 218
Barnard, Ann Mathews, 207, 216, 218
Barnard, Mrs. C., 71, 218
Barnard, Caroline Catherine, 55, 207, 218
Barnard, Catherine Elizabeth, 51, 54, 218
Barnard, Catherine L., 54, 71, 218
Barnard, Cato, 242
Barnard, Charles, 218
Barnard, Clifford Victoria, 218
Barnard, Edward, 48, 218
Barnard Elizabeth, 48
Barnard, Florence Augusta, 207, 218
Barnard, Frances Barnard, 50, 207, 218
Barnard, Godin G., 218
Barnard, Henrietta, 50, 208, 216, 218
Barnard, Henry J., 208
Barnard, I.M., 154
Barnard, Isabella Zenobia, 219
Barnard, Jack, 50, 51, 219
Barnard, James, 50, 51, 207, 219
Barnard, Jane Bradley, xx, xxi, xxii, 48, 50, 219
Barnard, Col. John, 48, 49, 209, 219
Barnard, John, xix, 9, 16, 38, 48, 49, 54, 208
Barnard, John Washington, 49, 208
Barnard, Sir John, 48
Barnard, Lucy, 49, 208, 219, 220
Barnard, Mary Ann, 50, 51, 75, 208, 219

Barnard, Mary Louisa, 48, 208, 219
Barnard, Mary S., 208
Barnard, Nathaniel Law, 208, 216, 219
Barnard, Robert, xxi, 48, 220
Barnard, Sarah, 220
Barnard, Susan Quarterman, 208
Barnard, Timothy, xxii, 48, 49, 211, 220
Barnard, Timothy Guerard, 55, 208, 213, 220
Barnard, Vernon Rosa, 209, 220, 223
Barnard, Virginia Clancy, 209, 220
Barnard, Virginia Margaret, 209, 213, 220
Barnard, William, 48, 207, 220
Barney, Hattie Hargroves, 231
Barney, Prince, 231
Barrett, Bridget, 211
Barry, Bishop John, 120
Barstow, Eben, 53, 71
Barstow, Elias Butts, 53, 68, 71, 74, 75, 209, 220
Barstow, John, 71, 220
Barton, James F., 238
Bateman, Oliver, 124, 125
Batson, Capt. Matthew Arlington, 178, 179, 180, 181, 182, 220
Battey, Grace, 231
Becu, Giles, 9
Bellilini, Caroline N., 54
Bergier, Fr. Gabriel, 120
Bertoia, Harry, 163
Bessett, William, 209
Betz, Jonathan Gasper, xx, xxii, 47
Betz, John Michael, xx
Bexley, Caroline E., 211
Bexley, Simon, 209
Bilbo, Henrietta, 209
Bird, James, 242
Bissell, H. M., 100
Bivens, Alice, 231
Bivens, Clara, 231
Bivens, Daniel, 231
Bivens, John, 231
Blackburn, Joyce, 186

Blois, Jane W., 176
Bolding, Andrew, 242
Bolton, Robert, xxi
Bonds, Lizzie, 231
Bonds, Shed, 231
Bones, Reuben, 235
Borshine, Charles, 242
Bosomworth, Mary Musgrove, 156
Bosomworth, Thomas, 156
Bourquin, Henry, 156, 165, 209
Bourquin, Mary Ann, 165, 209
Bowens, David, 193, 236
Bower, Mary, 43, 209, 216
Bower, William, 43, 209
Bowyer, H. L., 45
Boyd, Marion E., 41, 87, 95, 97, 203
Bradley, Jane, 48, 209, 220
Bradley, John, 209
Bradley, Richard, 9
Bradley, William, Jr., 48
Bradley, William, Sr., 48
Brady, R. A., 87
Bratton, Col., 89
Briggs, Charles D., 162
Brookes, Helen, 210
Brown, Abner, 241
Brown, Augustus, 242
Brown, Clara Bivens, 232
Brown, Dido, 236
Brown, George, 231
Brown, Capt. M. D., 192
Brown, Col. Philip P., 136
Brown, Prince, 242
Bruce, Thomas, xxi
Bryan, Amanda C., 110
Bryan, Conrad S., 209, 211
Bryan, Delia, 44, 209, 233
Bryan, Elizabeth, 191
Bryan, George Troup, 45, 209
Bryan, Hannah, 209, 212

Bryan, Hannah Georgia, 209, 214
Bryan, Jonathan, 43, 166, 209, 212, 216, 220
Bryan, Joseph, 1, 43, 44, 209, 220, 233, 246
Bryan, Josiah, 43, 210
Bryan, Mary, 43, 166, 212
Bryan, Mary Williamson, 44, 166, 216
Bryan, Thomas Marsh Forman, 45, 209, 210, 216
Bryant, Polydore, 242
Bryant, Seylon, 242
Buchenau, Margaret, 220
Buchenau, Nicholas, 108, 220
Buckman, Helen, 88, 250
Buckman, John, 88
Budreau, John M., 248
Budreau, Joseph Lindley, xvii, 248
Budreau, Joseph Lindley, Jr., 248
Budreau, Mary Louise Mingledorff, 248
Budreau, Mattie Woods, 248
Budreau, Remer Lane, 248
Bulloch, Archibald, 56, 128
Bumpas, Lloyd, 102
Bunting, John R., 238
Busbee, Gov. George, 165
Butler, Ed, 236
Butts, Eliza, 53, 209
Butts, Elias, 53
Butts, Harriet, 53
Butts, Lydia, 53
Cain, B. B., 99
Cain, H. T., Jr., xvii
Call, Alathea, 215
Call, Richard, 215
Caldwell, Henry W., xvii, 238
Caldwell, Lt., 12
Calhoun, Katherine M., 209
Campbell, Henry, 242
Campbell, Tunis G., 160
Campbell, William C., 109
Camuse, Anthony, xx
Canaday, Thomas, 210

Cant, John, 220
Carlin, Nicholas, 238
Carpenter, Bill (William Hiram), xii, 124, 185
Carr, Augustus, 241
Carswell, John Devine, 142
Carter, Louise, 85
Caruthers, Louisa Gibson, 23, 209
Caruthers, William A., 23, 209
Cassese, Anthony, 202
Cater, Ann, 213
Cater, William, 213
Chapeau, Armand, 88
Cheves, Langdon, 9
Chisholm, Anna, 86
Chisholm, Jacob, 242
Chisholm, Johnny, 231
Chisholm, Rena Bonds, 231
Claghorn, Mr., 81
Clark, Ann, 220
Clark, Helen, Walthour, 95
Clark, Nephew K., 250
Clark, William, 220
Clifton, Joe, 242
Cochran, Hugh, 43
Cochran, Janet, 43
Coe, Margaret, 211
Cohen, Percival Randolph, 142
Cole, Warren, 238
Coleman, Sam, 221
Colic, Ernest (see Kollock), 243
Collins, Barney, 238
Colt, William B., 238
Comer, B. B., 47, 140
Compton, H. Tayloe, 78
Compton, Spencer, 38
Conden, Levi, 238
Cook, Mrs. B. F., 143
Cooper, James, 238
Cooper, John, 209, 221
Copland, Aaron, 163

Copp, Capt. William Lenoir, 150, 151
Counihan, Joe, 87
Cowling, Betsey Herb/Hext, 2, 210, 211
Cowling, Slaughter, 2, 210, 211
Crafts, William, 190, 221, 235
Cramer, Ezekiel, 238
Crandie, Adam, xx, 9
Crawford, Capt. J. T., 11
Cullum, Frank, 33
Cumming, Sanney, 241
Curtis, Margaret, 111
Dale, Villa, 53
Dallas, Moses, 158
Danzler, Henry, 171
Davidson, Henry C., 221
Davis, John, 109
Dawsay, Mary Ann, 210
Dawson, E. J., 93, 94
Dawson, Richard, 221
DeGracia, Joe, 179, 182
DeLacey, Roger Hugh, 35
Delegal, Ann Rebecca, 210
Delegal, Catherine, 113, 114
Delegal, David, xxii, 210
Delegal, Edward, 210
Delegal, Jane, 110, 210
Delegal, Margaret Curtis, 111
Delegal, Philip, 108, 111, 112, 113, 233
Delegal, Robert, 109
Dell, Charles L., 110
Delong, Carlos, 238
Demere, Frances Ann, 221
Demere, Louis, 210
Demere, Mary E., 210, 221
Demere, Raymond, 16, 36, 210, 221
Demere, Raymond P., 210, 221
Demere, Virginia C., 221
Densler, David R., 210
Densler, Mary A. E., 210, 215
Densler, Susan, 210

Derr, Melvin J., 99
DeEcija, Capt. Francisco, 127
D'Estaing, Comte Charles Henri, 128
dePury, Jean Pierre, 52
Deveaux, James, 108, 146, 221
Deveaux, Jane, 154
DeVeaux, John H., 158, 221
Deveaux, Peter, 146
Desvergers, 30
DeVergers, Maxine J., 176
DeVillers, F. D. Petit, 153
DeVoe, Margery, 160, 221
DeWitt, Theodore, 100
Dews, John J., 210, 211
Dews, Mary, 210
Dews, Robert J., 211
Dews, William, xx, xxi, xxii, 211
Dilworth, John Hardee, 70, 71
Dixon, Charles H., 81, 82
Dixon, James, 210
Dixon, John, 242
Dixsee, James, 210, 221
Dixsee, Isabella Rogers, 210
Dixsee, Susannah Rogers, 210
Dougherty, Frances Elizabeth, 208
Douglas, Col., 12
Douglas, Henry, 192, 236
Downey, Ellen, 210, 211
Downing, Frank, 186, 187
Downy, John B., 221
Doyle, Richard, 242
Drayton, Bristow, 243
Driver, H. P., 236
Dukes, Joseph, 241
Dulmage, C. A., 13
Dunbar, Thomas, 166, 212
Dunbar, Tryphena, 166, 212
Duncan, Ann, 175
Duncan, Arthur, 175
Duncan, Bernice, 175

Duncan, Cinda, 175
Duncan, Daniel Z., 94
Duncan, Dr., 93
Duncan, Henry, 175, 176
Duncan, Henry Arthur, 172, 221, 233
Duncan, James A. , 94
Duncan, Margaret, 175
Duncan, Rita Mae (see Riley), 221, 232
Duncan, Rosa Lee (see Stoney), 175
Duncan, Sallie Johnson, 172, 221, 232
Duncan, William, 175
Dupon, Hampton, 109
Dupon, Stephen , 120
Dye, Sarah, 221
Eagan, Patrick, 191
Eagan, Michael, 191
Eagan, Thomas, 191, 236
Earle, John, 107
Eddy, James, 243
Edwards, David, 242
Elbert, Samuel, xxii
Elliott, Grey, xxii, 156
Elliott, Harriet Rutledge, 71
Elmgren, Gus, 179
Elmgren, Israel, 179
Elmgren, Yngve, 179
Elon, Benjamin, 243
Ennis, Johnny, 177
Espy, Leila W., 14
Everingham, John, 210
Fahm, Frederick, xxi, 210, 222
Fahm, Sophia , 210
Falk, Georgianna, 139
Falk, Joshua, 139, 236
Falligant, Claude, xxi, 47
Famble, Cornelia W., 231
Famble, Joseph, Jr., 231
Famble, Rev. Peter J., 160, 231
Farley, Mary, 128
Feely, Michael, 222

Fender, Harry, 236
Fenton, Col. W. M., 12
Ferguson, Henry, 242
Fincken, Theodore, 236
Finnesy, Henry, 160, 222, 233
Fleetwood, Green, 10, 210, 222
Fleetwood, John, 10, 240
Fleetwood, Rusty, 2, 130, 131
Fogarty, Eliza, 32, 223, 234
Footman, Mary White, 214
Forman, Delia, 43, 211
Forman, Florida Bryan, 45, 211
Forman, Thomas Marsh Bryan, 45, 46, 47, 211
Forrester, Mrs. Boston, 236
Fortson, Ben, 186
Forumi, Lucy R., 222
Forumi, Mary, 222
Foster, Bill, 103
Foster, Gen. J. G., 136
Frazier, Dr., 175
Frazier, William, 242
Friend, Georgianna Verdell, 210
Friend, Jacob, 210
Frye, William C., 54
Fulton, W. L., 207, 210
Funk, Arthur J., 179, 186
Gammert, Fred, 7, 78
Gammert, John, 78
Gammert, Marguerite "Margie" Merken, 78
Garbet, George, 222
Garbet, Mary Ann, 52, 211, 216
Gardner, John, 246
Garrett, Charles, 241
Gartelman, Catherine, 91
Gartelman, Mildred Katrina Louisa, 83, 84, 86, 91, 93, 94, 222
George, Susie, 232
Gibbons, Alfred, 242
Gibbons, Joseph R., 146
Gibbs, J. L., 243
Gibson, Daniel, 20, 223

Gibson, Louisa Catherine, 24, 211
Gibson, R. F., 240
Gibson, Richard Turner, 72
Gibson, Robert, 4, 9, 20, 21, 223, 234
Gibson, Robert T., 10, 11, 23
Gibson, Robert Stewart, 20, 23, 24, 211, 216, 223
Gibson, Sarah Stewart, 20, 211, 223, 234
Gibson, William, 20, 211
Gignilliat, Sallie, 212
Gilbert, Ann Ready, 211, 214
Gilbert, Mary Ann, 210, 211
Gilbert, William, xxi, 210
Giles, Jack, 242
Giles, William, 242
Giroud, Daniel, 7
Glynn, John, 190, 235
Gnann, David, 210
Gnann, family, 170, 233
Gnann, Joseph, 211
Gnann, Maria Sophia Reddick, 210
Godley, Margaret, 135
Goette, Albert, 74, 248
Goette, Annie Keys, 249
Goette, Catherine, 29, 32, 248
Goette, Clarence, 26, 27, 29, 248
Goette, John, 207
Goette, Joseph, 211, 222
Goette, Mary Amorous, 7
Goette, Mary Bernard, 248
Goette, Walter, 222
Golden, Betty, 231, 232
Golden, Esau, 231
Golden, Isaac, 231
Golden, Isaac Leon, 231
Golden, Jacob, 231
Golden, Louise, 232
Golden, Peter, 231
Golden, Sylvia, 231
Goldwire, Ann, 157
Goldwire, Benjamin, 158, 212

Goldwire, Benjamin, Jr., 157, 212
Goldwire, Elizabeth, 212
Gonzales, Gen. Ambrosio Jose, 66, 67, 68, 69, 71, 72, 74
Gordon, Bee, 17
Gordon, Jack, 243
Gradot, C. A., 236
Graham, Mrs. C. F., 142
Gray, Ellen, 222
Gray, Eliza M., 211
Gray, Johnny, 26
Gray, George Sweet, 29, 31, 211, 222, 240, 247
Gray, Mary Ann, 211
Gray, Tobias V., 29, 30, 211, 222
Green, Herbert, 39
Green, Joseph, 243
Green, Lonnie, 97
Green, Thomas, xxii, 237
Green, William, 231
Greene, Helen, 88
Greene, Henry C., 88, 91
Greenman, Francis H., 222
Greg, Roy, 180
Griffin, Archibald, 118
Grimm, Diedrich, 176
Gross, Bishop William H., 120, 121
Grover, Maj. Gen Cuvier, 136
Guerard, Catherine G., 208, 211
Gugel, Harriet, 211
Gunn, James, 166
Gwinnett, Button, 52
Haar, Ernest J., 47
Habersham, Joseph Clay, 115, 116
Hadger, Lt., 238
Haist, Elizabeth, 109, 222
Haist, George, 109, 222
Haist, George Jr., 109, 222
Hall, Jonathan, 28
Hall, Lyman, xviii, 28
Hall, Mary, 28
Hamilton, Gen. James, 70

Hamilton, S. Prioleau, 70
Hammond, Joe, 243
Handley, George, 166
Handy, Jamison, 47
Hardaway, Lewis, 243
Hardee, George Washington, 211
Hardee, Mrs. Margaret L., 222
Hardee, Mary T., 54
Harden, Ann Margaret, 29
Hargroves, Balaam, 231
Hargroves, Betty, 231, 232
Hargroves, Jacob, 232
Hargroves, Mary, 231
Harkinson, P. H., 238
Harris, Clayborn, 241
Harris, Stephen, 243
Harrison, James A., 162
Hartstene, Ann Margaret, 211
Hartstene, Benjamin, 222
Hartstene, Joachim, 28
Hartstene, Mary Ann, 29, 211
Harvey, Dennis, 91, 92, 93
Heak, R. L., 162
Heftl, Fr. Daniel, 121, 122
Helback, Adolph, 236
Helvenstine, Jacob, xx, 2
Helvenstine, Jeremiah, xx
Helvenstine, John, xx, xxi, 9
Henderson, Mary Elizabeth, 53, 211, 214
Herb, Betsey, 211
Herb, Catherine, 211, 222
Herb, Elizabeth, 176
Herb, Frederick, xxi, 170, 171, 211, 223, 247
Herb, George, 23, 170, 171, 211
Herb, John, 211, 222
Herb, Louise Carpenter, 211
Herb, Mary, 211
Herb, Mary Ann, 212
Herb, Sarah, 223, 234
Herb, Ursula Peters, 171, 211, 223

Hester, Ed, 186
Hext, Grady, 78
Hext, Hugh, 43, 211
Hext, Martha, 43, 211
Heyward, Elizabeth Pritchard, 57, 211, 223
Heyward, John, 211, 223
Heyward, Thomas Wilson, 64, 223, 233
Higgins, Martha, 128, 223
Hildreth, Lt., 144
Hinely, James J., 162
Hines, James L., 211
Hines, Mrs. V. R., 223
Hoffa, Jimmy, 102, 103
Holder, Preston, xvi
Holland, Albert, 54
Holmes, Tony, 237
Hopkins, Catharine T., 223
Hough, Mr., 140
Houston, G. Z., 243
Houston, W., 243
Houstoun, Hannah Bryan, 211
Houstoun, Henry Clay, 207
Houstoun, James, xxi, xxii
Houstoun, John, 43, 167, 211
Houstoun, Mary Arkwright, 207
Houstoun, Sir Patrick, 43, 211
Howell, Lymus, 243
Hoyt, John, 186
Hudnall, Matilda, 54
Hughes, John, 211, 223
Hughes, Mary Ann Gilbert, 211, 223
Hughes, Terrence, 223
Hull, Mr., 81
Hunter, Cassius, 30, 31, 32
Hunter, Frank O'Driscoll, 19
Hunter, Mrs. H. A., 223
Hunter, James, 240, 246
Hunter, John, 211
Hunter, Mary Ann Herb, 211
Hunter, William, 240

Hurburt, Paul, 243
Huse, Caleb, 159
Hutchison, Sam, 242
Isham, Ralph, 123
Jackson, Green, 242
Jackson, Nancy, 242
Jackson, Prince, 243
Jarvis, Jane, xxi
Jarvis, John, xxi, 108
Jeffreys, Mr., 26
Jemdal, Charles, 81
Jenkins, Mollie, 33
Jenkins, Sarah Turner, 35
Jenks, Robert, 242
Jennings, Aylmer, 238
Jennings, George, 238
Johnson, Pres. Andrew, 118
Johnson, Sallie (see Duncan), 172, 221
Johnston, Elizabeth Lichtenstein/Lightenstone, 114, 212, 223
Johnston, William Martin, 114, 212, 223
Jones, Austin, 243
Jones, Ernest R., 21
Jones, Henry Charles, 212
Jones, James, 212
Jones, L. T., 91
Jones, Noble, 55, 56
Jones, Gen. Samuel, 136
Jones, Sarah, 243
Judkins, Capt. J. J., 87
Judkins, Etta, 85
Kapple, D., 238
Keane, Jeremiah, 192
Kelly, V. E., 105
Kennedy, D. R., 139
Kessel, Adam, 79, 81
Keys, Annie, 86, 248
Killick, David J., 197
Kincaid, J. Leslie, 99
King, Harry, 36, 39, 41, 42, 61, 62
Kollock, Ernest (see Colic), 243

Kollock, George Jones, 157
Kreeger, Thomas, 212
Krieger, John, 212
Kuhn, Leonora Sipple, 82
Lachlison, Lydia, 132, 212
Lachlison, Robert, 132
Lacy, Daniel, 190, 223, 235
Lamar, Charles Augustus, 67
Lamar, Mirabeau, 67
Lane, Charles, 143
Lang, Hermann, 86, 88
Lang, Josie, 85
Lang, Lottie, 84, 85, 86, 224
Lang, Nicholas, 88
Lankenau, Clyde F., 177
Lankenau, Herman D., 176
Lankenau, Mary E., 176
Larner, Silas, 238
LaRoche family, 171
LaRoche, Mary, 178, 179
LaRoche, Isaac D., 178, 179
Lattimore, William, 95
Law, Ann P., 54, 212
Law, Martha J., 55, 212
Law, Nathaniel, 212
LeConte, Capt. John, 135
Lee, Robert Edward, 135
Lewis, Edith H., 54
Lewis, Huldah, 215
Lichtenstein, Elizabeth, 114, 212
Lichtenstein, John (see Lightenstone), 114, 212
Lightbourn, John, 224
Lightbourn, Margaret E., 224
Lightenstone, Beatrice Elizabeth, 114
Lightenstone, Catherine Delegal, 212, 223
Lightenstone, Elizabeth (see Lichtenstein), 114, 212
Lightenstone, Gustavus Philip, 114
Lightenstone, John (see Lichtenstein), 114, 115, 212
Lillibridge, Hampton, 109
Lippitt, Maxwell W., 95

Lloyd, Bonaparte, 242
Lominack, Loretto, 27, 28
Lopez, Gen. Narciso, 66, 67, 68, 71, 74
Lord, Melrose, 241
Lovett, Leon, 138
Lucas, Elizabeth, 4, 212
Lufburrow, Albert, 125
Lysaught, Chief Dennis, 144
Mackdonald, Adam, xix
MacKay, Patrick, 128
Mackey, William, 241
Madan, Robert, 224
Malcolm, Anna, 213
Mallory, Stephen, 159
Martin, Charles, 196
Martin, Charles (black), 232
Martin, Clyde, 232
Martin, Don, 78
Martin, Dorothy, 232
Martin family, 197
Martin, Judy, 78
Martin, Kate, 232
Martin, Nelson, 232
Martin, Patrick, 29, 30, 225
Martin, Paul, 231
Mathers, William H., 212
Matthews, Mamye L., 54
Maxwell, John, 243
Maxwell, Susan Jefferson, 212
Mayer, Adrian, 109
Mayer, John Hover, 224
Mayer, R. A., 179
Mayer, R. H., 47
McAllister, Matthew, 109
McCall, Sarah Ann, 207
McCann, Dr., xvii
McCarthy, Tom, 186
McClesky, George, 68, 213, 246
McDonald, Alexander, 157
McDonald, Rev. J. W., 148

McDonell, Edgar M., 11, 30, 212
McGinnis, Dr. E. S., 71
McGwiggins, Thomas, 160, 224, 233
McIntosh, George, 109, 224
McIntosh, Col. Lachlan, 106, 109, 224
McKinnon, John, 170
McLaws, U. H., 161
McNish, John, 109
McNish, T. W., 192, 246
McNulty, Capt., 69
McQueen, April, 241
McQueen, Harriet, 166
McQueen, Peter, 97
McQure, Thomas, 243
McWilliams, Samuel, 190, 224, 235
Meers, Raymond, 180
Mein, William, xxii
Meldrim, Peter W., 125, 203
Merken, Marguerite "Margie", 78, 84
Middleton, A. D., 179
Milledge, John, 107, 108, 114, 123, 224
Miller, Mary, 210
Miller, Samuel, 210
Mingledorff, Mary Louise (see Budreau), 175, 177, 248
Mingledorff, Walter Lee, Jr., 248
Mirault, Simon, 154
Mitchell, Katie Slee, 232
Mongin, Mr., 70
Mongin, Mary Ann Naylor, 208, 212
Mongin, Susan Frances, 53, 54, 208, 212
Monson, Karl, 179
Moore, Franklin, 238
Moore, Harriet, 208, 212
Moore, Thomas, 190, 224, 235
Mopson, Jack, 243
Mopson, John, 243
Morel, Ann Valleau, 22, 167, 224
Morel, Bryan, 157
Morel, Charles Harris, 224
Morel, Hannah Bryan, 224

Morel, Harriet McQueen, 166, 225
Morel, Henrietta Netherclift O'Brien, 166
Morel, Henry, 1, 166, 212, 225
Morel Ismael, 153
Morel, James S., 224
Morel, John I, xxi, 6, 39, 43, 156, 166, 212, 225
Morel, John II, 156, 157, 166, 212, 225
Morel, Jonathan, xxii
Morel, Mary Ann Bourquin, 156, 165, 166, 213, 225
Morel, Mary Bryan, 43, 167, 213, 225
Morel, Peter Henry, 157, 166, 167, 212, 224, 225
Morel, Sally Powell , 166
Morel, Tryphena, 166, 212, 226
Morel, Tryphena Dunbar, 166, 212, 225
Morgan, Maj. John L., 207
Morgan, Mary, 10
Morton, Valentine, 236
Moses, Eddie, 232
Moses, Phyllis Simmons, 232
Moss, Ozelle Walthour, 250
Moss, Virginia Walthour, 96, 250
Mouse, Lucy, 106, 107
Mouse, Thomas, 106, 107
Moxham, John, 235
Mulryne, Catherine, 128, 129
Murdock, Lisa Evans, 84, 85
Muse, Archibald, 225
Myers, Eli, 238
Myers, Henry, 29
Nation, Carry, 199
Newell, Mary Wylly, 229
Newton, Ellie, 231
Nicoll, James S., 190, 225, 235
Nieman, Leighton, 102
Nixon, President Richard M., 124
Norris, John, 135
Norton, Isaac, 53, 213
Norton, John Robert, 53
Norton, Leila, 22
Norton, Sarah Wilmington, 55, 226, 234

Norton, Tamar Waters, 213, 226
Norton, Thomas, 213
Norton, William, 107
O'Brien, Henrietta Netherclift, 166
O'Connor, Jerry F., 87
Odingsells, Anthony, 153, 154, 226
Odingsells, Benjamin, 115
Odingsells, Charles Spencer, xxi, xxii, 116, 153, 226
Odingsells, Lucy Ann, 153, 154, 155
Odingsells, Madeline, 153, 154, 155
Odingsells, Mary, 115, 226
Odingsells, Mary A., 226
Odingsells, Mary Susannah, 115, 226
Odingsells, Sarah Spencer, 115, 226
Odum, Dr. Eugene, 188
Oemler, Alan Norton, 53, 60, 213
Oemler, Armenius, 53, 58, 59, 64, 213, 226, 235
Oemler, Augustus Gottlieb, 53, 57, 58, 59, 60, 215, 226
Oemler, Charlotte Heyward, 53, 58
Oemler, Constantius Heyward, 53, 57, 58, 59, 64, 213, 233
Oemler, Elizabeth Latham, 53, 58, 213
Oemler, Frieda Rauers, 53, 226
Oemler, John, 53, 213
Oemler, Marianne, 53, 58, 226
Oemler, Mary Alexander, xvii, 53, 57
Oemler, Mary Teasdale, 53, 216
Oemler, John Norton, 53, 213
Oglethorpe, James Edward, xix, 48, 52, 106, 127, 165
Osborne, Andrew, 238
Osborne, Andrew J., 238
Osborne, J. H. H., 84
O'Malley, Mary Goette, 7, 29, 32
O'Sullivan, Mr., 69
Oswald, Fr., 121
Otto, Billy, 19
Page, Albert, 236
Palmer, Richard, 108, 124
Palmer, Thomas, xx, 9
Pape, Nina Anderson, 142
Parker, Andrew, 232

Parker, Clara, 232
Parker, Patience, 232
Parr, Newell Turner, x
Parsons, Charles, 249
Parsons, Charles, Jr., 249
Parsons, George, 147, 152, 249
Patterson, William, 50, 51, 215
Peatya————, 238
Pelot, Thomas P., 158, 159, 226
Pendarvis, Elizabeth, 43, 209, 226
Pendleton, Philip Coleman, 213, 215
Penrose, John, xx, 1, 4, 9, 10, 197
Perry, Florence, 231
Piechocinski, John Joseph, 138
Pinckney, Charles, 213
Pinckney, Elizabeth Lucas, 213
Pinckney, Jack, 97
Pinckney, Lizzie, 236
Pinckney, Robert, 97
Pindar, Sarah, 53
Pinder, Ann Margaret Tebeau, 213, 215, 246
Pinder, Joseph William, 213, 215, 240
Piper, Lewis, 238
Platen, Charles, 129
Plinstock, Thomas, 238
Poland, Capt., 138
Polk, Pres. Leonidas, 66
Pope, Tina, 75, 76, 77, 78
Potter Sarah W., 213
Pound, J. B., 101
Powell, J. D., 61
Powell, Joseph, 166
Powell, Sally, 166
Pratt, Capt. Minor, 12, 238
Prendergast, Margaret, 29
Preston, Henry, 213
Price, Eugenia, 186
Priester, Lawton M., 226
Pritchard, W. R., 54, 72, 213, 226
Proctor, Richard, 191

Prophet, James, 241
Provost, Ann T., 52, 213, 226
Provost, Peter, 52, 213, 215, 226
Provost, William, 213, 226
Provenzano, Anthony, 103
Purse, Dr., 93
Putnam, Anna Malcolm, 213, 215
Putnam, Augustus H., 213, 215
Putnam, Benjamin, 213, 215
Quarterman, L. S., 213, 227
Rahn, Ann E., 214
Rainey, Sarah Walthour, 250
Rauers, Frieda, 53
Ray, William S. "Billy," x, 32
Readick, Catherine, 214
Readick, Jacob, 154
Readick, Mary Salfner, 214
Readick, Peter, 154, 227
Readick, William, 214
Ready, Ann, 210, 214, 215
Reddick, Ann, 214, 215
Reddick, Ann E. Rahn, 214
Reddick, Maria Sophia, 212
Reddick, Sophia, 210, 215
Reddick, Susan Densler, 214
Reddick, William, 213
Reddick, William G., 176, 177
Reitter, Michael, 109
Rhines, Barton R., 87, 203
Richards, R. R., 60
Richardson, Lt., 12
Richardsone, Cosmo P., 227
Riley, Rita Mae (see Duncan), 171, 172, 173, 175, 176, 232
Rivers, Horace, 81
Robe, Francis, 106, 227
Roberts, Addie, 96, 227
Roberts, Robert, 243
Roberts, Samuel Capers, 78, 96, 227
Robertson, Susannah L., 227
Robider, Walter, 237

Roebling, Dorothy, 123
Roebling, Robert, 123
Rogers, Isabella, 210
Rogers, Susannah, 210
Roote, Judge, 172
Rosanova, Lou, 103
Rose, William, 132
Ross, Charles E., 118
Ross, Donald, 98
Ross, John, 179, 242
Rossignol, Harriet, 88
Rousakis, John, 186
Rowan, Lt. Robert, 137, 227, 233
Rowland, John Clark, 53, 54
Rowland, John T., 53
Rowland, William P., 54, 72, 208
Ruwe, Martha, 85
Ruwe, May, 85
Ryans, Walter S., 238
Saffold, John Barnard, 17, 19, 20, 227
Saffold, Joseph C., Jr., 17, 19
Saffold, Joseph Claghorn, Sr., 17, 215, 227
Saffold, Katherine Calhoun, 17, 215
Saffold, Katherine Miller Calhoun, 17, 214, 224
Saffold, Rex, 17
Saffold, Thomas Peter, 16, 227
Salfner, Mary, 214
Sanders, A. T., 140
Savage, John, 227
Scarborough, William E., 182
Schaad, Hans Joachim, 52
Schaad, Hans Joachim, Jr., 52
Schaad, Ann, 52
Schaad, Margareta, 52, 227
Schaad, Solomon, 52
Schaaf, Walter, 11, 24, 26, 27, 31
Schaeffer, Minnie, 85
Schloppi, Constantine, 238
Schwarz, George, 237
Screven, C. O., 214

Screven, Dick, 243
Screven, George P., 46
Screven, Hannah Proctor, 45, 227, 235
Screven, Henry, 243
Screven, James Proctor, 46, 51, 116, 191, 227
Screven, John, 45, 46, 59, 214, 227, 235, 240
Screven, Maj. John Richard, 45, 214, 227
Screven, Thomas F., 46
Seiler, Frank W. "Sonny", 170, 177, 178, 179, 180, 181
Sellmer, Charles Howard, 227, 233
Sellmer, Charles Marion, 227
Shad, Ann Catherine, xxi, 50, 51, 53, 214
Shad, Ann Christianna, 214
Shad, Annie, 214, 227
Shad, Armenius Oemler, 54
Shad, Catherine Elizabeth, 53, 214, 228
Shad, Daniel W. M., 54
Shad, Edward, 228
Shad, Elias Butts, 53, 228, 244, 245
Shad, Harriet, 51, 52, 53, 228
Shad, John Robert, 53, 215, 228, 244, 245
Shad, Margaret Norton, 215, 228
Shad, Mary Ann, 54, 214, 215, 229
Shad, Mongin, 56
Shad, Sarah, 55, 228
Shad, Savannah Schifelia, 54
Shad, Solomon Sigismund, 17, 51, 53, 57, 215, 228, 235
Shad, Solomon, Jr., 36, 53, 56, 57, 215, 228
Shadd, William, 240
Shaffer, Balthasar, 215
Shaffer, Harriet S., 228
Shaffer, Sarah, 215
Shellman, Cuffy, 243
Shillinger, Fred, 239
Shorts, Suzanne Batson, 182
Siegfrit, George, xx, xxi, 9
Simmons, Bella, 241
Simmons, Claw, 232
Simmons, John, 232
Simmons, Phyllis (see Moses), 232

Simpson, Matilda, 245
Sipple, Charles Henry, 73, 82, 84, 89
Sipple, Leonora, 82
Sipple, Louise, 86
Sisson, Charles, 192
Slee, Hattie, 231
Slee, Kate (see Mitchell), 231
Small, Celia, 97
Smart, H. P., 139
Smith, Anne Skidaway, 107
Smith, Fae Oemler, 55
Smith, Frances, 107
Smith, Rev. J. A., 148
Smith, L. H., 100
Smith, Thomas, 107
Smith, Walter D., 239
Solomon, Henry, 139
Solomon, Nathaniel, 139
Solomon, Tommy, 130, 131
Somerville, Eden, 129
Sowney, Mary, 32, 207
Space, Julian, 36
Spalding, Randolph, 69
Spencer, Joseph, 115
Spencer, Sarah (see Odingsells), 115
Spindle, B. L., 87
Spring, Hannah, 236
Spurbuck, George, 239
Squire, Taylor, 237
Stahmer, Carl F., 90, 91, 92, 93
Stahmer, Matilda, 86, 91
Stahmer, Millie, 86, 91
Stahmer, John William, Jr., 90, 91, 92, 93
Stahmer, John William, Sr., 86, 91
Stanley, Martha, 132, 215
Stark, Alathea, 215
Stark, Ebenezer, 115, 215
Steele, Charles, 243
Stevens, Henry, 228
Stewart, Fred, 228, 237

Stewart, Hartwell, 241
Stewart, Sarah, 20
Stewart, Matthew W., 51
Stibbs, Ann, 228
Stiles, Frank, 242
Stiles, Joseph, 242
Stillwell, Sarah Walthour, 95
Stone, George H., 87
Stoney, Rosa Lee Duncan, 175
Straight, William, 241
Symons, W. R., 116, 240
Tattnall, David, 97
Tattnall, Gene, 97
Tattnall, Henry, 172
Tattnall, Jack, 96, 97, 175, 228
Tattnall, James, 172
Tattnall, Josiah, 5, 9, 128, 129, 146
Tattnall, King, 241
Tattnall, Lizzie, 96
Tattnall, Mary, 128, 129
Tattnall, Sammy, 94, 97
Tattnall, Samuel, 97
Teasdale, Mary, 213
Tebeau, Ann Catherine Cecilia, 53, 216, 228
Tebeau, Ann Margaret, 53, 216, 228
Tebeau, Catharine Sarah Melissa, 213, 215, 228
Tebeau, Charles Watson, 229
Tebeau, Daniel, 239
Tebeau, Frederick, 215, 229
Tebeau, Huldah Lewis, 215
Tebeau, James, 52, 215, 229
Tebeau, John, 52, 215, 229
Tebeau, Mary Alice, 213, 215, 229
Tebeau, Susannah, 215
Thomas, Clarence, 161
Thomas, Mary Elizabeth, 215
Thompson, Christopher C., 215
Thompson, Mary, 10
Tice, 29, 32
Tilton, L. A., 229

Tilton, Millie E., 229
Tilton, Nathaniel O., 191, 229, 249
Tilton, Octavius L., 93, 229
Tiot, Sarah, 110
Tondee, Lucy Mouse, 106, 107
Tondee, Peter, 106
Torrey, Eleanor, 163
Torrey, Henry Norton, 163
Torrey, William F., 163
Torley, Alfred E., 215
Torley, Mary, 129, 215, 229
Trammer, Mrs. Otto, 76, 77
Treutlen, Ann, 216
Treutlen, Catherine, 52, 216
Treutlen, Frederick, 52, 56, 216, 230
Treutlen, John Adam, 52, 56, 216, 230
Treutlen, Margaret Schad, 215
Troup, George M., 215
Tucker, Capt., 12
Turnbull, Nicholas, 5, 146
Turner, Capt., 12
Turner, Elizabeth, 35, 229
Turner, Fannie E., 207, 215
Turner, Jesten, 35
Turner, John S., 11, 35
Turner, Lewis, 9, 35, 51, 215, 229
Turner, Lewis T., 35, 215, 229
Turner, Lucy C., 49, 215
Turner, Mary W. Newell, 230
Turner, Richard, 35, 230
Turner, Sarah, 35, 215
Turner, Sarah Caesar, 35, 215
Tyner, Keeland, 208, 215
Ulmer, A. C., 140, 142, 229, 237
Ulmer, Mrs. A. C., 140, 141, 142
Valleau, Fauconnier, 167
Vallotten, James, 229
Vandenstack, A., 239
Venghen, Catherine, 207

Verdell, Ann Reddick, 215
Verdell, Elizabeth, 230
Verdell, Georgianna, 215
Verdell, John, 215
Verdell, Josephalia, 230
Verdell, Maria, 230
Verdell, Peter, 215, 230
Verdell, Sophia Reddick, 215, 230, 233
Vincent, Hannah, xxi, 216
Vincent, Thomas, xxi, 39, 216, 230
Vinson, Mary Ann, 191
Wade, William, 120
Walcott, Jacob, 243
Walker, Mary Gertrude, 230
Wall, Samuel, 146
Wall, William, 146
Wallace, Hercules, 243
Walthour, A. M., 249
Walthour, Augusta 216
Walthour, George Washington, 216
Walthour, Henry Clayton, 96, 99, 249, 250
Walthour, Henry S., 88
Walthour, John P., 250
Walthour, Mary Ann, 216
Walthour, Ozelle, 250
Walthour, Sarah, 250
Waltower, Ben, 242
Walker, Amos C., 239
Walker, Gertrude, 230
Wanamaker, John, 161
Ward, John, 156
Waring, Antonio J., xvi
Waring, William R., 108, 117, 240
Warner, R. P., 179
Wasden, Wiley, 124
Wash, Amelia, 218
Wash, W. W., 53, 207, 216, 240
Washington, William, 243
Waters, Alicia, 110, 230, 233

Waters, John B., Jr., 110, 230, 233
Waters, John B., Sr., 110, 230
Waters, Joy, 22
Watson, Rena, 236
Watts, Robert, 146
Waver, Francis, 54, 215, 216, 247
Waver, M. N., 247
Webster, Charles E., 150
Weed, Henry D., 161, 162
Weeks, Elmo, 86
Wells, A. E., 179
Wesley, John, 134, 137
Wessels, Fred, Jr., 182
Wessels, Fred, Sr., 177
West, Alfred James, 230
West, Clifford, 163
West, Eleanor Torrey, 163, 164, 165
Weston, R. F., 179
White, Charles, 212
Whitaker, Josiah, 190, 230, 235
Whitfield, James, 55
Whiting, Ann Lucy, 35
Whiting, Elizabeth Turner, 35, 229
Whiting, Lewis T., 35, 229
Whiting, Lewis Turner, 35, 229
Whitney, Eli, 1, 6
Williams, Andrew, 232
Williams, Clarence, 232
Williams, Cribben, 31, 32
Williams, Cyrus, 232
Williams, Dan, 241
Williams, David D., 230
Williams, Helen, 232
Williams, James, 241
Williams, Jane, 230
Williams, John, 237, 241
Williams, Louise Golden, 232
Williams, Margaret C., 218
Williams, Peter, 242

Williams, Screven, 31
Williams, Stephen B., 51, 216
Williams, Steven, 171, 216
Williams, York, 243
Williamson, Mary, 43, 216, 230
Winkler, Tom, 241
Wilson, Lt. J. H., 12
Wilson, Peter, 230
Winn, Isaiah, 243
Wissel, Fr. Raphael, 120
Wolf, Georgianna Falk, 139, 236
Wolf, Joseph, 139
Wolf, Halle, 139 236
Wood, Virginia Steele, 6
Woods, Mattie, 248
Workman, Edward "Teddie, 140
Workman, Dorothy, 140
Workman, Frank, 140
Workman, Marjorie, 140
Workman, M. S., 140, 141
Wright, Helen, 232
Wright, Sir James, 108, 114, 128
Wright, John, 232
Wright, Martha, 243
Wright, Patience Parker, 232
Wylly, Col., 216
Wylly, Mary, 109
Wylly, Richard, 43, 216
Yonge, Daniel Fleming, 230, 234
Yonge, Elizabeth Oemler, 230, 234
Yonge, Henry, 39, 108, 109, 123
Youhill, W. H., 179
Younge, J., 129
Young, Alexander W., 162
Young, John, 171
Young, George, 241
Young, Isaac, xxi, xxii, 87, 128, 171
Young, Phillip, 243